Committees in Congress

THIRD EDITION

Christopher J. Deering and Steven S. Smith

CQ
PRESS

A Division of Congressional Quarterly Inc.
Washington, D.C.

Copyright © 1997 Congressional Quarterly Inc.

Printed in the United States of America

Cover design: Naylor Design Inc.

Library of Congress Cataloging-in-Publication Data

Deering, Christopher J.
  Committees in Congress / Christopher J. Deering, Steven S.
Smith.—3rd ed.
    p. cm.
  Includes bibliographical references and index.
  ISBN 0-87187-818-6
  1. United States. Congress—Committees. 2. United States.
Congress—Reform. 3. United States—Politics and government—
1945–1989. 4. United States—Politics and government—1989–
I. Smith, Steven S. II. Title.
JK1029.S64 1997
328.73'0765—dc21

                       97-2898

Committees in Congress

To the Mary Deerings
c.j.d.

To Barbara, Tyler, and Shannon
s.s.s.

Contents

Tables, Figures, and Boxes

TABLES

FIGURES

BOXES

Preface

Congressional committees have been and remain the central structural element of the United States Congress. Rule and practice in both the House and Senate make it extremely difficult to consider legislation that has not been reviewed by one or more committees. Career-oriented members find that committees, even more than parties, are essential to the achievement of personal political goals. Certainly committees, and the work that they do, increase the efficiency and efficacy of these institutions. But committees are not completely autonomous, and their power has been under siege in recent years. In the House, power has flowed away from the committees to party leaders. In the Senate, the shift has been to the rank and file.

Yet committees are extraordinarily resilient, as this third edition of *Committees in Congress* demonstrates. Indeed, the dramatic flow of power to House Speaker Newt Gingrich, achieved during the watershed 104th Congress, had reversed to favor committees and committee chairs as the 105th Congress began. And in the Senate, party leaders were searching for ways to limit the atomized power within that chamber—a move that is likely to increase the power of committees there. Finally, divided party government has fostered a rhetoric of cooperation that reflects recognition of the need for bipartisan policy development *within* committees. How far will all this go? It is hard to say. But we can be sure that whatever comes, committees will retain their place as central features of these two powerful legislative institutions. Whether they are the agents either of their parent chambers or of the two opposing parties or increasingly autonomous, understanding committees is essential to any understanding of Congress.

Although in broad form this edition of *Committees* is similar to its predecessors, several changes are worth noting. First, and most important, the debate about committee power that has emerged in the literature during the last decade has been given a more prominent position here. This debate—which juxtaposes distributive, informational, and partisan theories—has informed and enlivened the scholarship on Congress and on committees in many important ways. Indeed, it is fair to say that these contending approaches now dominate much of the literature on Congress. It is only appropriate, therefore, that they be introduced more clearly at the outset of this edition and revisited consistently throughout the text.

Second, previous editions of *Committees* featured a fairly exhaustive historical treatment of the origins and development of committees. In the interest of space, that review has been condensed to make room for a thorough discussion of the most recent round of reforms in the House and Senate.

And third, the second edition closed with a discussion of a series of reforms that had emerged during the late 1980s. In light of the events that transpired during the 103d and 104th Congresses, that discussion now requires revision. Chapter 2 features an account of the important reform efforts that emerged, but largely failed, in the 103d Congress and the significant alterations adopted by House Republicans and, to a lesser degree, Senate Republicans in the 104th Congress.

Authors of books of this sort inevitably roll up long lists of debts. For this edition, Roger Davidson (as always), Richard Forgette, Sarah Binder, Forrest Maltzman, Priscilla Regan, Paul Walbeck, and Lee Sigelman read all or parts of the manuscript, suggested important changes, and helped to improve this edition in many tangible ways. For this and for previous editions, Stanley Bach, Bill Connelly, Larry Evans, Paul Herrnson, George Kundanis, Walter Oleszek, Bruce Oppenheimer, Jack Pitney, Judy Schneider, Ken Shepsle, Barbara Sinclair, Jim Thurber, Joe Unekis, and Don Wolfensberger provided facts, data, ideas, guidance, and assistance of a sort that marks the scholarly community at its best. As with the previous editions, this edition has been enhanced in tangible and intangible ways by the American Political Science Association's Congressional Fellowship Program and by support from the Dirksen Congressional Leadership Research Center.

I am grateful to David Chambliss, Job Henning, and Mark Kugler, who put in long hours collecting documents and data for this edition. And Rachel Paine Caufield, Jason MacDonald, and Christine Nemechek did yeoman work in the midst of their busy schedules to collect much-needed data at the twelfth hour. I am indebted (and in debt) to them. Finally, it is time to thank John Zorotovich for providing me with a number of keen insights over the years.

This book would not exist if Jean Woy, formerly of CQ Press, had not placed her faith in two untested scholars back in 1981. Since then, a variety of people at CQ have shown continuing faith in the book. Brenda Carter, in particular, has extended that tradition. Tracy Villano edited the manuscript, Talia Greenberg guided the manuscript through final production, Rhonda Holland put together a thorough index, and Julie Rovesti prepared the promotional materials. I am grateful for their patience, professionalism, and encouragement.

Finally, although much of the data in this and previous editions are taken from archival sources, the willingness of present and former members of Congress and their staff to assist in a variety of ways was essential. At a time when access is increasingly difficult, the continuing generosity of many members and their aides is greatly appreciated.

C. J. D.
Washington, D.C.

CHAPTER 1

Committees in Congress

On January 4, 1995, the U.S. House of Representatives met under Republican control for the first time in forty years. During the course of the day, into the evening, and on past midnight, the new Republican majority eliminated three committees, altered committee jurisdictions, cut committee and subcommittee staff, lowered existing limits on subcommittee membership, restricted the practice of proxy voting, and established term limits for committee and subcommittee chairs. These changes—and there were others—marked the most dramatic alteration in the House committee system in two decades. That same day saw the U.S. Senate meet under Republican control for the first time since 1986. The Senate, with fixed rules spanning from one Congress to the next, quietly went about the business of shifting to Republican control. It made no changes in its committees, subcommittees, rules, or procedures. The single proposed rule change, one which would have made limiting debate easier, was rejected by a lopsided vote.

These contrasting responses to the same dramatic national election underscore the differences between two remarkable political institutions and the essential framework of committees that forms their cores. The politics of the United States Congress is vast, complicated, and endlessly interesting. But no vision of Congress would be complete without committees as a central feature. To some degree it is easy to take committees for granted. We are all familiar with them. Virtually every decision-making body, even of modest size, uses committees to make (and avoid making) decisions. At their simplest, committees are just formally constituted subgroups of a larger decision-making body. But regardless of how simple a committee may be, the student of decision making must always ask one basic question: how powerful is it?

Committees, of course, are the focus of this book. Because they are central to any understanding of Congress they are a logical and appropriate focus of study. In this chapter we begin by examining three different perspectives on committee power. We then describe the necessary features that define committees themselves. Several important questions emerge. First, how do we explain why committees exercise, or fail to exercise, power within the House and Senate? Second, what factors, both within Congress and external to it, condition committee power over time? And third, what are the mechanisms, formal and informal, that determine committee structures and procedures at any given point in time? It should be clear that, like other institutional features, congressional committees are dynamic rather than static. Indeed, in a variety of small ways committees change almost constantly. But occasionally change is dramatic, as was the case in the House at the outset of the 104th Congress. Thus, to understand committees and the ebb and flow of the power they possess, we need to appreciate how they have changed over time (see Chapter 2).

PERSPECTIVES ON COMMITTEE POWER

Decision-making processes in Congress represent an interaction of committees, parties, and the parent chambers. The relative importance of each to policy making varies over time. To develop an appreciation of their potential impact on policy outcomes, it is useful to consider three alternative perspectives on committee power: the distributive committees perspective, the party-dominated committees perspective, and the chamber-dominated committees perspective.[1] Each perspective is a highly stylized view of congressional decision making grounded in certain aspects of actual practice. After reviewing the three perspectives, we will consider conditions that lead Congress to adopt decision-making patterns that approximate one or another of these perspectives.

The *distributive committees perspective* holds that members of Congress self-select onto the various panels because of a keen interest in the legislation they produce. For example, farm state members join the agriculture committees, members from states with military bases or large defense contractors join the defense committees, and so forth. If non-committee members remain relatively indifferent to the policies produced by a committee, then that committee essentially becomes autonomous—determining policy within its jurisdiction, irrespective of the policy preferences of the parent chamber and parties.[2] Fully autonomous committees would have monopoly control over setting the agenda for their parent chamber in the issue areas within their jurisdiction.[3] They would have the ability to exercise negative power (blocking legislation by refusing to report it to the floor) and positive power (proposing legislation that the chamber is compelled to consider). Complete autonomy also requires that alternatives to committee recommendations be ineligible or routinely defeated and that committee recommendations be adopted.

While congressional committees never have been completely autonomous, the distributive committees perspective finds proponents in those who emphasize Congress's decentralized features. Supporting this perspective are the following observations: members whose constituencies care most about the jurisdiction of a particular committee tend to be assigned to that committee and dominate its decisions; once assigned to a committee, the "property right" norm allows committee members to retain their seat as long as they want it; and noncommittee members tend to defer to a committee when its legislation comes to the floor, primarily because there is little political incentive for them to do otherwise. The distributive committees perspective views policy as a product of the preferences of committee members and their constituencies, reflecting their biases. It depicts each chamber as a set of fairly autonomous, mutually deferential committees, allowing no real policy role for the floor, the parties, or party leaders.

The *party-dominated committees perspective* emphasizes the vital role of the parties in each chamber. Committee members are viewed as agents or instruments of their parties. Because they control appointment decisions, the parties have the capacity to shape the composition and policy outlook of their committee contingents. In addition, committees are dependent on party leaders for scheduling their legislation for floor consideration, giving party leaders an additional source of leverage within the committees. These ties create an implicit contract between the parties and their committee members that constrain committee behavior. As a result, the majority party has effective control over committee decisions. And because committee recommendations are constrained by the views of the majority party, committees lack autonomy.[4]

The *chamber-dominated*, or *informational*, *committees perspective* emphasizes the subordination of committees to their parent chambers. According to this view, committees are created to meet the needs of the chamber in its search for an effective division of labor in the development of expertise, the acquisition of information, and the organization of support staff. The charters of most committees are found in the rules of their parent chamber, which may abolish or restructure them at any time. Most important, committees must obtain majority support on the floor for their legislation and so must anticipate floor reactions to their recommendations. Rather than viewing committees as autonomous, this perspective considers committees to be highly constrained by chamber preferences. Committees are granted discretion only within narrow ranges of policy options and over legislative detail. This discretion may give committees leverage over individual noncommittee members, but it does not grant committees autonomy over matters of importance to chamber majorities.[5]

Each of these three perspectives on committee power has attractive features—both in actual practice and as scholarly models. In practice, a committee-dominated system allows Congress to manage a large workload by providing an effective division of labor that encourages the development of expertise among committee members. These members know their work will be respected and approved by others. As a model, it helps to explain many of the decentralized features of Congress that we commonly observe. In practice, a party-dominated system encourages the emergence of strong party leadership that can supervise the development of coherent, timely policy. This results in a high level of party accountability in congressional decision making. As a model, it helps to explain the growing strength and, in the House, the present-day dominance of the two congressional parties. Finally, in practice a chamber-dominated system preserves the equality of its members by sharing expertise widely and allowing all members a voice in important policy decisions. And as a model, it helps to explain why neither parties nor committees have absolute power and why policy decisions tend to represent centrist rather than extreme positions.

Taken to their logical extremes, these patterns would be catastrophic for effective policy making, and their associated models would perform poorly as explanations of committee politics. For example, if members were completely free to select their committee assignments some panels would be unmanageably large and others would be dangerously understaffed. Moreover, the legislative products they produced, when taken as a whole, would likely lack coherence. If, on the other hand, parties and chambers paid no heed to the assignment requests of members, they would lose the good will of those members by frustrating their career aspirations. If parties or chambers micromanaged the day-to-day affairs of the various committees, they would lose the efficiency gains achieved through delegation of authority and also undermine members' incentive for service on those panels. Finally, if parties or chambers routinely rejected the products that committees produced or altered them in ways totally contrary to committee intent, then the advantages of delegating authority to those panels would be lost.

None of these perspectives fully captures the nature of the relationships among committees, parties, and the parent chambers. Rather, each exaggerates the importance of certain features of congressional rules and practices. In fact, policy making through committees represents an admixture of these alternate models. For example, while self-selection and the property right norm are important to committee assignments, the parties do exercise great care in the appointment of members to certain committees. And while much legislation finds members quite indifferent and willing to defer to committee recommendations, there are key areas in which party leaders and the parent chambers show great interest and little deference. Finally, committees do make choices about what bills will look like, but in making those choices they also make calculations—however crude—about how their bills will be received on the floor. Most committee members want to deliver the goods—whether it be a project, contract, protection, or exemption. Thus, their efforts are geared toward meeting with success outside the committee on the chamber floor. In fact, we believe that the exercise of committee discretion, party influence, and chamber influence is visible in some degree on most major bills passed by Congress.

CONDITIONS SHAPING THE ROLE OF COMMITTEES

A fundamental issue of policy making is the degree to which the House and Senate rely upon committees, parties, and the floors of the parent chambers to make authoritative decisions for the institution. Because of our focus on the role of committees, we will view this issue as a question of the extent to which committee decisions are constrained or checked by the parties and parent chambers. Constraints on committee decisions are determined by the character of Congress's policy agenda, the distribution of policy preferences, and the institutional context. The effects of these factors can be summarized in several propositions.

THE POLICY AGENDA

The nature of the issues or policy problems that Congress faces affects how Congress makes decisions and the reliance it places on standing committees. In general, we argue that *the larger the agenda, the more separable the issues, the more frequently issues recur, and the less salient the issues, the more Congress relies on committees and the less it relies on parties or the parent chambers to make decisions.* Large agendas require a division of labor to handle the workload, and a system of powerful committees provides it. If the issues are not interconnected, then a system of committees handling mutually exclusive issues works well. Furthermore, if similar issues are raised frequently, then fixing committee jurisdictions can be done without concern that some committees will become superfluous, their members becoming inactive and powerless. Moreover, if issues concern only a few members, committees can make decisions without serious challenge on the floor. Conversely, more narrowly defined agendas, interrelated issues, rapidly changing policy problems, and widespread interest undermine committee autonomy and encourage active party and chamber involvement on most matters.

THE DISTRIBUTION OF POLICY PREFERENCES

When large numbers of members take an active interest in policy decisions, various alignments will shape the role of committees. The alignment of members is primarily a function of constituency preferences, although forces internal to Congress—the persuasiveness of a party leader, for example—can make a difference at times. Whatever the cause, *if the majority party is highly cohesive on the issues, and most issues are salient, then that party will be in a position to impose policy decisions by virtue of numbers, and a system of party-dominated committees will then develop.* If the majority party lacks sufficient cohesiveness, however, majority coalitions—perhaps different coalitions on different issues—may assert themselves on the floor and determine policy outcomes. That is, *when the majority party lacks cohesiveness, and most issues are salient, a system of chamber-dominated committees will develop.*

INSTITUTIONAL CONTEXT

Finally, the House and Senate are very different institutions. The root of much of this difference is size. The larger, more unwieldy House requires strong leadership and observance of formal rules. In the smaller, more manageable Senate, greater tolerance of individual initiative and resistance to committee- or party-imposed policy decisions is represented in rules that protect a senator's right to offer amendments on any subject and conduct extended debate—i.e., to *filibuster.* Such rules preserve the bargaining leverage that individual senators have when dealing with committee and party leaders. In general, *a chamber-dominated system will be more common in the Senate,* where floor procedures allow individual members to challenge committee and party actions more effectively. Therefore, *changes in policy agendas and political alignments that encourage committee-dominated or party-dominated decision making are not reflected as rapidly in the Senate as in the House.*

FORMS OF COMMITTEE POWER IN CONGRESS

An assessment of committee power in Congress must begin with an appreciation of the two principal forms of committee power, negative and positive.[6] Negative committee power is the ability to defend the status quo in the face of those who favor change. More bluntly, it is the power to do nothing. In the context of the committee–parent chamber relationship, negative power rests on a committee's ability to restrict the choices available to the chamber. In fact, the most common outcome for bills referred to a congressional committee is failure to report legislation to the floor—the exercise of negative power. Positive committee power is the ability to change policy in the face of those who would defend the status quo. In the committee–parent chamber relationship, positive power rests on the capacity of a committee to circumvent the floor or to convince some members to vote for the committee position contrary to their true policy preferences. The ability of committees to exercise each form of power rests, in part, on the rules and procedures of Congress, a subject we will return to later in this chapter. But it also involves other resources that committees can bring to bear in a legislative battle.

NEGATIVE POWER

Negative committee power has many sources in Congress. The most obvious is the ability to obstruct legislation by refusing to report it to the floor. This "gatekeeping" power is considerably stronger in the House than in the Senate. An 1880 House rule features strict language that compels the referral of legislation introduced in that chamber to the committee with appropriate jurisdiction.[7] This rule, in conjunction with written jurisdictions and permanent status, has long provided a foundation for House committee power by granting committees monopoly jurisdiction over designated policy areas (see Box 1-1). This foundation was weakened by a 1974 rule that allowed the referral of legislation to multiple committees. The Senate has adopted no similarly strict requirements. Senate standing committees are permanent with written jurisdictions; Senate rules simply give them "leave to report" bills and resolutions within that jurisdiction. By precedent, however, nearly all bills and resolutions introduced in the Senate are referred promptly and without quarrel to the committee with appropriate jurisdiction.

Committee gatekeeping power in the House is reinforced by a strict germaneness rule for floor amendments. There, though not in the Senate, floor amendments must be directly related to the provisions being amended. The rule makes it difficult to raise issues that are not addressed explicitly in a committee bill. In the Senate there is no limit on the content of amendments for most measures. As a result, senators may incorporate the text of whole bills as amendments to other bills. Indeed, relatively minor pieces of legislation may become the vehicles for the consideration and adoption of much more important legislation. In most situations, nongermane amendments may be prohibited only by unanimous consent.

Gatekeeping power in the House is not absolute. Mechanisms by which floor majorities may bring matters to the floor do exist. Examples are suspension of the rules, discharge petitions, and special rules. In addition, the House Rules Committee may report a resolution that, if adopted

Rules on Bill Referral

House Rule X, Paragraph 1

". . . all bills, resolutions, and other matters relating to subjects within the jurisdiction of any standing committee as listed in this clause shall . . . be referred to such committees. . . ."

Senate Rule XXV, Paragraph 1

"The following standing committees shall be appointed at the commencement of each Congress, and shall continue and have the power to act until their successors are appointed, with leave to report by bill or otherwise matters within their respective jurisdictions."

BOX 1-1

by majority vote, can discharge a measure from a committee and bring it to the floor for consideration. However, such mechanisms are difficult to employ without the support of the majority party's leadership.

Negative committee power is reinforced by other features of floor procedure. In both chambers, "depth" limitations reduce the number and degree of amendments to amendments that may be pending at one time, in the absence of a special rule or unanimous consent agreement that provides otherwise. In the House, measures are considered for amendment on a title by title or section by section basis. Sponsors may offer their amendments only when the appropriate section is debated, and only when they are germane to that section.

Committee bill managers—members who shepherd bills through the final stage of floor consideration—are allowed to offer amendments on behalf of their committee before other members are recognized. They are usually given precedence in offering second-degree amendments (amendments to amendments) as well. In combination, depth limitations and recognition privileges ensure that bill managers have an opportunity to offer alternatives to unfriendly amendments and thereby dilute their effects.[8]

Negative power is fortified by procedures of a more tactical nature, such as House special rules and Senate unanimous consent agreements. House special rules are resolutions from the Rules Committee that, if adopted by a majority vote, bring legislation to the floor and set limits on debate. Committees often seek and receive special rules that restrict amendments in some way. The Senate does not employ a similar proce-dure, although amendments and debate may be limited by unanimous consent. Because a single senator can prevent a unanimous consent request from being implemented, Senate committees are more vulnerable to unfriendly and unpredictable floor amendments.

Finally, domination of conference delegations by committee mem-bers reinforces a committee's ability to block unwanted outcomes or obtain acceptable compromises. This dominance coupled with the fact that conference reports cannot be amended on the floor leave committee members in a position to reverse decisions made in floor amendments, provided that the other chamber's conferees agree and that the final prod-uct is acceptable to House and Senate majorities. Such reversals may abate the damage done on the floor to a committee's original plan.[9]

Taken together, these elements of congressional procedure confer upon committees considerable negative power. Careful deployment of negative power gives committees important bargaining advantages that may be used to buy support for their legislation. In other words, negative power sometimes yields positive results. For example, a committee may threaten to block a measure important to a member if that member oppos-es another measure important to the committee. But there are practical limits on the ability of committees to translate negative power into posi-tive power in this way. Among other things, it might be expected that repeated hostage-taking strategies would produce a backlash, perhaps in the form of challenges to the procedures granting the negative powers in the first place.

POSITIVE POWER

Direct sources of positive committee power are few in Congress, at least relative to sources of negative power. Since early in the nineteenth centu-ry, committees have been able to report legislation at will.[10] With the exception of legislation having privileged status, however, the proposal power does not guarantee floor consideration of committee-reported mea-sures. Majority party leaders may refuse to schedule the legislation, and floor majorities may oppose motions to take up legislation. Even after a committee gets its bill to the floor, it must fend off unfriendly amend-ments and garner majority support. Avenues for circumventing the floor are very limited. Committee members sometimes manage to introduce new items at the conference stage, but even then a majority of both hous-es must approve the conference report.

To promote their legislative proposals successfully, committees often must employ extraprocedural resources, which can be substantial. First, committees sometimes gain tactical advantages over competitors because of their special role in gathering political and policy information. Committee members may selectively reveal that information to their chambers.[11] Committee leaders usually are better informed than their opponents about the politics and policy substance of issues within their committees' jurisdictions, which often allows them to make more persuasive arguments. Their informational advantage also may help them know where to expect support and opposition and the sources of unfriendly floor amendments. Second, committee staffs provide important support services, such as monitoring and anticipating actions on the floor, in the other chamber, and in conference; drafting defensive amendments strategically and rapidly; and soliciting the assistance of interest groups and others. And third, strong personal relationships between committee members and party leaders, other colleagues, and interested outsiders, developed during years of service in Congress, promote trust, garner support, and facilitate deal making.

Extraprocedural resources are important when there is some dissent from committee recommendations. Dissent means competition, and many committees' competitors have substantial political resources of their own. The president, party and faction leaders, and interest groups have access to large staffs, political and policy expertise, timely and relevant information, a network of political friends, and the ability to attract public attention, just as committee members do. These competitors can alter the policy preferences of members by changing the political costs and benefits of supporting committee recommendations. In the hunt for majority support in the House and Senate, committees sometimes find themselves outgunned by the opposition.

THE ULTIMATE WEAPON

Parent chambers retain the ultimate weapons against wayward committees: dissolution of their jurisdictions or their parliamentary privileges. All congressional committees are creations of their parent chambers and may be restructured or abolished by them. Committees are established and retained because they perform valued services for the chambers and individual members. In this light, committees are never truly autonomous decision-making units; rather, they must function in a procedural fashion and with a substantive effect generally consistent with the interests of their parent chambers. When the individual committees or the committee system as a whole become dysfunctional for a majority of members, chamber or party rules can be altered to remedy the situation.

In practice, committees wield great power, often somewhat independently of the preferences of their parent chambers. This is possible because threats to dismantle or reconstitute a committee usually are not

TABLE 1-1   Types of Congressional Committees

| Permanent? | *Legislative authority?* | |
	Yes	No
Yes	Standing committees, most subcommittees	Joint committees
No	Conference committees, ad hoc committees, some select committees	Most select committees, special committees, task forces

credible. A threat to strip a committee of jurisdiction normally is not taken seriously, if for no other reason than that it would set a precedent that members of other committees would not like to see repeated.[12] Alternative disciplinary tactics are often too unwieldy to be effective. A chamber could reduce a committee's budget, thereby diminishing its effectiveness, but such an action could limit the committee's ability to act in policy areas in which the committee and chamber are in full accord. The parties may strip individual members of their committee assignments in retribution for their activities and policy positions, but even this is not a practice that most members would like to make commonplace. In any event, a committee threatened by the parent chamber and parties could count on friends outside of Congress to come to its aid.

TYPES OF COMMITTEES

Throughout its history Congress has invented an array of committees—ad hoc, conference, select, special, standing, joint—and employed them for a variety of purposes. The House routinely uses a device called the Committee of the Whole to facilitate the process of considering legislation on the floor.[13] And both chambers have used what amount to committees under other names—task forces, for example. In fact, the formal names of committees often do not indicate the role they play. Two defining characteristics distinguish the basic types of committees: whether or not they have legislative authority (the right to receive and report measures) and whether or not they are permanent (existing from one congress to the next) (see Table 1-1).

In the modern Congress, committees have three primary powers: collecting information through hearings and investigations, drafting the actual language of bills and resolutions, and reporting legislation to their

Rule X: Establishment and Jurisdiction . . .

The Committees and Their Jurisdiction

1. There shall be in the House the following standing committees, each of which shall have the jurisdiction and related functions assigned to it by this clause and clauses 2, 3, and 4; and all bills, resolutions, and other matters relating to subjects within the jurisdiction of any standing committee as listed in this clause shall (in accordance with and subject to clause 5) be referred to such committee, as follows:

[The respective committees and their jurisdictions are provided for in subsequent paragraphs (a) Committee on Agriculture; (b) Committee on Appropriations; and so forth.]

(k) Committee on National Security.

(1) Ammunition depots; forts; arsenals; Army, Navy, and Air Force reservations and establishments.

(2) Common defense generally.

(3) Conservation, development, and use of naval petroleum and oil shale reserves.

(4) The Department of Defense generally, including the Departments of the Army, Navy, and Air Force generally.

(5) Interoceanic canals generally, including measures relating to the maintenance, operation, and administration of interoceanic canals.

(6) Merchant Marine Academy and State Maritime Academies.

BOX 1-2

parent chambers for consideration. All committees have the power to collect information. But some committees lack the formal authority to draft and report legislation to their parent chamber. Furthermore, not all committees are permanent. Standing committees carry over from one congress to the next by virtue of having been written into the rules of the House and Senate. These rules (see Box 1-2) name the committees, define their formal jurisdictions or responsibilities, establish procedures, and (in the Senate) prescribe their sizes. Nonstanding committees may carry over for more than one congress but, at least formally, cease to exist after a period of time specified by the parent chamber. The most important committees (and the primary focus of this book) are the standing committees and their subcommittees. These committees are both legislative and permanent, and they are the point of origin for most legislation.

... *Of Standing Committees*

(7) Military applications of nuclear energy.

(8) Tactical intelligence and intelligence related activities of the Department of Defense.

(9) National security aspects of merchant marine, including financial assistance for the construction and operation of vessels, the maintenance of the U.S. shipbuilding and ship repair industrial base, cabotage, cargo preference and merchant marine officers and seamen as these matters relate to national security.

(10) Pay, promotion, retirement, and other benefits and privileges of members of the armed forces.

(11) Scientific research and development in support of the armed services.

(12) Selective service.

(13) Size and composition of the Army, Navy, and Air Force.

(14) Soldiers' and sailors' homes.

(15) Strategic and critical materials necessary for the common defense.

In addition to its legislative jurisdiction under the preceding provisions of this paragraph (and its general oversight function under clause 2(b)(1)), the committee shall have special oversight function provided for in clause 3(a) with respect to international arms control and disarmament and military dependents education.

Source: Rules of the House of Representatives, United States House of Representatives, One Hundred and Fifth Congress, Robin H. Carle, Clerk of the House of Representatives, January 7, 1997.

Arguably the next most important committees are those that have legislative jurisdiction but lack permanent status. During the early congresses nearly all committees were of this type. After a bill or resolution had been debated, a small group of members was appointed as an ad hoc committee to draft final language and report back to the chamber. During most of its history Congress has not used ad hoc committees, instead preferring to create standing committees when new issues arose that required legislative action. In 1975, after an absence of nearly a hundred years, the House amended its rules to permit the Speaker, on his or her own initiative but subject to House approval, to create ad hoc or select committees. But they are rarely used.

Conference committees and (rarely) select committees also fall into the category of legislative, temporary committees. Conference committees

Creating Select Committees . . .

Rather than existing in the rules of the House or the Senate, special committees are formed by a simple resolution (or a concurrent resolution if they are bicameral). One of the most recent select committees to be established was the Senate Select Committee on the Whitewater Affair. Its purpose was to investigate a land deal in which President Bill Clinton and his wife Hillary had invested. The text of the resolution, adopted by a vote of 96 to 3 on May 17, 1995, opened as follows:

S. Res. 120

IN THE SENATE OF THE UNITED STATES

May 17 (legislative day, May 15), 1995

Mr. D'Amato (for himself and Mr. Dole) submitted the following resolution; which was considered and agreed to

RESOLUTION

Establishing a special committee administered by the Committee on Banking, Housing, and Urban Affairs to conduct an investigation involving Whitewater Development Corporation, Madison Guaranty Savings and Loan Association, Capital Management Services Inc., the Arkansas Development Finance Authority, and other related matters.

Resolved,

BOX 1-3

are appointed to resolve the differences between House and Senate versions of legislation. Because the Constitution in effect requires that the House and Senate pass identical legislation before a bill is sent to the president, conference committees are crucial to policy outcomes. (See Chapter 5 for further discussion of this role.) Within certain limits, these bicameral committees, composed of a delegation of senators and a delegation of representatives, have the power to consider, alter, and report legislation. Conference committees dissolve as soon as a chamber acts on the conference report.

Only four committees have permanent status but lack legislative authority. These are the four joint committees—Economic, Taxation, Library, and Printing—whose membership comprises both representatives

... *The Whitewater Affair*

SECTION 1. ESTABLISHMENT OF SPECIAL COMMITTEE.

(a) Establishment.—There is established a special committee administered by the Committee on Banking, Housing, and Urban Affairs to be known as the "Special Committee to Investigate Whitewater Development Corporation and Related Matters" (hereafter in this resolution referred to as the "special committee").

The balance of the resolution laid out a list of purposes. These sections authorized the special committee to investigate, hold public hearings, and study the conduct of White House officials, Justice Department officials, and Resolution Trust Corporation officials in the so-called "Whitewater Affair." The resolution further authorized the committee to investigate the "operations, solvency, and regulations of Madison Guaranty Savings and Loan Association . . . the activities, investments, and tax liability of Whitewater Development Corporation . . . [and] the policies and practices of the RTC and the Federal Banking agencies," as well as other matters.

The resolution authorizes committee members to hire staff and consultants, subpoena witnesses and evidence, grant immunity (subject to consultation with the special prosecutor), hold hearings, make a public report and recommendations to the Senate, spend up to $950,000 for the committee's activities, and "make every reasonable effort to complete, not later than February 1, 1996, the investigation, study, and hearings authorized by section 1." Finally, the resolution (Section 9 (b) (3)) provided: "After submission of its final report, the special committee shall promptly conclude its business and close out its affairs."

and senators, with the chairmanship rotating between members of the two chambers. The Joint Taxation and Joint Economic committees have some importance in policy making. As nonlegislative committees, their only "power" is their ability to analyze and publicize findings regarding current public policy issues. But Joint Taxation maintains a large expert staff that serves the two revenue committees—House Ways and Means and Senate Finance. And the Joint Economic Committee conducts hearings and studies on economic policy problems that often receive considerable attention. Library and Printing focus entirely on matters internal to Congress by overseeing, respectively, the Library of Congress and the Government Printing Office. In recent years, there have been proposals to drop some or all of these joint committees.

TABLE 1-2   Numerical Portrait of the Committee Systems of the 101st
(1989–1990) and 105th (1997–1998) Congresses

Types of committees	101st (1989–1990)		105th (1997–1998)	
	House	Senate	House	Senate
Standing committees	23	18	20	18
Subcommittees	139	86	86	68
Select committees	0	1	0	1
Special committees	4	1	0	1
Ad hoc committees	0	a	0	a
Joint committees	4		4	
Conference committees	93		58[b]	

[a] Senate rules do not permit ad hoc committees.

[b] Conference committees in the 104th Congress; final calendar for 105th Congress not available.

The final group of committees—typically designated select or special committees—is neither permanent nor legislative. Select and special committees are formed for a variety of purposes: to highlight important policy issues, to study or investigate pressing problems, to coordinate the development of policy that overlaps the jurisdictions of several standing committees, or simply as a reward from party leaders to members who have done them favors. Select committees have been used to examine and recommend reforms for the House and Senate. Two of these, the Bolling Committee and the Stevenson Committee, were instrumental in proposing House and Senate reforms during the 1970s. The best-known committees sometimes have been select committees. The Senate's Watergate Committee of 1973 (formally the Select Committee on Presidential Campaign Activities) and House and Senate select committees to investigate the Iran-contra affair are prominent examples. (See Box 1-3 for a more recent example.)

The names of committees can be misleading. For example, while the House and Senate Select Intelligence Committees at one time were neither permanent nor legislative, that is no longer true today. Both committees are now permanent and possess legislative authority. Interestingly, mention of the Senate Intelligence Committee cannot be found in the standing rules of that chamber; instead, it appears in the standing orders of that body. And while the House Intelligence Committee does factor in that chamber's rules, it appears off by itself in Rule 48 rather than with the other House committees in Rule 10. Pursuant to these standing orders and rules, both committees possess legislative and budget authority over various intelligence agencies—most notably the Central Intelligence

TABLE 1-3   Standing Committees of the 105th Congress (1997–1998)

Senate	House
Agriculture, Nutrition, and Forestry	Agriculture
Appropriations	Appropriations
Armed Services	National Security
Banking, Housing, and Urban Affairs	Banking and Financial Services
Budget	Budget
Commerce, Science, and Transportation	Commerce Science
Energy and Natural Resources	Resources
Environment and Public Works	Transportation and Infrastructure
Finance	Ways and Means
Foreign Relations	International Relations
Governmental Affairs	Government Reform and Oversight
Indian Affairs	
Judiciary	Judiciary
Labor and Human Resources	Education and the Workforce
Rules and Administration	Rules House Oversight Standards of Official Conduct[b]
Select Committee on Intelligence[a]	Select Committee on Intelligence[a]
Small Business	Small Business
Veterans' Affairs	Veterans' Affairs

Note: Senate committees are listed alphabetically; House committees are listed adjacent to corresponding Senate committee or Senate committee with encompassing jurisdiction.

[a] In spite of the Select in their names, the House and Senate Select Intelligence Committees are permanent and have legislative jurisdiction.

[b] The House Standards of Official Conduct Committee is permanent and has legislative jurisdiction. The Senate Ethics Committee does not have legislative jurisdiction and is therefore not included here.

Agency, the Defense Intelligence Agency, the National Security Agency, and some activities of the Federal Bureau of Investigation.

Subcommittees can also fall into each of these permanent/temporary, legislative/nonlegislative categories. Most of Congress's standing committees have created more or less permanent subcommittees.[14] And, for a time, the House Budget Committee had a set of standing nonlegislative subcommittees called task forces.[15] Conference committees provide a third variant on subcommittee categories: temporary, joint, legislative subcommittees. For example, recent congresses have seen conference committees formed to consider large, "temporary" appropriations measures (continuing resolutions) and other very large bills touching upon a wide variety of topics (omnibus bills). Some of these committees have been so large (as many as two hundred members) that they have broken up into numerous subcommittees for the sake of efficiency. Finally, committees have frequently created select or special subcommittees to study particular problems and report back to the full committees.[16]

Given the armada of committees existing in Congress at any given point in time (see Table 1-2), there is no feasible way to consider each type fully, let alone each committee at great length. Therefore, while we occasionally consider other committees, our primary focus here is upon those committees that share our two defining characteristics—permanence and legislative authority. A list of these panels appears in Table 1-3.

SOURCES OF COMMITTEE PROCEDURE AND STRUCTURE

The procedures and structural arrangements associated with the committee systems have varied a great deal during the two-hundred-year history of Congress. Indeed, they tend to change to some small degree at the beginning of each congress. Although more rare, dramatic change also has fundamentally altered the character of the two systems. Change may be achieved through a variety of mechanisms.

Article I, Section 5 of the Constitution states that "each house may determine the rules of its proceedings." As a result, House and Senate committees are principally, though not solely, the creatures of the separate sets of standing rules maintained by the two chambers—primarily Rules 10 and 11 in the House and Rules 24 to 28 in the Senate.[17] As we will see in the next two chapters, these rules frequently change from one congress to the next, respecifying committee size and occasionally altering jurisdictions or names. Such changes are driven by the majority party in the House and by bipartisan negotiations in the Senate. As it turns out, the two sets of rules are roughly parallel. Each prescribes about the same number of committees having similar jurisdictions and utilizing similar procedures. But nothing requires the House and Senate to adopt identical rules in creating and regulating their committee systems. In fact, House and Senate rules governing the committee systems have differed in important ways.

Chamber rules are not the only source of guidance for committee structure and procedures. Federal statutes, chamber party caucus rules, individual committees' written rules, and informal norms and folkways all help to define the House and Senate committee systems.

Statutes such as the Legislative Reorganization Acts of 1946 and 1970 have helped to shape the committee systems by creating new panels and legislative procedures. The two Small Business committees, the two Budget committees, the Senate Veterans' Affairs Committee, and all of the current joint committees were created by statute. Indeed, in retrospect we may well judge that the Budget and Impoundment Control Act of 1974, which created the two budget committees and is the source of much of the very complicated budget process now used by Congress, had a much bigger impact on Congress than any one or perhaps all of the other reforms enacted during the 1970s. This act, and follow-up reforms in the 1980s, fundamentally altered the relationship of the various committees of Congress (see Chapters 2 and 5).

While some party rules concern the organization of committees— limiting the number of House subcommittees, for example—their primary influence is procedural. These rules establish procedures for assigning members to committees, dictate how committee leaders are selected, limit the powers of full committee chairs, and, as in the case of House Democrats, even prescribe guidelines for the use of subcommittees. Party rules remain subordinate to the standing rules of the chamber and may not contradict them.

Individual committees also must adopt their own rules. These rules must be consistent with chamber rules, but they often go into greater detail about the chair's privileges and committee procedures. Meeting times, voting procedures, subpoena authority, referral of legislation to subcommittees, staff appointment procedures, and other topics are addressed in committee rules.

Finally, each chamber has evolved a set of recognizable, though unwritten, norms or folkways that constrain individual members' behavior and committees' performances.[18] The best known and most criticized of these was the traditional apprenticeship system prescribing that newer members be "seen but not heard" (see Chapter 2). A most conspicuous norm of the many not defined in formal rules is the use of seniority as the basis for selecting committee and subcommittee leaders.

These five sets of formal and informal rules—chamber rules, statutes, party rules, committee rules, and norms—have combined to define the

House and Senate committee systems. Change in any one of them can alter the function or power of committees. In the modern Congress, committees have considerable independence to conduct investigations, devise and revise legislation, and report recommended legislation to the floor. In fact, under current House and Senate rules, committees are obligated to survey policy developments and oversee the activities of executive and judicial agencies within their jurisdictions. Such independence has evolved over many decades. Yet policy-making autonomy is not guaranteed. The constitutional requirement that legislation be approved by a chamber majority binds committees to their parent chambers and parties. The extent to which chambers and parties have acted to limit the committees' exercise of policy-making discretion has varied greatly during the last two centuries. Committees acquired a remarkable degree of autonomy during the middle decades of this century, but that autonomy has been challenged in recent decades.

VARIATION AND CHANGE IN THE COMMITTEE SYSTEMS

Variation and change are conspicuous attributes of congressional committees. In the following chapters, we will see that the House and Senate committee systems differ in important ways, that there is substantial variation in the jurisdictions and roles of individual committees, and that the committee systems change constantly. When viewed in historical perspective, it also becomes clear that these internal changes are not simply the result of some inevitable bureaucratic process. To the contrary, it is important to recognize that events external to the institution, most particularly changes in partisanship and the policy agenda, play an important role in shaping committees. Although we will reach farther back from time to time, our primary concern is with variation among and changes in committees and the committee systems during the last three decades or so.

Many observers argued that the primary effect of changes made in the 1970s (changes detailed in Chapter 2) was to exacerbate the fragmented nature of congressional decision making. The increased number and independence of subcommittees caused the most stir, leading some observers to describe congressional decision making in the 1970s as "decentralized" and as "subcommittee government." Increasingly, it seemed, initial policy decisions were made within the subcommittees of Congress. Rather than complain about dictatorial full committee chairs, members came to decry the lack of "responsible leadership" and the presence of "runaway subcommittees." Decentralized decision making, critics charged, served to undermine further the efficiency and coherence of legislative policy making.

More recently, scholars and observers of Congress have remarked upon a trend toward recentralization (see Chapter 5). By the mid-1980s a more consolidated and interconnected policy agenda combined with more partisan political alignments to dramatically alter the context in which committees operated. The legislative workload contracted, core budget decisions constrained other policy decisions, and the parties were in a position to act more cohesively on key policy decisions. A process once dominated by fairly autonomous committees and relatively weak parties became a system of increasingly dependent committees and strong parties. Heightened partisanship, larger but fewer major pieces of legislation, the so-called "top down" budgeting process, expanded leadership powers, and more assertive leaders are all evidence of this trend in the postreform Congress.[19] In fact, today a debate has emerged as to whether committees have been too greatly compromised by overcentralization.

Whether centralized or decentralized, autonomous or dependent, past experience warns that it is unwise to render sweeping generalizations. The decline in committee power, for example, was greater in the House than in the Senate, where committees were less autonomous to begin with. But there is variation within each of the chambers as well. This is a central lesson of Richard Fenno's seminal work, *Congressmen in Committees*, a study of six House and six Senate committees in the 1960s.[20] Fenno discovered that committees differ in two vital ways: in the nature of their political environments, and in the personal goals of their members. Together, environments and members' goals shape relations among committee members, especially the formal and informal mechanisms devised for making committee decisions. As committee environments differ, so, too, do the demands placed on committee members. This relationship between environments and committee members is notable because it is the members' goals that dictate the nature of legislative products sought.

Not only do committees differ in important ways, as Fenno observed, but they also change in a variety of ways. Changes—particularly in policy agendas, membership composition, and committee members' attitudes and goals—may enhance, moderate, or even counteract the effects of formal alterations in committee structure and procedure. Taken together, this array of considerations means that patterns of centralization or decentralization among House and Senate committees may be quite varied.

NOTES

1. The alternative models parallel Fenno's scheme for characterizing the political environments of committees. See Richard F. Fenno, Jr., *Congressmen in*

Committees (Boston: Little, Brown, 1973), chap. 2. They also emphasize the locations in the legislative process that are central to the major styles of decision making noted by Smith. See Steven S. Smith, *Call to Order: Floor Politics in the House and Senate* (Washington, D.C.: Brookings Institution, 1989), chap. 1.

2. This literature is enormous and no lengthy genealogy is in order here. However, the roots of this perspective can be traced to Woodrow W. Wilson, before the turn of the century, to Oliver Garceau, E. Pendleton Herring, Peter Odegard, and E. E. Schattschneider before World War II, and to Grant McConnell and David B. Truman after World War II. The term is, of course, Theodore Lowi's. In the contemporary literature on Congress, Barry R. Weingast and William Marshall are perhaps most frequently associated with this position. See Weingast and Marshall, "The Industrial Organization of Congress, *Journal of Political Economy* 96 (February 1988): 132–163. In addition, see Kenneth A. Shepsle, "Institutional Equilibrium and Equilibrium Institutions," in *Political Science: The Science of Politics*, ed. Herbert Weisberg (New York: Agathon Press, 1986).

3. In the House, fixed, written jurisdictions and the 1880 rule change that required all legislation to be referred to the standing committee with appropriate jurisdiction would seem to be necessary, if not sufficient, conditions for such a model.

4. For further elaboration of a similar model, see D. Roderick Kiewiet and Mathew D. McCubbins, *The Logic of Delegation: Congressional Parties and the Appropriations Process* (Chicago: University of Chicago Press, 1991); and Gary W. Cox and Mathew D. McCubbins, *Parties and Committees in the U.S. House of Representatives* (Berkeley: University of California Press, 1993).

5. For further elaboration of a similar model, see Keith Krehbiel, *Information and Legislative Organization* (Ann Arbor: University of Michigan Press, 1991).

6. See Keith Krehbiel, "Spatial Models of Legislative Choice," *Legislative Studies Quarterly* 13 (August 1988): 259–319; and Smith, *Call to Order*, 168–196.

7. There is historical irony in this. Before 1880, and especially in the very early congresses, committees were the primary originators of most legislation. But this did not give them much power since they frequently had no choice but to report—favorably or not—to the floor. Following the 1880 rule, individual members formally gained a power they had been developing for some time, that of freely introducing legislation. The irony is that upon introduction they quickly lost control of their bills to the committee with appropriate jurisdiction. In 1880 House committees were guaranteed a first look at legislation in the House of Representatives. And that first look has more frequently than not also been the last for most bills and resolutions. On this important development see Joseph Cooper and Cheryl D. Young, "Bill Introduction in the Nineteenth Century: A Study of Institutional Change," *Legislative Studies Quarterly* 14 (February 1989): 67–105.

8. A formal treatment of these advantages in the House is provided in Barry R. Weingast, "Fighting Fire With Fire: Amending Activity and Institutional Change in the Post Reform Congress," in *The Postreform Congress*, ed. Roger H. Davidson (New York: St. Martin's Press, 1992), 142–168. Of course, second-degree amendments also may be employed by rank-and-file senators seeking to limit the options of others. If committee leaders do not anticipate such developments, they may discover that their opponents have gained a procedural edge.

9. The ex post veto, too, is an imperfect tool for committees. Its success is contingent on the willingness of the other chamber's conferees to agree to the change and of floor majorities in both chambers to support the conference report. The ex post veto can be undermined in a number of ways. For example, the floor may reject a conference report, send the report back to conference, reconstitute the conference delegation, bypass the conference through an exchange of amendments with the other chamber, discharge the conference, or use other means to limit the discretion of conferees. In addition, the preferences of the other chamber, its committee, and its conferees may severely restrict a chamber's conferees from repealing the decisions of its own floor. For background on the ex post veto, see Kenneth A. Shepsle and Barry R. Weingast, "The Institutional Foundations of Committee Power," *American Political Science Review* 81 (1987): 85–104; Keith Krehbiel, Kenneth A. Shepsle, and Barry R. Weingast, "Why Are Congressional Committees Powerful?" *American Political Science Review* 81 (1987): 929–945; and Steven S. Smith, "An Essay on Sequence, Position, Goals, and Committee Power," *Legislative Studies Quarterly* 13 (1988): 151–176.

10. For a formal treatment of the proposal power, see David P. Baron and John A. Ferejohn, "Bargaining in Legislatures," *American Political Science Review* 83 (1989): 1181–1206.

11. For a discussion of the long-appreciated importance of information advantages, see David Austen-Smith and William H. Riker, "Asymmetric Information and the Coherence of Legislation," *American Political Science Review* 81 (1987): 897–918.

12. In the 100th Congress, the Senate Budget Committee's charter was under serious threat. Many senators believed the committee should be supplanted by a committee composed of the leaders of the other standing committees. At least one candidate for majority leader supported the proposal. See David Rapp, "Budget Breaks Up in Acrimony," *Congressional Quarterly Weekly Report*, April 30, 1988, 1165–1166. For additional discussion of why changing jurisdictions may be difficult, see Melissa P. Collie and Joseph Cooper, "Multiple Referral and the 'New' Committee System in the House of Representatives," in *Congress Reconsidered*, 4th ed., ed. Lawrence C. Dodd and Bruce I. Oppenheimer (Washington, D.C.: CQ Press, 1989), 253–259.

13. The Committee of the Whole House on the State of the Union (and its counterpart, simply the Committee of the Whole, which handles private bills) operates under a reduced quorum and, through a series of other procedural devices, makes handling and especially amending bills much easier. The device can only be used for bills that have been through committee. For additional details on this procedural device see Walter J. Oleszek, *Congressional Procedures and the Policy Process*, 4th ed. (Washington, D.C.: CQ Press, 1995).

14. The current exceptions are the ethics committees in the two chambers and the Senate Budget and Select Intelligence committees.

15. While this was not the only time task forces had been used in this particular fashion, they were the only ones in persistent use in recent congresses. During the 99th Congress, for example, the House Administration Committee had a Task Force on Libraries and Memorials. It became a standing, presumably legislative, subcommittee in the 100th Congress.

16. None currently exist. The House Committee on Education and Labor (now called Education and the Workforce) long had a subcommittee called Select

Education that had legislative jurisdiction for miscellaneous educational issues.

17. House and Senate rules are actually rendered more formally with Roman numerals, but we have generally used Arabic numbers here for ease of reading. Committees are of sufficient importance in the House and Senate to be the subject of roughly one-third and two-thirds, respectively, of the total language in each chamber's rules. A tabulation of conference/caucus rules in the two chambers would show a similar pattern.

18. On the development of legislative norms in the Senate and House, respectively, see Donald R. Matthews, *U.S. Senators and Their World* (Chapel Hill: University of North Carolina Press, 1960); and Herbert B. Asher, "The Learning of Legislative Norms," *American Political Science Review* 67 (June 1973): 499–513.

19. See Davidson, *The Postreform Congress*.

20. Fenno, *Congressmen in Committees*. See also George Goodwin, Jr., *The Little Legislatures* (Amherst: University of Massachusetts Press, 1970).

CHAPTER 2

Evolution and Change in Committees

Between 1774 and 1788, the Continental Congress of the United States created more than 3,200 committees to aid in the transaction of its legislative business and run the affairs of government.[1] Since that time additional thousands of committees, subcommittees, joint committees, and other panels have come and gone. Even before the first American political parties had emerged, Congress was organizing its activity and augmenting its sometimes rudimentary structure by the addition of numerous subunits. From the Revolutionary War Claims Committee to Veterans' Affairs, from Levees and Improvements on the Mississippi River through Pacific Railroads to Aeronautics and Astronautics, the development of committees reflects our own national development.

In this chapter we address evolution and change in Congress's committee systems, examining how members, the parties and their leaders, and the chambers as collective decision-making bodies have benefited from and shaped the use of committees. Since they preceded party development, how did parties and party leaders cope with this rival source of power? As member service developed from brief tenures to long careers, what changes in the committee systems occurred to match this rise in ambition? As committees gained resources and informational advantages relative to party leaders and chamber colleagues, how much independence did they acquire and under what conditions? And, finally, to what extent have external political events shaped the use and evolution of committees?

An appreciation of committee history is vital to placing the current committee systems in proper context. Not only does an historical review illuminate the power and complexity of the modern committee systems, it also demonstrates how malleable legislative processes are in Congress. While past organizational decisions always influence future directions, Congress has shown a remarkable capacity to alter its decision-making processes in response to changing demands from its members and its political environment.[2] This chapter provides a basis for understanding how and when committees were established as independent agents within the House and the Senate and then traces the struggle within each chamber for, *and against,* committee autonomy.

While it is beyond the scope of the present text to document that history in detail, the student of committees should be aware of certain key developments and milestones in the establishment of the contemporary committee systems.[3] For this purpose, the history of Congress's committee systems can be divided, somewhat arbitrarily, into seven periods. The first four of these periods—Origins (1789–1810), Institutionalization (1811–1865), Expansion (1866–1918), and Consolidation (1919–1946) —saw the establishment of the modern committee systems; they are characterized briefly here. Each of the post–World War II periods—Committee Government (1947–1964), Reform (1965–1980), and Postreform (1981–1994)—and the most recent Republican reforms are considered at greater length. During each of these periods, important changes in the number and character of standing committees in the two chambers can be identified. The years that make up these seven periods are demarcated in Figure 2-1, which traces the number of standing, full committees throughout Congress's history. The essential features of the first five periods are summarized in Box 2-1, those of the reform period in Box 2-2, and those of the postreform period in Box 2-3.

DEVELOPMENT OF THE MODERN COMMITTEE SYSTEMS

Although Congress has made use of committees in a variety of shapes and sizes since its first session in 1789,[4] committees were not fully modernized until just before World War II. The modern committee systems took more than 130 years to become fully established. During that time committees grew in size and number and varied in the degree of power they held. Standing committees were used infrequently during the first period, that of the earliest congresses. Instead, fearing the prospect of independently powerful subgroups, carefully instructed select committees became the norm. These small groups, usually comprised of a bill's supporters,[5] ceased to exist once they reported back to their parent chambers. During the second period, the five decades preceding the Civil War, both chambers established a set of standing committees. Although seniority had yet to emerge and committees still lacked the privileged power to report bills to the parent chamber, relatively stable and identifiable jurisdictions had been established and continued from congress to congress. It is during this period that the roots of committee independence were put into place within each chamber.

From the end of the Civil War until 1918 standing committees proliferated in both chambers. During this time, partisan structures matured

FIGURE 2-1   Number of Congressional Standing Committees: 1789–1997

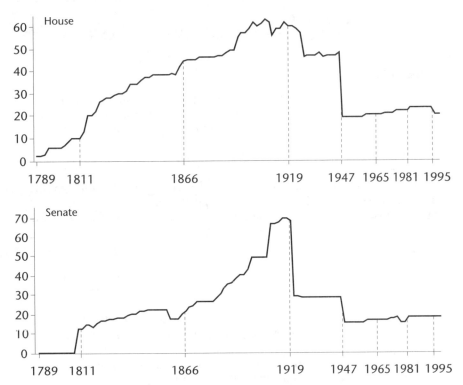

Sources: *The Congressional Directory;* Lauros G. McConachie, *Congressional Committees* (New York: Thomas Y. Crowell, 1898); *Annals of Congress; Register of Debates in Congress; Congressional Globe; Journal of the House; Journal of the Senate;* the *Congressional Record.*

Note: Graph smoothed between major points of change.

and the majority party became the dominant organizational element in each chamber—a circumstance that challenged committee autonomy. At the same time, members in both chambers became more likely to hold seats on committees from one congress to the next—the beginning of the so-called *property right* norm.[6] Another important change saw legislation from major House committees—starting with Appropriations and Ways and Means as early as 1865 but extended to other committees after 1880—given privileged access to the floor. Taken together these developments served to create tension between members and committee leaders on the one hand, who wished to see their independence enhanced, and party leaders on the other, who saw independent committees as a threat to party control. Also during this period the Rules Committee established

Congressional Committee Systems . . .

Origins: 1789–1810

- The House generally acts first in presenting legislation. Most important policy matters are initially examined in the Committee of the Whole, a parliamentary device that facilitates discussion through a committee of all members.
- Both House and Senate use select (or temporary) committees to fashion legislation once it has been debated on the floor.
- Early committees are chosen by chamber majorities, although the House moves quickly to committee appointment by the Speaker.
- The House and Senate create their first standing committees to handle recurrent policy or housekeeping matters.

Institutionalization: 1811–1865

- Both chambers abandon the use of select committees and establish permanent or standing committees. By 1860 there are 39 in the House and 22 in the Senate.
- Referral of legislation to Committee of the Whole is abandoned and committees are permitted to report legislation to the floor without prior approval.
- Most House committees are appointed by the Speaker, who uses the power to bolster the influence of that position.
- Committee chairs begin to emerge as institutional leaders with considerable influence on the content of legislation within their control.
- Clerks and offices are approved annually, and without controversy, for most committees.

Expansion: 1866–1918

- Number of committees expands to reflect changing political, economic, and social environment. By 1918 there are nearly 60 House and 74 Senate committees.
- Legislatively active committees, particularly those with appropriations responsibilities, begin to form subcommittees.
- The House Rules Committee becomes a tool of the leadership, chaired by the Speaker, with the power to pass "special orders" that determine floor agenda and conditions for consideration of specific bills.
- The seniority principle, which awards leadership posts to committee members with the longest continuous service, becomes widely followed in both the House and the Senate. Both parties establish a Committee on Committees to handle new committee assignments.

BOX 2-1

. . . Evolution and Change

- In 1910 a revolt in the House against Speaker Joseph G. Cannon solidifies the seniority "rule," limits the Speaker's power, and cements the power of full committee chairs within their own panels.

Consolidation: 1919–1946

- The House and Senate reduce the number of standing committees by eliminating many idle panels and incorporating other, more active groups into subcommittees within larger, full committees.
- The House and Senate Appropriations committees regain authority for all spending bills; one subcommittee for each of the annual appropriations bills is created.
- Committee leaders gain increased independence and influence even as formal party leadership structures are created; party leaders are denied committee leadership positions.
- In the House, the Appropriations, Rules, and Ways and Means committees become exclusive assignments for their members.
- Passage of the New Deal programs and World War II greatly enlarge the size and scope of government. Expansion of the authorization, appropriation, and oversight roles of Congress's committees is marked.

Committee Government: 1947–1964

- The Legislative Reorganization Act of 1946 reduces the number of committees to 19 in the House and 15 in the Senate.
- Committee staff and office space are provided on a permanent basis and committees are charged to exercise "continuous watchfulness" over the implementation of laws by the executive branch.
- Along with adherence to seniority, House and Senate committees develop the norms of apprenticeship and specialization to guide the participation of new and continuing members.
- Committee chairs gain effective control over their panels' agendas, structure, procedures, and policy outputs.
- With the number of full committees effectively capped, the number of subcommittees expands in both chambers to more than 100 in the House and more than 80 in the Senate.
- Virtually all legislation is now a committee product and committees have fully developed negative powers to bottle up any unwanted bills.

its critical agenda-making role. Prior to this point, committee bills, if they were not privileged, could only be considered in turn as they appeared at the top of the various House calendars. But the Rules Committee, then chaired by the Speaker, established the practice of passing special rules that, on a bill-by-bill basis, permitted the Speaker to move legislation directly to the floor. Thus, the Rules Committee took up a critical institutional role and came to be seen as an arm of the leadership.

Early in this century a revolt against Speaker Joseph Cannon of Illinois sharply reduced the Speaker's control over House committees and limited the concentration of power among top party leaders. This was done by denying the Speaker his position on the Rules Committee and, later, by denying the majority leader the chair of the Ways and Means Committee. The aftermath of that revolt, an era of consolidation, constitutes the fourth period, which lasted through the second world war. Most scholars and observers agree that the modern Congress was established by the second decade of this century.[7] By that time, 1922 to be precise, both chambers had stable standing committee systems, identifiable leadership structures, reasonably well established party organizations, an articulated fiscal policy-making system, recognized and accepted rules of floor procedure, and a budding infrastructure of professional and administrative staff. Likewise, the characteristics of the committee structure that emerged during that crucial period reflect, in most important respects, the committee system we have today. These characteristics include

- an internal structure with identifiable subcommittees;
- rule-determined jurisdictions that remain stable from congress to congress;
- legislative authority;
- fixed modes of member appointment;
- established leadership positions and methods of recruitment; and
- logistical support and resources necessary to do their jobs.

The Congress that emerged between 1910 and 1922 looked very much like the Congress we see today.

COMMITTEE GOVERNMENT: 1947–1964

Although Woodrow Wilson described Congress as "government by standing committee" back at the turn of the century, most observers agree that that description more accurately portrays the two decades that immediately followed World War II.[8] The period commenced with a landmark effort, the first Joint Committee on the Organization of Congress, to modernize and ready the Congress (and many other aspects of government)

FIGURE 2-2   Number of Congressional Standing Subcommittees: 1945–1997

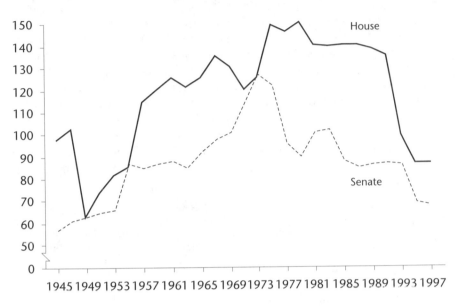

Source: U.S. Congress, Joint Committee on the Organization of Congress, *Background Materials,* 103d Cong. 1st sess. S. Prt. 103-55, 474–477; updated by the authors.

for the postwar era and passage of the Legislative Reorganization Act of 1946—also known as the LaFollette-Monroney Act.[9] Among other things, the act greatly reduced the number of standing committees, codified committee jurisdictions, provided each committee permanent (or statutory) staff, and consolidated Congress's oversight powers within the respective committees. The two chambers interpreted the law in a fashion to suit them, of course, by adding additional temporary staff, creating numerous subcommittees (see Figure 2-2), and allowing aggressive committees to expand their jurisdictions on an incremental basis. In concert, these changes helped committees gain a decisive informational edge over the parties and the rank-and-file members in the two chambers, and thus prompted a marked increase in the independence of committees. By themselves, however, these changes cannot explain why committees achieved the status and power they did during this era.[10]

    In addition, one must look to the institutionalization of certain norms—seniority, apprenticeship, and reciprocity—and to the voting coalitions, particularly the conservative coalition, that solidified in Congress during this period as sources for committee power.[11] Conservative southern Democrats held a disproportionate number of committee chairs during this era—a benefit bestowed by the *seniority* system. Less senior members, who were disproportionately northern and more liberal, were admonished to enter into a period of *apprenticeship* when it was best to be seen but not heard. Internal divisions within the Democratic party placed roadblocks on the liberal wing's desire to pass legislation and allowed the conservative wing to exploit its negative powers to halt legislation in committee. Thus, a relatively stable membership and nearly uninterrupted Democratic control reinforced committee power during this period. But as the liberal wing of the Democratic party slowly expanded, pressures for change began to build within the institution.

Committee chairs became a primary—though not the only—target for change. Why? Consider their power, as neatly summarized by George Galloway in 1953:

> Just as the standing committees control legislative action, so the chairmen are masters of their committees. . . . They arrange the agenda of the committees, appoint the subcommittees, and refer bills to them. They decide what pending measures shall be considered and when, call committee meetings, and decide whether or not to hold hearings and when. They approve the lists of scheduled witnesses and authorize staff studies, and preside at committee meetings. They handle reported bills on the floor and participate as principal managers in conference committees. They are in a position to expedite measures they favor and to retard or pigeon-hole those they dislike.[12]

This panoply of procedural authority ensured that committee chairs could maintain the upper hand in most disputes, but it did not make them absolute tyrants. Committee chairs of the era frequently were aggressive, colorful, and vain. Occasionally, they were unprincipled. But they always were highly goal-oriented.

Rep. Howard W. "Judge" Smith, Democratic chair of the House Rules Committee from 1955 until 1967, was among the most notorious of the independent committee "barons" of this era. Smith, who represented the same Virginia district that James Madison represented in the First Congress, was an undisputed leader of conservative southern Democrats who opposed, among other things liberal, virtually all civil rights legislation. The bespectacled Smith was not physically imposing. Rep. Richard Bolling, a Democrat from Missouri who would later chair the Rules Committee, described Smith as "[a] lean and stooped figure with a long and mournful face."[13] Smith never established a fixed meeting day for his Rules Committee, even though House rules prescribed the practice. He was known to go on "fishing trips" or disappear to tend to "barn fires" at his Fauquier County farm when important matters he opposed were up for consideration on the committee. Smith ruthlessly used the power of his committee to negotiate changes in legislation. He scheduled, or failed to schedule, committee meetings to shape legislation and the legislative agenda and served as a principal roadblock to civil rights legislation by becoming an independent center of power in the House of the late 1950s. Although Democratic House Speaker Sam Rayburn of Texas and President John F. Kennedy succeeded in gaining passage of a rule to expand the size of the committee in 1961, Smith continued to shape the legislative agenda until he was defeated in a primary in the fall of 1966.[14]

Smith was not the only committee baron to appear during this period. But he was emblematic of a particular species of chair that thrived during this era. And yet, for all their color, the "old bulls" as they are sometimes called should not be deified too hastily.[15] Their power was certainly real; their high-handedness was no myth. But they were not invincible. Most committee chairs ruled by active participation, skillful compromise, and judicious use of their procedural powers. Most had bipartisan majority support within their committees. And many had close working relationships with their minority counterpart on the committee. In the end, no chair could long resist overwhelming opposition. The fact is, during most of this period few chairs faced such opposition—a circumstance that changed as the middle 1960s approached.

REFORM: 1965–1980

By the late 1960s, members of Congress had begun to make concerted demands for major congressional reform. These demands were especially strong among junior members and some longstanding liberal Democrats who found their efforts to shape public policy stymied by their more conservative senior colleagues. The "reapportionment revolution," induced by the Supreme Court's one-person-one-vote ruling, began a wholesale shift to urban- and suburban-dominated congressional districts. These members, and the outsiders whose causes they supported, were concerned about issues that were not receiving active committee consideration and did not fall easily into existing committee jurisdictions. A nascent environmental movement, opposition to the Vietnam conflict, and a continuing interest in civil rights legislation placed new challenges before congressional committees. These Democrats, with the occasional support of their party leaders and minority Republicans, sought to improve their participation in congressional decision making by wholesale restructuring of legislative structures and procedures.

From the mid-1960s to the early 1970s, more than a half dozen reform missions were mounted in the House and Senate (see Table 2-1). The efforts of five of these—two bicameral committees, two bipartisan intrachamber committees, and one party caucus committee—are worthy

TABLE 2-1 Major Reform and Study Efforts, House and Senate (1965–1996)

House	Joint	Senate
Democratic Caucus Committee on Organization, Study, and Review (Hansen Committee) March 1970–October 8, 1974	Joint Committee on the Organization of Congress March 11, 1965–July 21, 1966[a]	Commission on the Operation of the Senate (Culver Commission) July 29, 1975–December 31, 1976
Select Committee on Committees (Bolling Committee) January 31, 1973–October 8, 1974	Joint Study Committee on Budget Control October 27, 1972–April 18, 1973	Temporary Select Committee to Study the Senate Committee System (Stevenson Committee) March 31, 1976–February 4, 1977
Commission on Administrative Review (Obey Commission) July 1, 1976–October 12, 1977	Joint Committee on the Organization of Congress (Boren–Hamilton Committee) August 6, 1992–December 17, 1993	The Study Group on Senate Practices and Procedures (Pearson-Ribicoff Group) May 11, 1982–April 5, 1983
Select Committee on Committees (Patterson Committee) March 20, 1979–April 30, 1980		Temporary Select Committee to Study the Senate Committee System (Quayle Committee) June 6, 1984–December 14, 1984

[a] Senate members of the Joint Committee continued their work as an intrachamber committee and filed an additional report on September 21, 1966.

of more detailed examination because they produced the most important committee reforms of the period.

THE LEGISLATIVE REORGANIZATION ACT OF 1970

The first major reform endeavor of the 1960s was designed to emulate the efforts that had resulted in the Legislative Reorganization Act of 1946.[16] The reformers' first strategy was to make a broad direct assault on congressional organization and procedure. On March 11, 1965, the second Joint Committee on the Organization of Congress was created to take a wide-ranging look at organizational reform. Among the major topics for study were committee procedures and organization, committee staff, legislative research support, floor procedures, lobbying regulations, fiscal controls and procedures, and the role of political parties.[17]

In its final report, based on lengthy hearings during the 1965 session, the Joint Committee made reform recommendations in every area except the role of political parties. Despite quick Senate action, the Joint Committee's final recommendations took five years to be signed into law. The objections of powerful House interests to several proposed reforms were responsible for this delay. When finally enacted into law, the Legislative Reorganization Act of 1970 contained none of the provisions recommended by the Joint Committee regarding seniority, electronic voting, or lobby reform, but did include a series of procedural reforms. Among other things, the act required committees to make public all recorded votes, limited the use of proxy votes, allowed a majority of members to call meetings, and encouraged committees to hold open hearings and meetings. Floor procedure was affected, too—primarily by permitting *recorded teller votes* (a voting procedure where members file past "tellers" who record their votes for or against a pending question) during the amending process and by authorizing (rather than requiring) the use of electronic voting.[18]

The Legislative Reorganization Act of 1970, despite its somewhat limited effects, remains an important milestone in legislative reformers' efforts. It marks the end of an era when powerful committee chairs and other senior members could forestall structural and procedural changes that appeared to undermine their authority. And it marked the beginning of nearly a decade of continuous reform in Congress, providing the opening wedge for further committee change.

HOUSE REFORMS: THE HANSEN AND BOLLING COMMITTEES (1970–1974)

The Legislative Reorganization Act of 1970 contained important lessons for members interested in reform. It demonstrated clearly that most of the

Major House Committee . . .

Committee reforms of the 1970s occurred incrementally, with some later reforms extending or amending changes adopted earlier in the period. The first two sets of changes noted here (Hansen I and II) were the product of the Hansen Committee and were changes to the Democratic Caucus rules. Hansen III was also the work of that panel, but became a substitute for House rule changes proposed by the Bolling Committee. Caucus IV was another set of Democratic Caucus rule changes. Though not listed here, changes adopted by the Republican Conference mirrored (and frequently preceded) those of the Democrats.

Hansen I (1971)

- Democrats limit their members to holding one legislative subcommittee chair.
- Subcommittee chairs are allowed to select one professional staff member for their respective subcommittees.
- The system for electing full committee chairs and committee members is altered so that nominations are presented one committee at a time.
- A request by ten or more members initiates debate, a separate vote, and, in the event of a defeat, a new nomination by the Committee on Committees for each chair nominated.

Hansen II (1973)

- Automatic votes on committee chairs are permitted, with a secret ballot to be provided on the demand of 20 percent of the caucus.
- The Democratic Committee on Committees (formerly comprised solely of Democratic members of the Ways and Means Committee) is expanded to include the Speaker (who now chairs the group), the majority leader, and the caucus chair.

BOX 2-2

reforms desired in each chamber were fundamentally different. In fact, the Senate simply was not experiencing the same level of pressure for reform as the House. Therefore, the earlier bicameral efforts gave way to intrachamber reform movements in the House. Another half-decade would elapse before serious Senate reforms would be attempted.

House reformers' strategies targeted committees and the power of committee chairs. As noted in Chapter 1, committee structures and procedures are the result of two sets of rules: the standing rules of the parent

. . . Reforms of the 1970s

- A twenty-three-member Steering and Policy Committee is created within the caucus.
- Procedures are adopted allowing the caucus to demand more open rules for floor deliberations.
- The "Subcommittee Bill of Rights" is adopted. Reforms include guaranteed referral of legislation, "bidding" for subcommittee seats, and fixed jurisdictions for subcommittees.

Hansen III (Bolling substitute) (1974)

- No committees are eliminated; Small Business is given standing status.
- Multiple referral and early organization are retained from the Bolling plan.
- Committees over fifteen members are to establish at least four subcommittees.
- Committee staff sizes are increased.
- One-third of House committee staffs are guaranteed to the minority.
- Proxy voting is banned in committee.

Caucus IV (1974)

- Ways and Means Democrats are stripped of role as Committee on Committees.
- The Ways and Means Committee is expanded from twenty-five to thirty-seven.
- Appropriations Committee subcommittee chairs are elected by caucus.
- Speaker nominates Democratic members of the Rules Committee.

chamber and those of the two party caucuses. House standing rules focus on the jurisdictions and formal legislative authority of each panel. But they are generally silent regarding the selection and powers of committee leaders and members. Instead, these requirements are written into the caucus (or conference) rules of the two parties. As a result, House reforms of this period were developed by two separate but closely linked efforts.

Within the Democratic party caucus, reform efforts were spearheaded by the Committee on Organization, Study, and Review, an eleven-member group chaired by Julia Butler Hansen of Washington (hence, the Hansen Committee). This committee was first authorized by the Democratic Caucus in March 1970 and produced substantial reform packages that were passed by the Caucus in January 1971 and again in early 1973.[19] Not least among these changes, which were designed to enhance the influence of party leaders and link committee leaders more tightly to the Caucus, were rules that forced each committee chair to face the party Caucus for election by a secret ballot. (See Box 2-2 for a summary of the major committee reforms.)

The initial successes of the Hansen Committee coincided with a bipartisan leadership effort to create a House select committee to study the basic structure of the chamber's committee system. This bipartisan committee, the House Select Committee on Committees, was chaired by Democrat Richard Bolling of Missouri.[20] The committee's proposals ignited a firestorm of opposition because they threatened to alter fundamentally a pattern of committee jurisdictions that had developed over decades.[21] Much to the committee's dismay, these proposals were referred by the Democratic Caucus to a hastily resuscitated Hansen Committee for review. It was the Hansen Committee's substitute reform package, stripped of all but minor jurisdictional tinkering, that ultimately passed the House in October 1974.[22] The Caucus also adopted further substantial changes to its own rules during the party organizing caucus of December 1974. And in a *coup de grace,* the Caucus, bolstered by seventy-five "Watergate babies" elected in 1974, exploited its new rules to depose the senior committee chairs of the Agriculture, Armed Services, and Banking committees—W. R. Poage (D-Texas), F. Edward Hébert (D-La.), and Wright Patman (D-Texas), respectively.[23]

By 1975 the House committee system and the means by which the ruling Democrats organized and operated that system had been altered dramatically. Committee jurisdictions were redrawn in minor ways. Party leaders had new authority to refer legislation to more than one committee—a change that more aggressive leaders would use as leverage on committees in the 1980s. Democrats on the House Ways and Means Committee no longer comprised their party's Committee on Committees. Members faced strict limits on the number of committee and subcommittee chairs they could hold. Subcommittees were bolstered by the "subcommittee bill of rights."[24] And rules and procedures for selecting committee and subcommittee chairs—dramatically exploited in the dismissal of Poage, Patman, and Hébert—forced these individuals to be more responsive to their colleagues.

Reform efforts did not cease, but a watershed period for reform had drawn to a close. In 1977 the House Commission on Administrative Review (the Obey Commission, named after Democrat David R. Obey of

Wisconsin) produced a report recommending a wide range of procedural innovations and further investigation of the committee system. The report was rejected by the House on a procedural vote. And in 1979 a new Select Committee on Committees (the Patterson Committee, named after California Democrat Jerry Patterson) was formed and given a year to renew the study of the committee system.

The House was clearly in no mood for more reform. It rejected the Patterson Committee's proposal to consolidate energy jurisdiction into a single House committee and opted instead simply to rename the powerful Interstate and Foreign Commerce Committee the Energy and Commerce Committee. No jurisdiction was taken from other House committees that considered energy issues, but the House rules were changed to give the "new" Energy Committee a general oversight jurisdictional grant over energy problems.

Finally, it must be noted that the successive waves of reform that flowed over the House substantially increased the power of Democratic leaders. The resuscitated Steering and Policy Committee placed the Speaker, acting also as Democratic party leader, at the vortex of party politics and organization. Such influence in committee assignments had not been seen since that power was handed to the Democratic floor leader (then chair of the Ways and Means Committee) in 1911. Add to this the power to appoint Democratic members of the Rules Committee, to refer bills to multiple committees, to create ad hoc committees, and to appoint additional staff to the Steering and Policy Committee, and, at least on paper, the leader rivaled anything seen in the House since 1910. But these were not unalloyed advantages. Substantial power had also been handed to the middle managers of the House—the subcommittee chairs. And this would act as a brake on leadership power and influence. Nonetheless, these powers would prove important during the next two decades as committees, parties, and chambers continued to compete with one another.

THE CONGRESSIONAL BUDGET AND IMPOUNDMENT CONTROL ACT OF 1974

In 1972, after nearly a decade of inter- and intrabranch wrangling over budget formulation, fiscal policy making, and executive impoundment of funds, Congress created a joint committee to study new budget mechanisms and procedures. Members of the Joint Study Committee on Budget Control were drawn almost entirely (28 of 32 members) from the House and Senate Appropriations committees, the House Ways and Means Committee, and the Senate Finance Committee.[25] Budget reform legislation was referred to the House Rules Committee and (sequentially) to the Senate Government Operations and Rules and Administration committees.

These committees approved budget reform measures in late 1973 and early 1974 that subsequently were passed by both chambers. After further changes were made in the House/Senate conference, the bill was signed into law on July 12, 1974, less than two years after the first serious calls for reform.

The budget process created by the 1974 act was added to the existing committee structure, providing new mechanisms for integrating the work of appropriations, revenue, and authorization committees and producing a congressional budget for each fiscal year. House and Senate Budget committees were created, an analytical staff (the Congressional Budget Office) was established, and a timetable was fixed for constructing a budget for each fiscal year. Each year two budget resolutions, required by the act, would set spending targets in broad programmatic categories, set total revenues, and stipulate the deficit (or surplus) and total federal debt. The first resolution, to be adopted in May, was intended to provide guidelines for money committees during the summer months. The second resolution, to be adopted in September, would be binding. A *reconciliation* process was created to settle any differences between the fiscal decisions of the summer months and the second budget resolution before the start of the fiscal year on October 1. In addition, the reform included a procedure for congressional review and a veto of presidential *deferrals* (delays) or *rescissions* (cancellations) of appropriated funds—making presidential impoundment of funds more difficult.

By virtually all accounts, the Budget Act was one of the most important congressional initiatives of the post–World War II period. Its effect on the relations among the budget, authorizations, revenue, and appropriations committees has been substantial. The appropriations committees' decade-long shift from "guardians" of the federal purse to "claimants" of the purse was cemented. Budget constraints and the new time limits partially reoriented authorizing committees toward greater oversight. And economic conditions and changes in the budget process forced the revenue committees into a much more active role in tax policy. These changes often strained relations among committees. Properly managed, though, the new budget process held out the possibility of much more coherent and centralized fiscal policy making. But this would be achieved only through significant alterations in committee relationships.

SENATE REFORMS: THE STEVENSON COMMITTEE (1977)

For most of this period, the Senate committee structure remained remarkably unchanged, although pressures for reform continued to build. By 1976 the Senate was ready to create its own reform committee. The Senate's major committee reform effort originated within a bipartisan group of relatively junior members. Their concerns, which were similar to those of House reformers, stimulated several changes during the first half of the 1970s: open markup sessions, some committee staff assistance for junior members, and secret-ballot elections for committee chair nominees. Nonetheless, most members saw the need for further improvement. As in the House, these early reforms failed to deal with overlapping jurisdictions, poor committee scheduling, multiple committee and subcommittee assignments, and unequal committee workloads.

These problems were especially acute in the Senate because of the larger number of committee assignments held by each member (about 17 committees and subcommittees per senator) and the added burden of their status as national figures. Indeed, the Commission on the Operation of the Senate (the Culver Commission) recommended in 1976 that the Senate adopt designated days for floor and committee business and computerized committee scheduling to ameliorate these very problems.

Following several unsuccessful attempts to stir members' interest, a resolution was adopted on March 31, 1976, creating a twelve-member, bipartisan Temporary Select Committee to Study the Senate Committee System.[26] The committee, chaired by Adlai Stevenson (D-Ill.), and cochaired by William Brock (R-Tenn.), was given just eleven months to make its recommendations. The Stevenson panel sketched three alternative committee plans: a minimal-change plan, a twelve-committee plan organized along functional lines, and a five-committee scheme containing sixty standing subcommittees. These proposals drew the attention of chamber colleagues and outsiders. Realizing the Senate was not yet ready for a radical restructuring of its committees, the Stevenson Committee quickly settled on the twelve-committee plan and reported its recommendations to the Senate.[27]

Stevenson introduced a resolution (S. Res. 586) embodying those recommendations on October 15, 1976. In the November 1976 elections, the chairs of three standing committees designated to be abolished were defeated.[28] And in December, Stevenson and Oregon's Bob Packwood, who replaced Brock as cochair after the latter had been defeated in his bid for reelection, won an agreement from key members of the Rules and Administration Committee facilitating prompt consideration of the reform resolution. The parties delayed making new committee assignments until deliberation on the resolution was completed. Stevenson reintroduced the reform resolution (now S. Res. 4) at the beginning of the next congress, and it was referred to the Rules and Administration Committee. S. Res. 4 was approved unanimously by the committee and passed the Senate on a vote of 89–1. Only Quentin Burdick (D-N.D.), who was in line to chair the abolished Post Office Committee, voted against the resolution.

By the time the Senate had finished its work, the committee reorganization plan had evolved from an innovative restructuring to a moderate, yet significant, realignment of the old committee system. Nearly all of the Senate's select and special committees had been abolished, along with the Aeronautical and Space Sciences Committee, Post Office Committee, and District of Columbia Committee. Wholesale jurisdictional changes involving energy, the environment, science and technology, human resources, and government affairs had been achieved. Limits were placed on the number of assignments (3 committees and 8 subcommittees) and the number of chairs (4 committees and subcommittees in the 95th Congress and 3 in the 96th Congress) that senators could hold.[29] The reforms also expanded minority staffing and computerized committee scheduling in a further effort to help relieve overburdened senators.

At each successive phase, plans of the Stevenson Committee had been weakened by members fearful of losing jurisdiction. Despite this, a substantial alteration remained, which in structural terms far exceeded the House's achievements. By contrast, the Senate made essentially no changes in either party or chamber procedures. Selection of committee and subcommittee leaders remained strictly dictated by seniority. And with the exception of reducing the number of votes required to limit debate (the *cloture* process), the Senate left its longstanding rules for considering legislation intact. On these matters, the House Democratic Caucus had made more substantial progress. For a time, at least, the reform process was dead. For members, pundits, and scholars alike the question now became: What effects would these reforms have on Congress and its two committee systems?

POSTREFORM COMMITTEES (1981–1995): DECENTRALIZATION AND INDIVIDUALISM

With reforms in the House and Senate complete, both chambers settled in for a period of consolidation and the inevitable discovery of unintended consequences of change. In the House, most scholars agree that subcommittee government replaced committee government as the operative form of governance.[30] Accommodationist party leaders expanded committees to meet members' demands for desirable committee positions. Wary committee leaders expanded the size and number of subcommittees to accommodate members' political and policy goals. And subcommittees supplanted the full committee as the primary locus of decision making. For some, however, these reforms had gone too far towards decentralizing the House. And the reforms had done much to increase the formal powers of party leaders. Scholars began to characterize this period as the *postreform*

Salient Features of the Postreform Congress

- Increased centralization of formal leadership powers is established.
- Floor challenges to committees via amendment increase but success remains limited.
- Seniority norm is weakened but not eliminated.
- Legislation is packaged into larger "omnibus" measures or "megabills."
- Leaders use authority to accommodate members' demands for positions on specific committees.
- Increased interparty conflict accompanies rising party support scores.
- Apprenticeship becomes active rather than passive as new members seek to descend learning curve more quickly.

BOX 2-3

era. According to Roger H. Davidson, the postreform Congress featured fewer but larger bills, a more hierarchical structure, stronger party leaders, and increased partisanship.[31] (For a summary of features of the postreform Congress, see Box 2-3.)

In the Senate, individualism—an extreme form of decentralization that empowered each participating senator—took hold as the apprenticeship and reciprocity norms declined.[32] Floor leaders found themselves "janitors in an untidy chamber."[33] Filibusters were on the rise, interparty conflict increased, and showhorses seemed to outnumber workhorses in a sea of major-league egos. Although Senate leaders enjoyed none of the increased power of House leaders, they, too, used megabills or omnibus legislation as tool to achieve legislative victories. Complicated time-limitation agreements and elaborate legislative bargains became their stock in trade.

The urge to reform did not disappear entirely, particularly among purists. During ensuing congresses the Patterson (1979–1980), Pearson-Ribicoff (1982–1983), and Quayle (1984) groups (see Table 2-1 on page 34) were established to consider items left unattended by the earlier reform efforts. Issues included jurisdictional realignment, scheduling, and floor procedure. But no notable reforms resulted from these efforts.

As the nation became more determinedly Republican and conservative in broad national terms (reflected in the Republicans' strong hold on the presidency), the persistence of Democratic congressional majorities and the dominance of senior leaders created friction within the institution. This friction was bothersome for Republicans during the Speaker-ship of Thomas P. "Tip" O'Neill (D-Mass.), especially once O'Neill decid-ed to thwart the legislative initiatives of the Reagan administration. O'Neill began to put his new powers and resources to work. He exploited the Rules Committee to structure floor debates to Democratic advantage. He utilized the leadership's role in the budget process to recapture ground lost to Republicans early in the Reagan administration. And he exploited the revitalized Steering and Policy Committee to monitor committee activities. As a result, both parties became more cohesive internally. But party cohesion became even more pronounced and the interparty warfare more visible, visceral, and confrontational during the brief Speakership of Texas Democrat Jim Wright, who succeeded O'Neill in 1987.[34]

Wright had few friends in either party in Congress. He was aggres-sive, partisan, and bent on winning floor victories. To this end he exploit-ed House rules, meddled in committee politics, and hampered the efforts of the minority party at every opportunity. But it was the wrath of con-servative Republicans that proved his undoing. Backbench members of the so-called Conservative Opportunity Society took up the Wright chal-lenge and returned his fire. One of them, Republican Newt Gingrich of Georgia, succeeded in getting the House Ethics Committee to examine a lucrative book deal that Wright had arranged. In the end, Wright was forced to resign his seat in the middle of 1989.

He was replaced by the conciliatory Majority Leader Thomas S. Foley of Washington, whom most people believed could calm the partisan war-fare. He could not, and the partisan friction continued against a backdrop of ethics problems. Republican president George Bush added to this mix a string of successful vetoes, and gridlock emerged inside the Beltway. The friction was similar in some respects to that of the 1960s, when liberal legislators felt stymied by their conservative opponents on the Hill. In the earlier period, however, the shifting political coalitions could work out their differences within the party caucus (via the Hansen Committee) or through the inevitable working of the Senate's will. As the decade of the nineties began, however, no such solution presented itself. The pressures building in Congress were primarily partisan and ideological, but they were exposed by structural and procedural characteristics within both chambers. It is not surprising, therefore, that reformers seized upon mechanisms for change that had worked in the past. But neither is it sur-prising that they failed in their efforts until partisan change came about.

THE PHONY WAR AND PRELUDE TO CHANGE

On July 31, 1991, Rep. Lee H. Hamilton, a Democrat from Indiana, and Rep. Bill Gradison, a Republican from Ohio, introduced House Concurrent Resolution 192 (H. Con. Res. 192), which proposed the creation of a third Joint Committee on the Organization of Congress. Companion legislation (S. Con. Res. 57) was introduced by Oklahoma Democratic senator David L. Boren and Republican New Mexico senator Pete V. Domenici on that same day and received a Rules Committee hearing the following November. But the proposals were received coldly by the leadership and committee chairs in both chambers and languished for almost a year.

Near the end of 1991 a General Accounting Office report revealed that thousands of checks had been drawn against insufficient funds by House members using a 150-year-old "bank" created for their convenience. At nearly the same time an inquiry by a U.S. attorney uncovered abuses in the House post office. Together, these two scandals effectively scuttled Congress's dwindling public reputation and reinforced critics' images of the institution as petty, corrupt, and outdated. By March 1992, with ethics storms raging throughout the institution, Speaker Foley endorsed the Boren-Hamilton-Gradison-Domenici plan, which then slowly began to make its way through committee.

By early spring of 1992 change on Capitol Hill seemed certain. Members were retiring in record numbers. Some had become frustrated with legislative life while others were afraid of electoral repercussions from bounced checks. Many were induced by a lucrative retirement buyout. In an article titled "Hill Upheaval," *National Journal* reporter Richard Cohen wrote:

> Get ready for something entirely new on Capitol Hill. Some details remain uncertain pending November's elections, but the bottom line seems unmistakable: The House is facing its greatest upheaval since the 1950s and possibly the New Deal.[35]

Under such circumstances serious reform efforts might be expected to get off the ground. The leadership decided to support creation of the Joint Committee. The Democratic Caucus's Committee on Organization, Study, and Review—under the direction of Louise M. Slaughter of New York—began investigating possible rules changes. And House Republicans began working on an aggressive set of reforms designed to modernize the chamber.

Despite these conditions, there was still reason to doubt that reform had a chance. Janet Hook of the *Congressional Quarterly Weekly Report* put it this way:

> . . . the obstacles to major change are monumental. Many Democratic leaders are lukewarm. Powerful committee chairmen are downright hostile. Even among junior lawmakers, the interests vested in the status quo are legion. Many members wonder if it is worth the trouble to even try.[36]

Hook went on to quote Rep. Butler Derrick, a South Carolina Democrat and Rules Committee member, who said: "We'll never get any of it done."[37] Still, both chambers forged ahead, and on August 6, 1992, H. Con. Res. 192 was cleared by the House and Senate.

As predicted, the elections of 1992 produced an enormous class of new members, many of whom had campaigned against Washington and in favor of government reform. Unlike their relatively inexperienced predecessors of the early 1970s, however, this was a group of veteran state-level politicians for whom positions of power within the new Congress were as important as any changes that might be pushed through. They were not, to be sure, opposed to reform. But they coveted positions on quality committees (Appropriations and Ways and Means, for example) and membership on party committees (such as the Democratic Steering and Policy Committee).

Although content with the status quo, wary Democratic leaders used the Slaughter group to draft a set of possible reforms rather than enter into the organizing sessions emptyhanded. On December 8, 1992, the Caucus adopted most of these changes by eliminating sixteen subcommittees, limiting "special order" speeches and "one-minute" speeches, dropping old-fashioned teller votes, restricting access to certain privileged parliamentary motions, making challenges to sitting committee chairs easier, and establishing a twenty-member Speaker's Working Group on Policy Development. This last was a compromise between members of the Democratic Study Group, who sought to further curb the power of standing committee chairs, and the chairs themselves, who wished to maintain their considerable independence in agenda formation. The limitations on "special order" and "one-minute" speeches were later shelved for further study when Republican outrage over these proposals reached a fevered pitch. Several additional changes were ignored, defeated, or delayed. Democrats sidestepped a proposal to establish term limits for committee and subcommittee chairs, stalled the elimination of the House's five non-legislative select committees, and delayed the adoption of a rule that would have granted four House delegates and the resident commissioner of Puerto Rico voting rights on the House floor.

THE BOREN-HAMILTON COMMITTEE

House Concurrent Resolution 192 created a twenty-eight-member, bipartisan Joint Committee on the Organization of Congress, with Hamilton, Boren, Domenici, and Gradison as its bipartisan leadership group. (Gradison later resigned his House seat and was replaced by California Republican David Dreier.) From the outset, the Joint Committee was replete with contradictions and conflicts. An early House-Senate disagreement led to a prohibition against initiating work officially until after the November 1992 elections. But the committee was required to report no later than December 1993. It was directed to "make a full and complete study of the organization and operation of Congress," including the committee systems, House-Senate relationships, executive-legislative relationships, and the powers and duties of congressional leaders. But it was given only very modest resources to achieve this. The House Democratic contingent was neither pronouncedly pro-reform nor anti-reform. It would take its cues from senior Democrats who had no particular stake in reforms. House Republicans, by contrast, represented the activist "new guard" and pressed hard for dramatic changes. The divergent partisan interests became even more pronounced when Republican leaders appointed the hard-charging Dreier to replace the retiring Gradison. Finally, while some interchamber problems existed on Capitol Hill, the primary reform targets were unique to each chamber, making the Joint Committee structure ill-suited to achieve reform.

Given these circumstances, it is hardly surprising that the Joint Committee was a failure. The committee's lengthy hearings, symposia, surveys, public appeals, academic consultations, roundtables, and so forth netted the usual set of reform proposals. As always, different reforms attracted different constituencies within and without Congress. Most importantly, partisan differences divided the House's committee members from the outset. And interchamber differences hampered the whole committee's ability to proceed beyond the incremental tinkering that everyone supported to the "blue sky" proposals that almost no one supported. These stumbling blocks became increasingly insurmountable as the committee's report deadline drew near. Each chamber held its own markup and produced its own draft legislation.

In the end, there was simply no consensus for a specific set of changes. And, in what became an oft-repeated mantra, reformers, journalists, and pundits alike noted that "House and Senate leaders just weren't interested." Absent leadership commitment, shared interbranch concerns, and some bridge across a widening partisan chasm, reform efforts simply failed. Even the Joint Committee's final report was a "yours-mine-ours" production with each chamber producing its own volume in the three-volume set that also included a joint report on the contemporary structural and procedural characteristics of the institution.[38]

REPUBLICAN RULE AND THE 104TH CONGRESS

Partisan change, the missing ingredient to reform, was provided in dramatic form by the 1994 midterm elections. As with the 1992 elections, a large class of new senators and representatives was assured due to numerous retirements. More importantly, however, a seemingly distant yet plausible chance for a Republican takeover of both the Senate and House hung in the air. Journalists, political pundits, and even scholars talked about a Republican victory in serious terms.

THE CONTRACT CONGRESS

The congress elected in 1974 will always be known as the Watergate Congress and the Class of 1974 as the Watergate Babies. In much the same way the congress elected in 1994 is likely to be remembered as the Contract Congress in recognition of its introduction of the "Contract with America." The Contract was a ten-point platform masterminded by House Republican Whip (and soon-to-be Speaker) Newt Gingrich in an attempt to nationalize the notoriously local character of congressional elections. If elected, Gingrich and his fellow partisans promised, the Republican House would vote on each item in the Contract in the first 100 days of the new congress. Furthermore, Gingrich boasted that a sweeping set of changes within the institution—point one of the Contract—would be passed on the first day of the new session. The Republicans followed through on both counts.

The House of Representatives of the 104th Congress came to order at 10:58 A.M. on January 4, 1995, and did not adjourn until 2:42 A.M. January 5.[39] After a good many ceremonial activities, the Republican House adopted a set of landmark rules changes, just as promised. These changes, listed in greater detail in Table 2-2, included reform of the House committee system, term limitations for a number of House leaders, alterations in floor procedure, and a series of administrative changes designed to cut costs and depoliticize House operations.

It should be noted that the package of rules changes had taken shape over a rather extended period of time and amounted to a "bill of particulars" authored by House Republicans. As previously noted, Republicans believed that the House Democrats had grown complacent with their role as the majority party. Indeed, Gingrich and his colleagues frequently used very strong language to describe the Democratic hegemony. Details of the reform plan were worked out during the House Republican Conference's organizing sessions in December 1994. During these meetings—the Democratic Caucus held its own organizing sessions—the Republicans selected their new leaders, appointed committee leaders and established committee rosters, and molded the set of rules changes that would be presented on the House floor on opening day.

To the casual observer, the elimination of 3 committees (District of Columbia, Merchant Marine and Fisheries, and Post Office and Civil Ser-

TABLE 2-2 Major House and Senate Reforms of the 104th Congress (1995–1996)

House	Senate
Six-year term limits for committee and subcommittee chairs	Six-year term limits for committee chairs
Eight-year term limit for Speaker	Six-year term limits for Republican party leaders other than floor leader and president pro tempore
Elimination of three standing committees and some jurisdictional shifts	Senators prohibited from "reclaiming" seniority upon return to a committee on which they previously served
Most committees (Appropriations, Government Reform and Oversight, and Transportation excepted) limited to five subcommittees	Secret-ballot elections for committee chairs in committee and party conference; majority leader can nominate chair in case of conference rejection
Joint referrals eliminated; Speaker gains enhanced authority over split and sequential referrals, including authority to designate a "lead" committee with deadline for reporting	GOP to adopt a formal legislative agenda prior to beginning of each Congress and prior to selection of committee chairs
Rolling quorums prohibited	
Proxy voting in committees prohibited	
Majority party leaders given enhanced authority over committee chair selection	
Members' assignments cut back to two full committees and four subcommittees	
Verbatim transcripts of hearings and meetings required	
Members' committee votes to be published	
Subcommittee staff hired by the full committee chair	
Committee staff reduced by one-third; House Oversight gains authority to establish committee staff sizes	
Motion to recommit with instructions guaranteed	
Motion to rise from Committee of the Whole reserved to the majority leader	
Three-fifths floor vote required for measures that raise income tax rates	

Sources: For the House, David S. Cloud, "GOP, to Its Own Great Delight, Enacts House Rules Changes," *Congressional Quarterly Weekly Report*, January 7, 1995, 13–15; for the Senate, David S. Cloud, "GOP Senators Limit Chairmen To Six Years Heading Panel," *Congressional Quarterly Weekly Report*, July 22, 1995, 2147.

vice),[40] 31 subcommittees, and the attendant loss of 484 committee and subcommittee seats would be the most visible changes. These reductions were reinforced, and in some ways made easier, by new limits on the number of committee assignments (2) and subcommittee assignments (4) that members could hold. Somewhat less visible to the public was a series of relatively minor changes in committee jurisdictions that affected financial institutions, transportation, and nonmilitary nuclear issues. Republicans also made good on their promise to cut back substantially on staff; they established caps one-third below those permitted in the 103d Congress and forced a long list of so-called legislative service organizations—nonlegislative issue groups supported by members' office allowances—out of House office space. In this way Republicans were able to reduce the congressional bureaucracy and realize budget savings at the same time.

Another series of changes that went largely unmarked by the public increased the power of the new Republican Speaker while reducing the power of committee and subcommittee chairs. Full committee and subcommittee chairs now have term limitations (three two-year terms) that will permit them less independence and further weaken the seniority system in the House. The Speaker, who also has a term limit (of eight years), gained additional influence in the committee assignment and chair selection process. (As we will see in Chapter 4, Speaker Gingrich used this power at once to elevate less senior colleagues to chairs on three important committees—Appropriations, Commerce, and Judiciary.) Committee chairs suffered some additional loss of power with a ban on proxy voting, the elimination of so-called rolling quorums (which allowed committees to operate with less than a majority present), and reinforcement of certain open committee rules that prevent work from being done in executive session. Committee chairs were not total losers, however. They gained the authority to appoint subcommittee staff and, if they were willing to work with party leaders, the authority to work out the details of "Contract" legislation.

In the short term, at least, there is no mystery about the actual and intended consequences of these reforms. The corporate party leadership, and the Speaker in particular, gained substantial power at the expense of committees and committee chairs. Leadership control of the agenda, fewer staff, diminished procedural powers, more open committee procedures, reduced protection on the floor, and the ultimate threat of simply being dismissed by party leaders have already transformed the balance of power in the House. Even the new Republican chairs, after a wait in the wilderness of minority status, acknowledged their backseat to the leadership's control. Quipped Henry Hyde (R-Ill.), chair of the Judiciary Committee, "I'm just the *subchairman.*" In so saying, Hyde was acknowledging that the leadership-dominated schedule of the first hundred days had given the new committee leaders very little leeway.[41]

Unlike the Democratic practice of altering their caucus rules, many of these important changes (terms limits and committee limits, for example) were written into the standing rules of the House and not simply into the Republican Conference rules. Thus, if the Democrats do not like the rules, and they regain control of the chamber, they will be put in the somewhat awkward position of having to repeal these "reforms."

CONTINUITY AND CHANGE IN THE SENATE

Although Republicans also regained control of the Senate in the 104th Congress, the new majority party (which in that chamber had only been out of power for eight years) simply went about the business of switching offices and hiring new (but somewhat fewer) staff. There were no dramatic rules changes, no elimination of committees, and no challenges to the authority of the party leaders.

Nonetheless, the seeds for change, which had been planted several congresses earlier, were beginning to take root in the Senate as a core group of conservative Republican senators, many with previous House experience, began to chafe at the slow pace of the highly decentralized upper chamber. On March 2, 1995, these members became agitated when Mark Hatfield of Oregon, chairman of the Appropriations Committee, voted against a constitutional amendment requiring a balanced budget. The amendment failed by a single vote. Backbench conservatives advocated stripping Hatfield of his chair for his failure to support an otherwise unified Republican party. Though no action was taken against Hatfield, the disgruntled senators did convince Majority Leader Robert Dole (R-Kan.) to appoint a Republican task force, headed by Connie Mack of Florida, to study possible changes in the Conference's rules. Two months later, Mack's task force returned to the Conference with eight proposed rule changes designed to substantially reduce the power of the committee chairs, enhance the power of the floor leader, and improve the leverage of rank-and-file members within the party.[42]

On July 19, 1995, the Republican Conference voted on these proposals. It adopted term limits for most leaders and chairs, a secret-ballot procedure for electing committee chairs, a procedure for establishing a formal GOP legislative agenda, and a rule to limit committee members from reclaiming seniority upon their return to committees they had abandoned. Republican committee leaders, like their House counterparts, are now limited to three two-year terms as chair of a full committee. This limitation also was extended to each of the Republican party leadership positions, except the floor leader and the largely ceremonial president pro tempore. The task force also recommended that the floor leader be given the power to nominate committee chairs—a process currently handled within committees and strictly according to seniority.

This proposal was defeated. The reformers did succeed in pushing through a secret-ballot procedure for the election of the committee chairs that would allow the leader to present a nominee in the event that a committee's choice failed to gain a majority from the Conference. The new Republican agenda is not binding upon members of the Conference, but it is supposed to be adopted prior to the selection of the committee chairs.

The changes didn't appeal to all the senators. Orrin G. Hatch (R-Utah) was nonplused, responding: "Whatever they want to do." But others wanted more. "It didn't go as far as I wanted, but we got the secret ballot," said Sen. John McCain (R-Ariz.).[43] Though modest, the rules changes move the Senate closer to the House in terms of the relations between committee leaders, party leaders, and the party groups. Secret ballots allow dissatisfied senators to "send a message" to their colleagues. Term limits force rotation—although the levels will depend greatly on the party's electoral fortunes. Seniority wasn't overthrown. The leader didn't gain dramatic new powers. Prior to the 105th Congress rumors circulated that one sitting chair, John H. Chafee (R-R.I.), and one heir apparent, James M. Jeffords (R-Vt.), might be challenged by more conservative colleagues. Neither challenge materialized, partly because Majority Leader Trent Lott (R-Miss.) discouraged the moves, but the threat was clear and Lott's move to protect his colleagues leaves them beholden in some way. As the leader of the task force, Connie Mack, put it: "Basically, it's to enhance the leadership's authority and to encourage team play."[44]

COMMITTEES AND PARTIES IN CONGRESS

The United States Congress is formed by a marriage of two structures—the committee structure and the party structure. Because the committee structure was developed prior to the party structure, it has some precedence in the system. Yet as our treatment of evolution and change in the committee systems has shown, tension between these two structures remains. It is this tension that distinguishes the U.S. Congress from its parliamentary cousins. In parliaments, the party structures—and their attendant caucuses—dominate the process of policy making. Only episodically has party strength in the United States been sufficient to permit some comparisons between our system and those of other nations. During the Jeffersonian period, for example, and after the revolt against Speaker Joseph Cannon, the party caucus became a focal point for power and policy development.

But American parties also are comparatively weak. During this century they have been able to sustain an electoral drive and a policy focus that allows them to govern in the manner of European parties for only brief periods (the 1910s, 1930s, and, perhaps, mid-1990s, for example). More often, that energy is lost to a decline in electoral fervor and changes in the policy agenda that don't fit well into the existing party superstructure. At those times—and they are more the rule than the exception—Congress has fallen back upon a system of relatively independent and autonomous committees to transact its business. Thus, the history of the modern Congress reflects an ebb and flow of power between parties and committees.

At present, of course, it is party that is in ascendance. The disgruntled but energized former minority party is attempting to work its will within institutions grown accustomed to the longstanding rule of the Democrats.[45] For the new majority Republicans, eager to achieve their own policy goals, the old rules are simply impediments best swept aside. Senate traditions make this more difficult there than in the House, but generational and partisan shifts—along with the replacement of "old guard" leader Robert Dole by aggressive House transfer Trent Lott—may pave the way for further changes there as well. Regardless, the partisan tide is now running against committee power, with the result that committees have lost the autonomy they enjoyed for three decades before the 1980s.

NOTES

1. For background on committees in the First Congress see Calvin Jillson and Rick K. Wilson, *Congressional Dynamics: Structure, Coordination, and Choice in the First American Congress: 1774–1789* (Stanford: Stanford University Press, 1994), esp. chap. 4.
2. See Frank R. Baumgartner and Bryan D. Jones, *Agendas and Instability in American Politics* (Chicago: University of Chicago Press, 1993), 1–24.
3. The interested reader should refer to the first edition of this book, which carried a detailed discussion of committee development. In recent years, congressional scholars have produced excellent theoretically driven work on congressional development. See, for example, Gerald Gamm and Kenneth Shepsle, "Emergence of Legislative Institutions: Standing Committees in the House and Senate," *Legislative Studies Quarterly* 14 (1989): 39–66; Joseph Cooper and Cheryl D. Young, "Bill Introduction in the Nineteenth Century: A Study of Institutional Change," *Legislative Studies Quarterly* 14 (1989): 67–105; Sarah Binder, "Partisanship and Procedural Choice: Institutional Change in the Early Congress, 1789–1823," *Journal of Politics* 57(1995): 1093–1117; Sarah Binder, "The Partisan Basis of Procedural Choice: Allocating Parliamentary Rights in the House, 1789–1991," *American Political Science Review* 90 (March 1996): 8–20; Jonathan N. Katz and Brian R. Sala, "Careerism, Committee Assign-

ments, and the Electoral Connection," *American Political Science Review* 90 (March 1996): 21–33; Thomas W. Skladony, "The House Goes to Work: Select and Standing Committees in the U.S. House of Representatives, 1789–1828," *Congress & the Presidency* 12 (Autumn 1985): 165–187; and Joseph Cooper, *The Origins of the Standing Committees and the Development of the Modern House* (Houston: Rice University Studies, 1970), 8–17. For additional detail on this first period, see Skladony, "The House Goes to Work." On the subject of bill introduction, consideration, and reporting, see Cooper and Young, "Bill Introduction in the Nineteenth Century." On the Senate, see Walter Kravitz, "Evolution of the Senate's Committee System," *Annals of the American Academy of Political and Social Science* 411 (January 1974): 28; and George L. Robinson, "The Development of the Senate Committee System," Ph.D. dissertation, New York University, 1954, 20–21.

4. Committees existed during the Continental Congress, the Constitutional Convention, and in the emerging state legislatures, so their use in the First Congress was by no means a novel institutional structure. As with much else in the new nation, committees were borrowed and adapted to suit the purposes of the new government.

5. As Thomas Jefferson's *Manual of Parliamentary Practice* so aptly put it, "The child is not to be put to a nurse that cares not for it." House Doc. 95–403, 95th Cong., 2d Sess., 1979, Sect. XXVI.

6. Jonathan N. Katz and Brian R. Sala have linked this change to ballot reforms that took place near the end of the nineteenth century. See "Careerism, Committee Assignments, and the Electoral Connection," *American Political Science Review* 90 (March 1996): 21–33.

7. As we have noted, the balance of power between party leaders and committee leaders was quite well established in the aftermath of the revolt against Cannon. Based on this, Morris P. Fiorina's claim that the modern House dates from the events of 1908–1911 is quite correct. But the House and Senate had yet to establish—through the Budget and Accounting Act of 1921—a modernized fiscal policy-making process or the trimmed-down committee system that we know today. Without doubt, the balance of power established in the post-Cannon House and the remaining structural and procedural touches of the early twenties gave us a truly modern Congress. Fiorina's argument, and an encapsulated summary of the Cannon revolt, can be found in note 5 of Chapter 1 in *Congress—Keystone of the Washington Establishment* (New Haven: Yale University Press, 1977), 95–96.

8. Woodrow Wilson, *Congressional Government* (Boston: Houghton Mifflin, 1885), 102.

9. Sen. Robert W. LaFollette of Wisconsin and Rep. Mike Monroney of Oklahoma were co-chairs of the Joint Committee on the Organization of Congress that produced the Reorganization Act.

10. For a critical assessment of the 1946 act and the post-1946 congressional power structure see Roger H. Davidson, "The Legislative Reorganization Act of 1946," *Legislative Studies Quarterly* 15 (1990): 357–373.

11. On norms in the Senate see Donald R. Matthews, *U.S. Senators and Their World* (New York: Vintage, 1960); for norms in the House see Herbert B. Asher, "The Learning of Legislative Norms," *American Political Science Review* 67 (1973): 499–513. Also see Barbara Hinckley, *The Seniority System in Congress* (Bloomington: Indiana University Press, 1977), and Nelson W. Polsby, Miriam Gallaher, and Barry Spencer Rundquist, "The Growth of the Seniori-

ty System in the U.S. House of Representatives," *American Political Science Review* 63 (1969): 787–807.

12. George B. Galloway, *The Legislative Process in Congress* (New York: Thomas Y. Crowell, 1953), 289.

13. Richard Bolling, *House Out of Order* (New York: E. P. Dutton, 1966), 81.

14. One of the first things Rules Committee members did after Smith's departure was to established a regular Tuesday/Thursday meeting schedule. For a treatment of the Rules Committee during this era see James A. Robinson, *The House Rules Committee* (Indianapolis: Bobbs-Merrill, 1963).

15. See Lawrence C. Dodd and Bruce I. Oppenheimer, "The House in Transition: Change and Consolidation," in *Congress Reconsidered*, 2d ed., ed. Lawrence C. Dodd and Bruce I. Oppenheimer (Washington, DC: CQ Press, 1981), 40.

16. While the Legislative Reorganization Act of 1970 heralded major reform, the earlier expansion of the Rules Committee in the 1960s was perhaps the first notable reform of this period. It should also be noted that in early 1965, after Republican Gerald R. Ford of Michigan had been elected minority leader, a series of reforms was implemented within the Republican Conference.

17. The Joint Committee approach would be used once again in 1992 with the creation of the Boren-Hamilton Committee. As with its predecessors, the 1992 Joint Committee achieved little in the way of true reform. The Boren-Hamilton Committee is treated later in this chapter.

18. "Legislative Reorganization Act: First Year's Record," *Congressional Quarterly Weekly Report*, March 4, 1972, 485–491.

19. "House Reform: Easy to Advocate, Hard to Define," *Congressional Quarterly Weekly Report*, January 20, 1973, 69–72.

20. An in-depth history of the Bolling Committee is provided by Roger H. Davidson and Walter J. Oleszek in *Congress Against Itself* (Bloomington: Indiana University Press, 1977).

21. See "Jurisdiction Overhaul Recommended for House," *Congressional Quarterly Weekly Report*, December 22, 1973, 3358–3366; and U.S. Congress, House, Select Committee on Committees, "Committee Reform Amends of 1974," 93d Cong., 2d sess., March 1973, House Rept. 916.

22. Davidson and Oleszek, *Congress Against Itself*, 250.

23. On the role of the "Class of '74," see Burdett Loomis, *The New American Politician* (New York: Basic Books, 1988), 31–36.

24. For a summary of subcommittee reforms during this period, see Christopher J. Deering and Steven S. Smith, "Majority Party Leadership and the New House Subcommittee System," in *Understanding Congressional Leadership*, ed. Frank H. Mackaman (Washington, D.C.: CQ Press, 1981), 264.

25. Allen Schick, *Congress and Money: Budgeting, Spending, and Taxing* (Washington D.C.: Urban Institute, 1980), 53–71.

26. This account of the Stevenson Committee is drawn from Judith H. Parris, "The Senate Reorganizes its Committees, 1977," *Political Science Quarterly* 95 (Summer 1979): 319–337; and Roger H. Davidson, "Two Avenues of Change: House and Senate Committee Reorganization," in *Congress Reconsidered*, 2d ed., ed. Dodd and Oppenheimer, 120–128.

27. The Select Committee had no legislative authority, so it could not report legislation to the floor. Therefore, upon completion of a report, a resolution embracing suggestions of the committee had to be formally introduced, referred to the Rules Committee, and reported back to the chamber before floor consideration.

28. The members were Frank Moss of Utah, who chaired the Aeronautical and Space Sciences Committee, Gale W. McGee of Wyoming, who chaired the Post Office and Civil Service Committee, and R. Vance Hartke of Indiana, who chaired the Veterans' Affairs Committee. As it turned out, Veterans' Affairs survived while the District of Columbia Committee, chaired by Thomas F. Eagleton of Missouri, was eliminated.

29. It is important to note that these changes were seriously compromised by special exceptions written into the Senate's standing rules for virtually every senator. In the 98th Congress, for example, these exceptions ran on for seven pages at the end of Rule XXV, which defines the jurisdictions of the standing committees and the membership limitations.

30. See for example, Roger H. Davidson, "Subcommittee Government: New Channels for Policy Making," in *The New Congress*, ed. Thomas E. Mann and Norman J. Ornstein (Washington, D.C.: American Enterprise Institute, 1981): 99–133; Steven Haeberle, "The Institutionalization of Subcommittees in the U.S. House of Representatives," *Journal of Politics* 40 (1978): 1054–1065; Christopher J. Deering and Steven S. Smith, "Subcommittees in Congress," in *Congress Reconsidered*, 3d ed., ed. Lawrence C. Dodd and Bruce I. Oppenheimer (Washington, D.C.: CQ Press, 1985): 189–210; and Lawrence C. Dodd and Richard L. Schott, *Congress and the Administrative State* (New York: Wiley, 1979).

31. Roger H. Davidson, "The Emergence of the Postreform Congress," in *The Postreform Congress*, ed. Roger H. Davidson (New York: St. Martin's Press, 1992), 14–15.

32. The "individualism" characterization is Randall B. Ripley's. See Ripley, *Power in the Senate* (New York: St. Martin's Press, 1969). On developments in the Senate during this period, see Barbara Sinclair, *Transformation of the U.S. Senate* (Baltimore: Johns Hopkins University Press, 1989).

33. The phrase comes from the title of Roger H. Davidson's chapter, "Senate Leaders: Janitors for an Untidy Chamber?" in *Congress Reconsidered*, 3d ed., ed. Dodd and Oppenheimer, 225–251. He in turn attributes the reference to former Republican floor leader Howard H. Baker, Jr., of Tennessee.

34. Wright's rise and fall are treated at length in John M. Berry's *The Ambition and the Power: A True Story of Washington* (New York: Viking, 1989).

35. Richard E. Cohen, "Hill Upheaval," *National Journal*, May 23, 1992, 1222.

36. Janet Hook, "Extensive Reform Proposals Cook on the Front Burner," *Congressional Quarterly Weekly Report*, June 6, 1992, 1579.

37. Ibid.

38. U.S. Congress, Joint Committee on the Organization of Congress, *Organization of Congress: Final Report*, H.Rept. 103–413/S.Rept. 103–215, 3 vols. (Washington, D.C.: Government Printing Office, 1993). For a discussion of these latest reform efforts, see the essays in James A. Thurber and Roger H. Davidson, *Remaking Congress: Change and Stability in the 1990s* (Washington, D.C.: Congressional Quarterly, 1995).

39. These times and other tidbits can be found in Elizabeth A. Palmer, "Minute-by-Minute Through the GOP's Momentous Day," *Congressional Quarterly Weekly Report*, January 7, 1995, 10–11.

40. The committees did not disappear altogether, of course. The District Committee became a subcommittee on Government Reform and Oversight, Merchant Marine and Fisheries was split between the Resources and the Trans-

portation committees, and Post Office and Civil Service became two sub-committees, also on Government Reform and Oversight.

41. Richard E. Cohen, "The Transformers," *National Journal*, March 4, 1995, 531.

42. Helen Dewar, "Senate GOP Urged to Shift Power, Solidify Policy Positions in Advance," *Washington Post*, May 17, 1995, A21; and David Hosansky, "GOP Conference Will Consider Limits on Seniority System," *Congressional Quarterly Weekly Report*, May 20, 1995, 1392. For an in-depth treatment of reform and the new Republican majority, see C. Lawrence Evans and Walter J. Oleszek, *Congress Under Fire: Reform Politics and the Republican Majority* (Boston: Houghton Mifflin, 1997).

43. Hatch and McCain's quotes are from David S. Cloud, "GOP Senators Limit Chairmen To Six Years Heading Panel," *Congressional Quarterly Weekly Report*, July 22, 1995, 2147.

44. Lott's defense of Chafee and Jeffords was reported by (among others) Richard L. Berke in "Trent Lott and His Fierce Freshmen," *New York Times Magazine*, February 2, 1997. Mack's quote is from Hosansky, "GOP Will Consider Limits on Seniority System," 1392.

45. For additional discussion of the interplay between partisan goals and procedural change, see Sarah A. Binder and Steven S. Smith, "Acquired Procedural Tendencies and Congressional Reform," in *Remaking Congress*, ed. Thurber and Davidson, 53–72.

CHAPTER 3

Member Goals and
Committee Assignments

In 1981 Rep. Jim Wright of Texas was the Democratic majority leader, chief lieutenant, and heir apparent to Speaker of the House Thomas P. "Tip" O'Neill of Massachusetts. By virtue of his position as majority leader, Wright also served as the vice-chair of the Democratic Steering and Policy Committee—the group of Democrats charged with placing their party's members on the various committees. During this process—one that can create ingrates and enemies just as easily as friends—Wright made a fateful decision. Phil Gramm, a conservative, second-term Democrat and fellow Texan, wanted to join the Budget Committee. Wright decided to back his candidacy even though other, more liberal members of the Steering Committee vigorously opposed the appointment. Although he must have had misgivings, Speaker O'Neill deferred to Wright, and Gramm joined the Budget Committee for the first congress of Ronald Reagan's first term as president.

In the following months, Gramm conspired with committee and House Republicans to author a series of budget proposals in direct opposition to the Democratic leadership. Gramm co-sponsored key Republican proposals, defected on key votes, and, according to some, leaked information about the Democratic budget strategy to minority Republicans. Gramm was not alone in these activities. Southern Democrats, including a significant number of Wright's fellow Texans, delivered the votes necessary to defeat the majority Democrats and pass President Reagan's landmark economic initiatives. But two of the initiatives bore Gramm's name, and he was the most visible of the cross-over Democrats. Wright felt betrayed. Liberal Democrats were angry. Many wanted Gramm immediately removed from the committee—if not worse.

Gramm *was* punished, but not severely. Democratic leaders faced a dilemma. If they treated Gramm and the other defectors too harshly they might bolt for the Republican party and endanger the Democrats' longstanding control of the House. Republicans had, after all, just gained control of the Senate for the first time since 1955. So after allowing him to retain his committee positions throughout the 97th Congress, the leadership simply dropped Gramm from the Budget Committee in 1983. By then, however, the damage had been done. Democratic leaders had learned a costly lesson about the importance of committee assignments and the tension that exists between accommodating their colleagues' committee requests and the necessity of keeping winning coalitions together. Gramm, however, wasn't through.

Shortly after being denied reappointment to the Budget Committee, Gramm resigned his seat, declared himself a Republican, and reentered the House after a special election. He was promptly appointed to the Budget Committee by his new party colleagues.[1] In 1984 he "retired" from the House and ran successfully for the Senate. In the infinitely more accommodating Senate, Gramm joined the Armed Services Committee and the Banking, Housing, and Urban Affairs Committee during his first two congresses as a senator. Toward the end of his first term as a senator, and now in his third congress, Gramm dropped Armed Services and picked up appointments to the Appropriations Committee and the Budget Committee, where he remained through the 103d Congress (1993–1995). When Republicans regained control of the Senate in 1994, however, seats on the much-coveted Senate Finance Committee became available. In the Senate, where seniority is paramount, only one thing could prevent Gramm, a presumptive presidential candidate, from joining the committee—a more senior colleague making the same request. The Senate's Republican leader, Bob Dole of Kansas, who also hoped to be president, tried to find just such a person to displace Gramm. In the end, however, no one could come to Dole's assistance and, after some delay, Gramm joined the panel. (For details on later events, see Box 3-1 on p. 70).

The adventures (or misadventures) of Phil Gramm's search for committee assignments in the House and Senate illustrate the variety of forces—external, internal, partisan, and personal—that come together during the process of assigning members to committees. The driving force behind this process is a set of personal goals that each member brings to Congress after he or she is elected. Leaders, parties, and the parent chambers are obliged to consider these goals and, in the end, accommodate, alter, or deny them.

Committee assignments are important to individual members. Indeed, in many ways they determine the character of a member's career. But because they shape the composition and policy decisions of committees, they also are important to the leaders charged with running the two chambers and to the party groups that organize so much of the legislative activity. It is for this reason that most theories of committees, and committee power, advanced by scholars begin with consideration of committee assignments. Put simply: they make a difference. If members were completely free to choose their committee assignments, then membership patterns would be a perfect reflection of the demand patterns of members and their constituencies. But some committees would be unacceptably large, and others tiny or even nonexistent. By contrast, if committee assignments were controlled closely by party leaders, then committees might be more partisan in their makeup and in their subsequent decision-making patterns.

The actual situation, of course, falls somewhere in between. And the two patterns are neither mutually exclusive nor exhaustive. Leaders' needs may match members' needs fairly well during periods of relatively sharp partisanship. But at times they also may diverge, a circumstance that can create tensions between members and leaders if the latter fail to accommodate the demands placed upon them. As a practical matter, leaders must pick and choose. They need not accommodate each member's assignment requests. But they need to be sufficiently responsive to ensure that the bulk of their colleagues continue to support them.

In this chapter we focus first on the goals that lead members to request certain committee assignments. Why do members request the committee assignments they do? What does this tell us about how members perceive the panels they serve on? And how might their goals affect the way committees operate? Next, we examine how committee jurisdictions vary. Committees are clearly not equal. But how are they different and what do these differences mean to the members who serve on them? In particular, how do jurisdictions affect committee agendas and environments and what affect might this have on members' choices and goals? We then take a look at the mechanics of the committee assignment process. In Chapter 2 we saw that party leaders have gained substantial influence in the committee assignment process during the last two decades. But are party leaders free to appoint members to whatever panels they please, or must they heed the requests that members make? As noted in Chapter 1, we are also interested in the extent to which committees represent the interests of the chambers, the concerns of the parties, or the preferences of the committees themselves. In conclusion, we consider some evidence on the distribution of these preferences among the various committees.

THE IMPORTANCE OF COMMITTEE ASSIGNMENTS

Most new members of Congress arrive in Washington with a pretty clear idea of what committee assignments they will pursue. Some have professional backgrounds or experiences that lead them toward particular committees. Others, indeed most, know there is a fairly clear pecking order to the two committee systems and hope to land a spot on one of the premier panels. At the outset of the 104th Congress, freshman representative Phil English (R-Pa.) won a coveted spot on the House Ways and Means Committee. But this is not an everyday event. "I was stunned when I was selected," English said.[2] Still others feel compelled to join certain committees regardless of their own predilections—like the House member who said that he had not chosen his committee assignment on Agriculture, he was "sentenced to it." Only a handful, albeit an ever-diminishing handful, reach Washington without having given any thought to their committee assignments.

Members think seriously about committee assignments because they realize their importance to their personal political goals. As we will see, these goals animate their activities once they have joined their committees. For nearly all members appropriate committee assignments are essential to a successful stay on Capitol Hill. And all committees are not created equal in the members' minds. As Rep.-elect Gene Green (D-Texas) put it in 1992: "If they say, 'What do you want?' I'll say the moon and the stars"[3]—in this case, Appropriations, Commerce, Rules, and Ways and Means. Committees present members of Congress with different opportunities and attractions. Decisions about which committee assignments to pursue—and pursuit it is since there is no guarantee of assignment to a desired committee—are personal and vary from member to member. Perceptions about what advantages particular committees offer also vary. But almost all members of Congress agree with Rep. Charles E. Schumer (D-N.Y.): "It's the most important decision you can make. If you're on a good committee, you'll enjoy legislating and accomplish something. If you're on a bad committee, you won't enjoy it here."[4]

The significance of personal political goals for understanding committee differences was established by Richard Fenno in *Congressmen in Committees*.[5] Through interviews with members of twelve congressional committees during the late 1950s and 1960s, Fenno identified three goals that motivated members' committee activity: reelection, good public policy, and influence within the chamber. Fenno found that committees did indeed attract members differentially according to members' personal goals, a finding that later was corroborated by Charles Bullock's interviews with House freshmen of the 92d Congress (1971–1973)[6] and our own interviews of the 97th (1982–1983) and the 100th/101st (1987–1990) Congresses.

Our House and Senate figures for the 97th and 100th/101st Congresses were calculated from the responses of junior members or their knowledgeable staff to the questions, "What committees did you want to serve on (after you were first elected to your chamber)?" "Why?"[7] These responses include committees that members may not have requested formally, because they believed such requests would be denied, but which they viewed as attractive nevertheless. Unfortunately, there are no directly comparable data available for the Senate in an earlier congress. The 1948–1971 Senate figures that we use here were collected by Bullock from the archived papers of two former members of the Senate Democratic Committee on Committees.[8]

Since Fenno's work, scholars have disagreed about which of the three goals motivates most members most of the time. In our view, however, such a choice is both unnecessary and oversimplified. Members differ and members' goals differ. Based on our interviews with members and their senior staff, it seems reasonable to conclude that most members have multiple goals that motivate their committee requests and their subsequent committee activity. Regardless, it seems incontrovertible that the set of goals Fenno discovered remained valid throughout the 1980s and the 1990s. In the discussion that follows, we have replaced the *reelection* label used by Fenno with *constituency* because members mention a richer set of constituency-oriented motivations than *reelection* suggests. Even so, the vast majority of constituency-oriented motivations are defined in terms of electoral needs.[9] Overall, such motivations are the most frequently mentioned reasons for preferring particular committees. Policy interests are a close second and influence or prestige a distant third, especially in the Senate.[10] And while mixed motives are characteristic of members of both chambers—appearing in 62 percent of our House interviews and 75 percent of our Senate interviews for the 100th/101st Congresses—multiple motives are infrequently expressed for the same committee. Usually only one goal is emphasized for each committee of interest, and several committees are mentioned for different reasons. Of the separate committee mentions in the 100th/101st Congress interviews, 86 percent were associated with only one goal in the House and 79 percent were associated with only one goal in the Senate (up from 77.4 percent and 73.4 percent, respectively, in the 97th Congress). Thus, these findings continue to corroborate Fenno's assumptions about members' calculations when considering their options for committee assignments.

Whether a member seeks a committee berth for purposes of serving constituency concerns, good public policy, or chamber influence, his or her interest is grounded in the committee's substantive jurisdiction. The relevance of a committee's activities to any member's personal goals therefore may increase or decrease as a function of formal jurisdictional changes. And the perceived opportunity to pursue certain goals can change as political events outside members' control affect a committee's informal agenda.

MEMBER GOALS IN THE HOUSE

Member and staff responses to questions about committee preferences are reported in Table 3-1. The data show that, in making the important decision about which committee assignments to pursue, House freshmen distinguish among committees based on personal aspirations and goals. Interestingly, the survey also indicates that only a handful of committees attract members who share nearly identical motivations.

INFLUENCE AND PRESTIGE COMMITTEES

The Rules, Appropriations, and Ways and Means committees remain distinctively prestigious in House members' eyes. When describing them, House members use terms and phrases such as "important," "powerful," "*the* committee," "where the action is," and "the mover-and-shaker committee"—descriptions similar to those Fenno heard for Appropriations and Ways and Means in the 1960s. A fourth committee, Budget, has almost reached a position of parity with the traditional troika. Driven largely by the importance of budget deficits on the national agenda, and augmented by several centralizing trends in national policy making, Budget must now be ranked among the most powerful of House standing committees.

As we will see shortly, these committees impact every member of the House. They are the only committees that both parties have designated "exclusive."[11] This means that members assigned to them may not sit on other standing committees (with the exception of Budget, as explained below). What makes these committees unique is their attractiveness to House members beyond their value for serving constituents or pursuing personal policy interests. Their importance in House politics dictates that attention be given to each in turn.

THE RULES COMMITTEE.   Membership on the House Rules Committee is widely coveted but rarely sought. This small but powerful group has the capacity to influence virtually all legislative matters within the chamber. Members know that a seat there will allow them the opportunity to participate in every important decision that comes before the House. Why, then, do so few members seek an appointment? The answer is tied to the importance of the committee to the party leadership. At present the principal leader of each party controls the assignment of his party's members to this panel—a procedure designed to ensure that the committee is closely guided by the wishes of party leaders. Today, therefore, members who wish to be appointed to the committee must have strong party credentials and be willing to labor in relative obscurity for the rewards of sitting on this powerful committee.

TABLE 3-1   Committee Preference Motivations for New House Members (92d, 97th, and 100/101st Congresses)

Committee type	Constituency			Policy			Prestige		
	92d	97th	100/101st	92d	97th	100/101st	92d	97th	100/101st
Prestige committees									
Appropriations	5	5	7	3	6	4	7	11	4
Budget	—	0	0	—	4	2	—	5	2
Rules	1	0	0	0	1	0	0	3	1
Ways and Means	1	0	2	0	6	8	5	7	4
Policy committees									
Banking	1	14	4	9	17	10	1	1	0
Education and Labor	5	3	2	7	2	6	0	0	0
Energy and Commerce	3	9	6	16	13	3	1	0	0
Foreign Affairs	1	2	0	4	8	8	0	0	0
Judiciary	0	0	1	7	3	3	0	0	0
Government Operations	0	0	1	0	9	2	0	0	0
Constituency committees									
Agriculture	10	15	8	3	7	1	0	0	0
Armed Services	5	11	9	3	7	3	1	0	0
Interior	7	12	2	4	2	1	0	0	0
Merchant Marine and Fisheries	3	5	7	0	0	0	0	0	0
Public Works	7	4	6	1	2	1	0	0	0
Science, Space, and Technology	0	9	8	1	5	3	1	0	0
Small Business	—	13	3	—	4	0	—	0	0
Veterans' Affairs	5	2	8	0	1	0	0	0	0
Unrequested committees									
District of Columbia	0	1	0	0	1	0	0	1	0
House Administration	0	0	0	0	0	0	0	0	0
Post Office and Civil Service	1	1	1	0	0	0	0	0	0
Standards of Official Conduct	—	0	0	—	1	0	—	0	0
Select Intelligence	—	—	0	—	—	1	—	—	0

Sources: (92d) Charles S. Bullock III, "Motivations for U.S. Congressional Committee Preferences: Freshmen of the 92d Congress," *Legislative Studies Quarterly* 1 (May 1976): 201–212; (97th and 100/101st) author interviews.

Note: Committee names reflect titles used in the 101st Congress.

The prestige and influence of the House Committee on Rules reside in its power to propose *rules*—which come in a variety of forms and are sometimes called special orders—for the consideration of legislation on the floor.[12] Unlike the smaller Senate, which tolerates flexible floor procedures, the House more carefully structures its floor activity. Without special rules, House floor debate would be sheer chaos. Because rules are required to bring nearly all important legislation to the floor, to limit debate, and often to limit amendments, Rules members are in a position to block or expedite legislation important to individual members of the House. The committee's reach is as broad as that of any committee in Congress, despite its otherwise limited jurisdiction. And its decisions are salient and often controversial within the chamber. Thus the Rules Committee is ideally suited to the member seeking influence and prestige within the House. With its small size (only thirteen members in the 105th Congress), the Rules Committee is truly elite.[13]

By most accounts, the contemporary Rules Committee has been restored to its turn-of-the-century status as "the Speaker's committee." It was Bruce Oppenheimer who first noted that reforms implemented by House Democrats in the early 1970s firmly established the committee as an arm of the House leadership.[14] For an entire era prior to this, the committee had operated quite independently of House leaders and was dominated by a coalition of conservative Democrats and Republicans frequently united in opposition to the agenda of the increasingly liberal Democratic party. But the 1970s' reforms saw party loyalty become a primary criterion for the precious few openings on this powerful committee. Under the new Democratic rules, the Speaker became responsible for nominating his party's committee members and the committee chair. For obvious reasons, Speakers have been very careful about whom they appoint. Barbara Sinclair quoted one committee Democrat as follows:

> When Tip [Speaker of the House, Thomas P. O'Neill (D-Mass.)] asked me to go on the Rules Committee, he said to me, "_____, now if you take this, I expect you to support me on the committee and, if every once in a while you can't, to make sure it doesn't influence the outcome on the committee."[15]

The new Republican majority has adopted essentially the same appointment procedures to ensure that their party leaders retain influence over the flow of legislation to the floor of the House.

Over the years the source of influence and prestige for the Rules Committee, as articulated by its members, has changed in important ways. Oppenheimer noted, for example, that Rules members of the 1970s began to view themselves as "field commanders" for party leaders, a role perception that has been strengthened since that time.[16] In this role, Rules members serve as additional sets of eyes and ears for their party leadership. They often spot legislation that poses political problems for the party and draw the attention of elected party leaders to it. Majority party leaders consult with Rules members on nearly all major pieces of legislation—not only to inform them of leadership preferences for a rule, but also to seek information and advice about legislative strategy. As a result, Rules members' influence and prestige are closely tied to that of the party leadership.

The Rules Committee of the 1980s also fashioned a creative role for itself by structuring new types of rules. Prior to this, the committee's practice had been to grant simple open rules that permitted unlimited germane amendments. In so doing it served as the House's gatekeeper for access to the floor. Bills were either granted rules, or they were not. Two trends forced the committee to refine its role. First, the informal norms that had restrained members' amending behavior began to erode. Second, there was a marked trend toward larger, catch-all legislation—called *omnibus* bills— that frequently touched upon a very wide array of policy matters. This latter trend reduced germaneness as a barrier to floor amendments. With neither individual norms nor germaneness serving as a barrier, most bills became the target of numerous floor amendments. In response to entreaties from committee chairs and party leaders, the Rules Committee began to fashion a variety of complex, restrictive rules that had the effect of constraining amending behavior.[17] This change is important because it marks a shift from committee involvement in macro-level decisions— determining whether or not a bill gets to the floor—to micro-level decisions—determining when and how a bill may be amended when it gets to the floor. Thus, members of the committee are now involved in the details of legislative design to a much greater degree than they once were.

Finally, the Rules Committee of the 1990s has become even more closely tied to the leadership team and functions as the primary agent for partisan control of the agenda. Both parties now ensure that their leaders control appointments to this committee, with the majority party retaining its traditional outsized majority. The majority party uses the committee to structure the most important decisions that are made on the House floor. Having long chafed under restrictive rules written when in the minority, the Republicans promised more open floor procedures when they captured a majority in 1994. They point to their adoption of a greater proportion of open or modified open rules during the first part of the 104th Congress (72 percent to the Democrats' 44 percent during the 103d Congress) as evidence of their success.[18] At the same time, though, they have imposed much stricter time constraints on floor debate—thus limiting the period allowed for amendments—with, according to minority Democrats, essentially the same restrictive effect. (For more on special rules, see Chapter 5.)

THE APPROPRIATIONS COMMITTEE.   The Appropriations Committee has been and remains one of the most desirable committee assignments in the House. And yet, with the exception of panels that simply have been abolished, no other committee has been more affected by internal and external changes. Thus, while Appropriations remains among the elite committees in the House, members are drawn to the panel by a more diverse set of motivations. Reforms and agenda changes since the mid-1970s, and more recently the dramatic shift in partisan control, have affected the relative significance of the three goals for Appropriations members. At bottom, however, the committee's appeal is easy to understand. Appropriations member Norman Dicks (D-Wash.) put it quite simply: "It's where the money is. And money is where the clout is."[19]

The committee's jurisdiction over spending bills makes it attractive to members seeking dollars for district programs and projects and to members interested in federal fiscal policy. But more important, the committee's significance in national fiscal policy making and its importance to noncommittee members looking for district funding also make membership valuable to those members seeking influence and prestige within the chamber.[20] "Appropriations is the key spot. Members need you and come to you for help. If you're not on Appropriations, you are really at the mercy of other people," said Mickey Edwards (R-Okla.).[21] During the past two decades a series of changes has altered the ability of committee members to influence fiscal policy. At the same time, the importance of fiscal policy on the national agenda has boosted the appeal of committee membership.

First, Democratic rule changes in the early 1970s—open committee meetings, the bidding process that allowed members to select their own subcommittees, and the independent election of subcommittee chairs by the entire party caucus—reduced the power of the full committee chair and encouraged members to be more constituency oriented. Second, the erosion of the Appropriations Committee's control over expenditures, which was well under way in the late 1960s, was exacerbated in the 1970s and 1980s by creation of the new budget process and a separate Budget Committee. Third, an upsurge of policy-related interest in Appropriations occurred as federal spending became a more salient national issue in the late 1970s. This has been especially true for conservative Republicans, who even in the 1960s occasionally sought the Appropriations Committee for policy reasons.[22]

By the mid-1980s and into the 1990s a noticeable tension had emerged between the less senior but more conservative contingent of Republicans on the committee and the more liberal group of senior Republicans.[23] At the outset of the 104th Congress, Republican Speaker Newt Gingrich passed over several more senior Republicans in hand-picking budget "hawk" Robert L. Livingston (R-La.) to lead the panel. And when the time came to appoint new members to the committee, the more senior members of the Republican party shied away, as only five of these asked to fill one of the eleven openings available to the new majority party. According to Livingston, "Not too many senior Members wanted a job here. They saw that this was going to be a committee that was going to cut funds and not add."[24] Four of the five apparently received slots as seven of the eleven new committee members were freshmen.

Included among that group of first-term members was former math teacher and deficit fanatic Mark W. Neumann, a Republican from Wisconsin. In addition to this appointment to the committee, Neumann also received a coveted slot on the powerful Defense Appropriations subcommittee. Unfortunately for Speaker Gingrich and Chairman Livingston, Neumann proved to be more independent-minded in his pursuit of deficit reduction than the leadership had wished. Neumann opposed an emergency defense spending bill, first in subcommittee and later on the floor. Then in September 1995 he offered a floor amendment to the regular Defense Appropriations bill that would have prohibited U.S. troops in Bosnia without congressional approval. The amendment failed, but so did the bill. The leadership blamed Neumann. Livingston was furious. "He [Livingston] called me into his office and started screaming at me," Neumann told a reporter. "It got so bad two Capitol police officers came to the door to see if anything was wrong."[25] The Speaker took an even more unusual step. He removed Neumann from the Defense subcommittee—a punishment that pushed the House Republican newcomers contingent into virtual revolt.

On balance, then, House Appropriations has become somewhat less attractive for reasons of prestige and influence (although these still dominate), decidedly more attractive to conservative, policy-oriented members, and slightly less attractive to constituency-oriented members.

THE WAYS AND MEANS COMMITTEE.   The House Ways and Means Committee long has been considered one of the most—if not the most—powerful and prestigious committee in Congress.[26] Throughout the 1960s and early 1970s, Ways and Means' small size (twenty-five members), its huge, nationally salient jurisdiction (taxation, trade, Social Security, health insurance, public assistance, and unemployment compensation), and, for Democrats, its function as the Committee on Committees combined to make it especially attractive to influence- and prestige-oriented members. Much of the committee's legislation, and nearly all of its tax legislation, was considered on the House floor under closed rules on the theory that tax bills were too complex and important for uninformed outsiders to tamper with. The Ways and Means chair for two decades, Wilbur D. Mills of Arkansas, was described as the most powerful member of Congress. A renowned expert on tax policy, Mills operated the committee with a strong hand, controlled staff and paperwork, closed markups, appointed no subcommittees, and was committed to the apprenticeship-seniority norm.[27]

Not surprisingly, Ways and Means became a chief target for reform in the 1970s. Along with other House committees, Ways and Means was forced to open its hearings and meetings to the public. The Democratic Caucus established a procedure to make it easier to have an amendment to a Ways and Means bill considered on the floor. The Caucus also initiated a change in chamber rules requiring committees with more than twenty members to establish subcommittees. This rule change was targeted specifically at Ways and Means, which was the only committee without subcommittees (except for the Rules Committee, which fell below the twenty-member minimum). Hence, the committee was forced to create five subcommittees, its first since Mills's second term as chair. And, bowing to demand for committee positions, the Caucus dramatically expanded the committee to thirty-seven members. Finally, Ways and Means Democrats were stripped of their committee assignment authority. Perhaps the only bright spot was that it, like other House panels, escaped any major changes in its jurisdiction, despite the earnest attempts of reformers.

Reforms and agenda changes have somewhat diminished the attractiveness of Ways and Means membership. For Democrats in particular, the loss of the committee assignment function was a blow.[28] For all members the value of membership was deflated by the committee's expansion. Counterbalancing this, however, were the expanded opportunities for participation in subcommittees and the continued centrality of budget, trade, and health issues on the national agenda. Policy goals, always important to at least some Ways and Means members, have gained added importance in recent years.[29] And even though few members mention the committee for constituency reasons, there are opportunities to be of service to local or regional interests. Finally, most members are far from dismayed at the proliferation of generous political action committees (PACs) who give a disproportionate share of their campaign contributions to members of the tax committees.[30] (See Box 3-1 for an example of PACs' fund-raising clout.)

BUDGET COMMITTEE.   The House Budget Committee resembles Ways and Means in member motivation (see Table 3-1). Members seek assignments due to its recognized power and broad policy impact: "I've been very fortunate in my career, getting on Ways and Means in my first term," noted Frank J. Guarini (D-N.J.). "But I've never been on any other committee. The Budget Committee affords a huge panorama for all our nation's problems."[31] Unlike Appropriations, Rules, and Ways and Means,

Plenty to Go Around

Raising money to finance his campaigns has been easy for Rep. Charles B. Rangel, D-N.Y. Since his first election to Congress in 1970, he has only once faced a significant challenger.

Most of his expenses are for standard party-machine functions, such as printing fliers and campaign posters for Democrats down the ticket. But this election cycle [1996] Rangel collected more than $1.35 million in contributions to four different campaign committees, according to preliminary Federal Election Commission (FEC) Reports. He raised money primarily from New York sources to help the Democrats' nationwide efforts to win back the House.

Rangel took in about nine times the amount raised by Ways and Means Committee Chairman Bill Archer, R-Texas, according to FEC records, which say he took in about $153,000. However, Archer does not accept contributions from political action committees (PACs) and does not make contributions to other candidates. He has a campaign war chest of more than $700,000, according to the Center for Responsive Politics, which tracks campaign finances.

Rangel admits that his recent success as a fundraiser had little to do with his own re-election. Rather, business groups were scared that they would be in disfavor if they failed to support Democrats and the party regained control of the House. Rangel leveraged that fear in his fundraising calls. "I was campaigning to be chairman of the Ways and Means Committee. I don't know how well I would have done if I was campaigning to become the ranking member," he says.

Rangel's strategy was simple: He got lists of donors to the National Republican Congressional Committee (NRCC), "and I would call right behind them and say, 'I see you donated to the NRCC. I know in the interests of good government, you would like to donate to the DCCC [Democratic Congressional Campaign Committee], too.' "

Of the $915,000 he had raised by mid-September [1996], 60 percent came from PACs. The most generous contributions came from the financial services sector, including insurance, investment, and banking industries, which donated more than $147,000. Labor union PACs gave $138,000.

Rangel also took money from tobacco companies, even though they have been criticized for targeting cigarette advertising in minority neighborhoods. He insists the contributions have not influenced his votes on tobacco-related issues, although he has opposed excise taxes on tobacco. . . .

Source: Alissa J. Rubin, "Plenty to Go Around," *Congressional Quarterly Weekly Report,* December 7, 1996, 3336.

BOX 3-1

however, Budget has not traditionally been regarded as a prestige committee.

A major contributing factor to Budget's odd combination of power and limited prestige is the restricted tenure of its members.[32] The Congressional Budget and Impoundment Control Act of 1974 provided that the committee be composed of five members from Appropriations, five from Ways and Means, and fifteen (later seventeen) members of other House committees. Each member's service was limited to four years in any ten-year period, a limit that was extended to six years in 1979. Consequently, Budget members do not have the opportunity to develop long-term chamber influence by virtue of membership on the committee or the prestige that might come with that influence.

The Budget Committee also suffers from its nonexclusive jurisdiction.[33] The committee's main function, writing budget resolutions, entails making judgments about expenditures and revenues that fall under other House committees' jurisdictions. As a result, Budget exercises independent discretion only by directly challenging the decision-making autonomy of other House committees. Until 1981 the Budget Committee minimized direct conflict with other committees by setting spending targets at levels that permitted most of them to act freely, without violating the ceilings.[34] In 1981, faced with President Reagan's budget-cutting program, the committee produced resolutions forcing most House committees to find programmatic ways to reduce projected spending sharply, a move that stimulated efforts to revamp the budget process in the 98th Congress.[35] To the extent that Budget is successful in influencing policy, it appears to create more enemies than admirers in the House.

Lance LeLoup discovered in interviews with Budget members between 1975 and 1978 that Budget Democrats saw their major goal as ensuring that the new budget process worked.[36] While Budget Republicans were motivated strongly by their policy goal of reducing federal spending and deficits, Democratic members acted to establish a firm institutional footing for the new budget process and the new committee. Keeping the process alive meant avoiding direct conflicts with other powerful House committees whenever possible. LeLoup concluded that Budget Democrats in the mid-1970s should be classified as process-oriented rather than as policy- or influence-oriented. In fact, two or three Democrats had developed an excellent reputation for their expertise in understanding the details of budgeting and the budget process. He found, as we have, that members do not mention motivations related to reelection chances as a reason for their interest in Budget.[37]

During the 1980s the committee became even more integral to House politics as the budget process moved to center stage. The committee is now the first congressional step in the budget process after receipt of the president's annual budget. Indeed, by the late 1980s pressure again mounted to delimit the committee's power as Appropriations Committee members fought encroachments on their traditional authority and budget resolutions became ever more detailed. This goal was partially achieved in the Budget Enforcement Act of 1990, which established new rules limiting the committee's micro-level budget authority—a change that shifted power modestly back in the direction of appropriators.[38] In fact, the whole budget process raises important questions about the change in the level of committee autonomy. These are treated in more detail in Chapter 5.

The common thread of underlying change in the Rules, Appropriations, Ways and Means, and Budget committees is procedural reform. The first three committees were directly affected by the democratizing reforms of the 1970s. Rules became more closely tied to an elected party leader, the Appropriations chairs lost the ability to dictate subcommittee memberships, and the Ways and Means chairs lost their stranglehold over committee deliberations. In addition, Ways and Means lost its vital sources of influence to the Democratic Caucus. Yet few jurisdictional changes directly affected these committees, and informal agenda changes were not major factors. In each case, the net effect was a recognition on the part of committee members that their influence within the House was reduced as their decision-making autonomy was weakened. Nevertheless, each committee continues to occupy a highly influential position within the House decision-making structure. As such, each retains great attractiveness in the eyes of the members seeking appointments of prestige and influence.

POLICY COMMITTEES

Policy committees are defined by the predominance of members attracted to them by issue-based motivations (see Table 3-1). Policy-oriented members are not disinterested in reelection and they frequently seek membership on a second committee that has a more obvious tie to particular demographic characteristics of their districts. Members motivated by an interest in particular policy areas, or perhaps merely an interest in becoming involved in important issues, see things somewhat differently than their prestige- or constituency-oriented colleagues. Salient national issues are attractive because the policy-oriented member seeks to contribute to the shape of important policies. If they are conflict-ridden issues, so be it. Conflict, after all, often reflects the importance and complexity of the issues. Thus policy decisions with concentrated perceived costs, but only diffuse benefits, do not keep the policy-oriented member away from a committee facing such decisions. And the broader the committee's jurisdiction, the better it is for a member attracted to challenging issues.[39] Policy-oriented members generally have fairly well-established positions on major issues. They are more likely to be labeled as liberals or conservatives. Most importantly, they are likely to seek membership on committees with policy impacts that go well beyond the boundaries of their own districts.

For the policy-oriented member, participation is important. It is therefore not surprising that the 1970s reforms had the greatest impact on policy committees (see Chapter 2 for details). At that time, liberals felt that power was too frequently concentrated in the hands of a minority of conservative members. Newer, more policy-oriented members became frustrated by their incapacity to help shape and pass legislation. These members had sought and received appointments to committees with desirable jurisdictions. But once on those committees they faced procedural roadblocks that prevented them from achieving their political goals. Banking, Commerce, Foreign Affairs, and Government Operations were particularly mired in the procedural red tape that left newer members unable to pursue more vigorously policy interests already motivating their committee activity. Some members perceived externally imposed reforms as the only way to achieve their personal policy goals.

For members interested in the leading issues of the late 1960s and the 1970s—the environment, energy, urban development, civil rights, housing, labor, and a variety of foreign policy issues—the committees on Commerce, Judiciary, Education and Labor (now called Education and the Workforce), Banking, Foreign Affairs (now International Relations), and, increasingly, Interior (Resources) presented attractive opportunities. During the 1980s, some of these same committees lost their attractiveness to liberals as budget woes, Republican control of the White House, and a national swing toward conservatism altered the national agenda. Indeed, majority party Democrats on some committees spent little time passing bills and much more time using the negative power of committees to kill legislation favored by Republicans. As a result, the Democrats found it necessary to recruit members to serve on Judiciary, Education, and Foreign Affairs—forcing them to grant waivers to Caucus rules limiting the number of committees on which member could serve. In contrast, Republicans interested in crime, balanced budgets, privatization, deregulation, school prayer, and other elements of the emerging conservative agenda found membership on these same committees attractive. By the early 1990s, health care legislation had become the most hotly contested non-fiscal policy issue, with numerous committees and subcommittees scrambling for jurisdictional control.

While the list of committees attracting policy-oriented members has remained remarkably stable, some shifts in desirability have occurred. From the 1960s to the 1970s, for example, changes in the national agenda burnished the reputation and attractiveness of the Energy and Commerce Committee (which has since dropped Energy from its title) to the point where vacancies on the panel were nearly as hotly contested as the prestige committee slots. That situation reversed somewhat in the late 1980s, though, as the committee receded from public view and its agenda took on a more distributive bent.[40]

Two committees warrant brief additional comment. First, Government Operations has been among the top choices of members requesting policy committees only since the early 1970s. Continuing budget crises and repeated procurement scandals helped to buoy member interest in slots there—an interest enhanced by its categorization by the two parties as a nonmajor committee. Now called Government Reform and Oversight, this panel features an expansive oversight and investigative authority that is particularly attractive at a time when new authorizing legislation is extremely rare. In addition, the committee's jurisdiction has been expanded to include matters once under the purview of the now-abolished Post Office and Civil Service Committee. Post Office, which appears with other unrequested committees in Table 3-1, has generally been considered a constituency-oriented committee. Thus, the addition of this new jurisdiction—and three new subcommittees at a time when the House was otherwise dramatically cutting subcommittees—may well give a more constituency-oriented cast to the new Government Reform panel.

Second, the Education and Workforce Committee—formerly Employment and Educational Opportunities (1995–1996) and Education and Labor (1947–1994)—has regained some of its attractiveness to policy-oriented members. Beginning in the late 1970s and for most of the 1980s the committee had trouble filling its vacancies.[41] Declining union membership and the ascendance of a more market-oriented Republican agenda left the committee with diminished appeal. Moreover, its partisan approach left it isolated within the chamber. By the early 1990s, however, educational reform issues and the partial resuscitation of big labor had re-energized the panel, rekindling an interest among members. Because it remains one of the most partisan committees in the House, it retains the characteristics that are hallmarks of a policy-oriented panel.[42]

CONSTITUENCY COMMITTEES

Members motivated by constituency-oriented concerns describe their committee assignments almost as extensions of their districts. Time and again, members (or their senior staff) tell us about the character of the district rather than the nature of the issues when they reflect upon their motivations for seeking these committees. Members see their districts as military districts, as farm districts, or as port districts, for example. Unlike policy committee members (who define their committees as holding companies for various important or contentious issues), constituency-committee members see a connection to the folks back home: they're farmers, fishermen, loggers, retirees, veterans, ranchers, or whatever. And although members are extremely reluctant to say so, they evince no personal or intellectual excitement about the issues considered by these panels. One member characterized his service on what is now the Transportation and Infrastructure Committee as follows: "As far as I can see, there is really only one basic reason to be on the . . . Committee . . . certainly not for intellectual stimulation. Most of all, I want to be able to bring home projects to my districts."[43]

A committee with jurisdiction over programs that have concentrated benefits (for one's constituents) but widely dispersed costs (taxes, consumer prices) is well suited to these needs. Such a committee is typically one with a narrow jurisdiction over programs of interest to a limited number of members and constituencies. Thus, a committee with low national salience, high local salience, low conflict, and a narrow jurisdiction is especially attractive to constituency-oriented members. These committees are the classic pork-barrel committees of the House. The committees' products are readily identifiable by their names (further elaborated in most cases by their subcommittee arrangements), with a clear set of constituent consumers for their products.

Seven House committees attract members primarily for constituency-oriented reasons. These are the Agriculture, Armed Services (now National Security), Interior (Resources), Public Works (Transportation and Infrastructure), Science, Small Business, and Veterans' committees. An eighth committee, Merchant Marine and Fisheries, was abolished at the start of the 104th Congress. One additional committee, Post Office and Civil Service, also was district-oriented, but was desired by so few members that it is listed in the "unrequested" category in Table 3-1. It, too, has been abandoned.

The most striking characteristic of member goals in the constituency committees is their stability. Only one of these committees, Science, has changed markedly in its desirability to members during the past twenty years. The others have retained moderate attractiveness for the same balance of reasons observers noted fifteen or twenty years ago. Several of these committees feature quite distinctive patterns of regional representation—patterns we would not expect to see in the absence of self-selection (see Table 3-2). With very few exceptions, neither agenda changes nor procedural reforms have had a major effect on the goal orientation of constituency committees. Most new issues retain a district orientation for the committees' members. The constituency orientation is not surprising for committees whose jurisdictions involve clear benefits for limited constituencies—highways, airports, harbors, water projects, military installa-

TABLE 3-2 Regional Representation on Selected House Committees: 89th/90th, 96th/97th, 99th/100th, and 103d/104th Congresses (Percent from Each Region)

Region	House seats per region				Agriculture				Resources				Merchant Marine			
	89th/ 90th	96th/ 97th	99th/ 100th	103d/ 104th	89th/ 90th	96th/ 97th	99th/ 100th	103d/ 104th	89th/ 90th	96th/ 97th	99th/ 100th	103d/ 104th	89th/ 90th	96th/ 97th	99th/ 100th	103d[a]
East	25	24	22	20	11	5	2	3	24	14	11	12	33	31	31	27
South	24	25	27	29	36	27	33	36	12	12	12	11	21	23	31	42
Border	6	6	6	5	4	4	7	6	9	8	7	5	7	10	10	8
Midwest	29	30	26	24	34	39	35	33	24	18	16	11	19	13	8	4
West	16	15	20	21	15	25	23	22	32	48	54	61	19	23	20	19

Note: Regions: *East:* Conn., Del., Maine, Mass., N.H., N.Y., Pa., R.I., Vt.; *South:* Ala., Ark., Fla., Ga., La., Miss., N.C., S.C., Tenn., Texas, Va.; *Border:* Ky., Md., Okla., W.Va.; *Midwest:* Ill., Ind., Iowa, Kan., Mich., Minn., Mo., Neb., N.D., Ohio, S.D., Wis.; *West:* Alaska, Ariz., Calif., Colo., Hawaii, Idaho, Mont., Nev., N.M., Ore., Utah, Wash., Wyo.

[a] The House Merchant Marine and Fisheries Committee was disbanded at the beginning of the 104th Congress and much of its jurisdiction transferred to the Resources Committee. Data here is for the 103d Congress only.

tions, commodity supports, small business loans, and veterans' medical programs are typical. Of course, dramatic shifts in agendas are not likely to occur on constituency committees with very narrow jurisdictions. Likewise, procedural reforms alone do not make these committees any more attractive to members without relevant constituency interests or to members seeking committees for reasons of policy or chamber influence.

The most dramatic change to constituency committees during recent years involved the abolition of the Merchant Marine and Fisheries Committee in 1995. The disbanding of Merchant Marine and Fisheries had an impact on the two constituency-oriented committees that received its areas of jurisdiction. The Resources Committee now has the natural resource elements—the Fisheries part, that is—of the former committee, and the Transportation and Infrastructure Committee now has jurisdiction over the Coast Guard, merchant marine, and navigational elements— the harbors part—of the former committee. For some members this poses a vexing choice because they need to decide whether the fisheries components or the harbor components are of greater interest to their constituents. Regardless, the Resources and Transportation committees will now be sought by members from coastal districts, who will then gravitate to the Subcommittee on Fisheries, Wildlife, and Oceans on the Resources Committee or the Subcommittee on Coast Guard and Maritime Transportation of the Transportation Committee, depending on their constituents needs.

UNREQUESTED COMMITTEES

In addition to the Post Office and Civil Service Committee and the District of Columbia Committee—whose jurisdictions have been transferred to Government Reform and Oversight—three House standing committees are rarely requested by new members of Congress. The first, Standards of Official Conduct, is a special case because of its unique jurisdiction over ethics violations by House members. As one party leader described it, "anyone who wants a seat on Standards doesn't deserve a seat on Standards." This comment reflects the discomfort felt (or that ought to be felt) by members sitting in judgment of colleagues' behavior. The second committee, House Administration, once had complete control of House office accounts and supplies. This gave the committee special intrachamber influence when the infamous Wayne L. Hays was chair, but the committee's ability to dispense goodies was substantially reduced after Hays resigned in the midst of the Elizabeth Ray sex scandal and in the wake of House reforms in its accounting and personnel procedures in 1976. During the 1980s, the committee retained a certain amount of cachet among relatively senior members who were appointed, at the direction of the leadership. But it also became the target of Republican attacks on the entrenched Democratic party. At the outset of the 104th Congress, Republicans reoriented the committee toward downsizing and modernizing the House and renamed it the House Oversight Committee. Aside from its internal management responsibilities—which includes everything from barbers and groundskeepers to the Capitol Hill police—the committee retains its authority over campaign finance legislation. This, however, is insufficient to attract newer members.

The third committee, Select Intelligence, also is a special case. Like the Budget Committee, membership on this panel is limited to no more than six years in a ten-year period. Members are recruited to the panel by party and issue leaders within the chamber. By and large, it is policy-oriented members who are willing to serve on the committee. Membership has modest advantages for those who wish to be "in the know" about international affairs but comes with a heavy burden of secrecy attached to most of its work. New members of Congress rarely consider joining the panel upon their arrival on Capitol Hill.

MEMBER GOALS IN THE SENATE

Member goals are less easily characterized in the Senate than in the House for three reasons. First, mentions of chamber influence or prestige are less common in the Senate. In fact, for no Senate committee was this objective the most frequently mentioned motivation (see Table 3-3). Second, reelection and other constituency-oriented motivations are of greater concern to Senate respondents than House respondents, despite the fact that senators are up for reelection only once every six years. As a result, a number of Senate committees whose House counterparts are clearly policy-oriented are also constituency-oriented to a substantial extent. The desire to be reelected leads to a greater emphasis on publicity in the Senate than in the House, perhaps as a consequence of senators' larger and more diverse constituencies and their greater dependence on the electronic media for communicating with their constituents. For many senators, the publicity emphasis makes it more difficult to differentiate personal policy interest from reelection interest because both goals often entail attracting public attention to an issue. (See Box 3-2 for an example of the mix of motives that may come into play when choosing committee assignments.)

Third, and most compelling, distinguishing committee types in the Senate is difficult because senators display less certainty and intensity about their motivations for preferring particular committees than do representatives.[44] The lack of intensity among the Senate respondents in the

Dole Search Fails:
Gramm Going to Finance Panel

Sen. Phil Gramm, R-Texas, will assume the GOP seat on the pivotal Finance Committee being vacated by Bob Packwood of Oregon, whose resignation [in the face of an Ethics Committee recommendation for his expulsion] takes effect October 1 [1995].

For Gramm, the committee is the logical place to pursue his fondness for tax cuts, for downsizing programs, and, not least, for showing up Majority Leader Bob Dole, R-Kansas, as both lawmakers compete for the GOP presidential nomination. But Gramm's input may be limited because he likely will join the panel after it has completed its initial work on the deficit-reducing or reconciliation package.

"My guiding light on the Finance Committee will be cutting taxes and cutting spending," Gramm said.

Gramm pointedly took issue with budget cutters who favor reducing the size of the tax cuts in the Republican budget plan and in favor of deficit reduction. "I'm committed to a tax cut. I will oppose any effort to make the cut temporary or to reduce its size," he said.

Dole, who announced Gramm's selection Sept. 29 [1995], has been trying to line up a more senior member to take the slot, but none was willing to give up other assignments to make the move. Dole used similar tactics to deny Gramm a seat earlier this year.

Gramm was able to take the post after Arlen Specter, R-Pa., passed up his chance to take the seat. Specter, by virtue of his seniority, had first choice, but decided to remain on Appropriations. The Gramm appointment still must be approved by the Senate GOP Conference. . . . Gramm plans to give up his seat on Appropriations, where he chairs the Commerce, Justice, State, and Judiciary Subcommittee. Sen. Ben Nighthorse Campbell, R-Colo., [who switched from the Democratic to the Republican party only a few months earlier] is a leading candidate for Gramm's Appropriations slot.

Source: Jackie Koszczuk and David S. Cloud, "Dole Search Fails: Gramm Going to Finance Panel," *Congressional Quarterly Weekly Report*, September 30, 1995, 2967.

BOX 3-2

97th and 101st Congresses also reflects the larger number of opportunities the Senate committee system offers its members to pursue their goals. First, as mentioned earlier, nearly all senators receive a seat on one of four top committees. (Traditionally, these have been Appropriations, Armed Services, Finance, and Foreign Relations, with Foreign Relations lagging in

TABLE 3-3   Committee Preference Motivations for New Senators (92d, 97th, and 100/101st Congresses)

Committee type	Constituency 92d	Constituency 97th	Constituency 100/101st	Policy 92d	Policy 97th	Policy 100/101st	Prestige 92d	Prestige 97th	Prestige 100/101st
Policy committees									
Budget	—	1	1	—	4	6		0	0
Foreign Relations	3	1	0	19	5	2	2	0	0
Governmental Affairs		1	0		3	0		0	0
Judiciary		2	0	9	7	2		0	0
Labor	2	3	0	4	4	1		0	0
Mixed policy/ constituency committees									
Armed Services	4	4	4	4	6	4		0	0
Banking		2	1		3	6		0	0
Finance	4	8	1	13	9	2		4	1
Small Business	—	4	1	—	4	0		0	0
Constituency committees									
Agriculture	4	13	8		2	2		0	0
Appropriations	31	6	3	15	3	3	2	2	3
Commerce	13	5	5	5	2	3		0	0
Energy	4	6	3	2	3	2		0	0
Environment	5	5	2	4	1	2		0	0
Unrequested committees									
Rules and Administration	—	0	0		0	0		0	0
Veterans' Affairs		2	2	3	0	0		0	0
Select Intelligence	—	—	0	—	—	0	—	—	0

Sources: (92d) Charles S. Bullock III, "Motivations for U.S. Congressional Committee Preferences: Freshmen of the 92d Congress," *Legislative Studies Quarterly* 1 (May 1976): 201–212; (97th and 100/101st) author interviews.

recent years.) Although there is no formal rule to the contrary, senators of both parties only rarely receive assignments to more than one of these committees.[45] Second, senators' larger number of committee assignments permits them to pursue more easily both state and personal policy goals. By 1996, for example, the average senator had three standing committee assignments as compared to slightly more than two in 1955.[46] Third, several Senate committees have larger jurisdictions than their House cousins—a circumstance somewhat diminished by the House's elimination of three committees in 1995. This allows senators on those committees to pursue a wider range of personal political objectives. And fourth, it is easier for Senate noncommittee members to influence a committee's decisions. This greater permeability is reinforced by the Senate's more open and flexible floor procedures, which make it easier for noncommittee members to amend bills after they are reported to the floor, to filibuster, or to place a hold on a bill. (In recent years, senators have been able to ask the majority leader to delay action on a bill; the majority leader has felt bound by their requests—sometimes as a matter of courtesy, but more often to avoid tying up the floor proceedings with a filibuster.)[47] Senators simply are in better bargaining positions than their colleagues in the House.

POLICY COMMITTEES

Of the five Senate committees containing a majority of members who are policy-oriented in their approach (see Table 3-3), Foreign Relations is the most exclusively policy-oriented. Members of Foreign Relations mention such things as "personal interest," "my previous job sent me to Central America often," "I wanted to broaden my experience," and "no real political reason" when commenting on why they sought appointments to the committee. For at least a couple of decades now, Foreign Relations members have not considered the committee especially powerful or prestigious within the Senate.[48] As one committee member said,

> Well, you know, it is fun to hobnob with foreign leaders and discuss world affairs, but it doesn't get me any place with my Senate colleagues. . . . Foreign Relations doesn't have much legislative jurisdiction that's important to other senators—it's nothing like Finance or Appropriations.

Senate Budget members also listed policy goals as prime motivators for their committee activity, particularly because budget issues figured prominently on the national agenda. "Where the action is" was a phrase used by three junior committee members during the 97th Congress. By the 104th Congress, the centrality of budget deficits continued to attract members. As with the House Budget Committee, the Senate Budget Committee's lack of direct substantive jurisdiction over programs and the congressional budget process's high level of aggregation do not permit its members to take much positive action on behalf of constituents or colleagues. Yet some senators do believe that Budget membership allows them to protect programs important to their states.[49]

Senate Governmental Affairs is much like House Government Operations in its members' policy motivations. Although in 1977 Governmental Affairs gained jurisdiction over areas that have a constituency orientation in the House (civil service, postal service, District of Columbia), the committee's main attractions are its broad oversight authority and issues such as government regulation and intergovernmental relations. Committee leaders of both parties take pride in the committee's moderate political composition and have sought to maintain it during recent congresses.

No chamber influence or prestige is gained by membership on Governmental Affairs, but some members perceive electoral value accruing to them from publicity they receive in oversight hearings.

Senate Labor and Human Resources and Senate Judiciary also are similar to their House counterparts in their policy orientation. Both attract members of ideological extremes who push their personal policy views on divisive issues. Senate Labor differs from House Education and the Workforce in that it has additional jurisdiction over health issues, which senators see as a constituency-oriented policy area. Labor lost a strong constituency-oriented area, veterans' affairs, when the Veterans' Affairs Committee was created in the early 1970s. Senate Judiciary, like House Judiciary, is a difficult assignment for some members because of the salient social issues under its jurisdiction. At least four members attempted to leave Judiciary in the early 1980s for that reason. Not surprisingly, Senate party and committee leaders have had difficulty attracting members to these two committees over the last few years. In both cases, ideological factionalism within the parties has been a stumbling block to finding "acceptable" members.

Just after the 1992 elections, for example, Judiciary Committee chairman Joseph Biden (D-Del.) flew to Chicago to beg newly elected senator Carol Moseley-Braun (D-Ill.) to join his committee. Just the previous year, Biden had presided over the tension-filled confirmation hearings for Associate Supreme Court Justice Clarence Thomas—made infamous by the circus atmosphere created by charges of sexual harassment leveled by Anita Hill. The hearings left the all-male, all-white Judiciary Committee shell-shocked. Moseley-Braun was unenthusiastic about joining the committee and recalls saying to Biden: "Joe, you just want Anita Hill on the other side of the [hearing] table."[50] Moseley-Braun relented and spent the 103d Congress on the committee with fellow first-term senator Dianne Feinstein (D-Calif.). But in the very next Congress she dropped her Judiciary seat when she gained a spot on the Finance Committee.

MIXED POLICY/CONSTITUENCY COMMITTEES

Senators seeking assignment to the Finance, Armed Services, and Small Business committees express an even mix of policy- and constituency-related goals. A fourth committee, Banking and Urban Affairs, has become increasingly more policy-oriented based in recent congresses (see Table 3-3). In the case of Finance, no change has occurred in the blend of members' motivations since the 1960s, when Fenno concluded that its members "emphasize about equally the pursuit of policy and reelection goals." Senators find the committee's jurisdiction over tax, trade, and Social Security matters both personally interesting and useful for reelection. In contrast to Fenno's findings, however, a few members of the 97th Congress, both within the committee and outside it, viewed Finance as an influential and prestigious Senate committee. These senators clearly perceived Finance's tax jurisdiction as salient to the entire chamber, and several of them mentioned Finance members' ability to do favors for noncommittee members in writing tax legislation, applying terms such as "powerful," "influential," and "prestigious." Many senators identify Finance as the most powerful and prestigious Senate committee.

Armed Services and Small Business also are seen as useful for both policy and constituency reasons. The Senate Armed Services Committee, like its House counterpart, can have a great impact on those states housing military installations and personnel and defense contractors. For this reason, members from these states find it attractive. On the policy side, a large number of Senate Armed Services members have strong and usually conservative policy views that coincide with their constituencies' interests.[51] Even so, the Senate committee's largest contingent is composed of members with insignificant state connections to the defense establishment but who possess a personal policy interest in the committee's activities.

Our 1982 interviews showed Senate Banking to be more constituency-oriented than its House counterpart. According to one member at that time, the committee had lost some of its appeal to liberal activists when issues such as urban decay and redevelopment slipped from the national agenda during the 1970s. Since then, the committee has been buffeted by agenda changes and the political scandal surrounding the savings and loan crisis and bailout. Not the least of these, of course, was the so-called Keating Five Scandal in which two senior Senate Banking Committee members and three other senators were investigated by the Senate Ethics Committee for dispensing favors to savings and loan executive Charles R. Keating, Jr., in exchange for campaign contributions.[52] Although this episode and the whole savings and loan scandal chilled members' interest in joining the committee in the late 1980s and very early 1990s, it has since regained its appeal (on both sides of the Hill). It remains, along with the Finance Committee, one of the most lucrative committee assignments for members interested in donations from political action committees. Urban and housing issues still attract members for state-oriented reasons, but personal interest in the committee's issues appears more pronounced, with the committee's jurisdiction being described as "interesting," "intellectually stimulating," and "educational."

Finally, Small Business has had legislative jurisdiction only since 1977. While interest in Small Business is very low, it is somewhat attractive to members as a third (or nonmajor) assignment. The committee has limited legislative jurisdiction and a narrow but geographically dispersed constituency outside the Small Business Administration. It does attract members who are looking for another state-oriented committee and who have a small business background.

CONSTITUENCY COMMITTEES

Five Senate committees attract members primarily for constituency-related reasons. (A sixth committee, constituency-specific Veterans' Affairs, was viewed so undesirable as to be placed in the "unrequested" category.) All five have exhibited little change in member goals during the past twenty years.

Senate Agriculture is the chamber's most purely constituency-oriented committee. Like its House counterpart, Senate Agriculture's membership is disproportionately southern and midwestern, with the midwestern bias having emerged in the 1970s and maintained into the 1990s (see Table 3-4). Throughout this time period some 70 percent of the committee's members have come from these two regions. The Energy and Natural Resources Committee (Interior before the 1977 reforms) holds primarily state-related interest for senators and, like House Interior, retains a distinct western bias in its composition. But world events and the regrouping of energy jurisdiction in 1977 have changed its geographic composition. A handful of senators from energy-poor states have been attracted to Energy and Natural Resources to protect their states' interests in the face of energy shortages and rising energy prices. Also, the addition of domestic atomic energy production, coal, and other energy matters to the committee's jurisdiction has attracted senators seeking to serve state interests. While energy issues have enticed to the committee several senators with personal policy interests in energy, for the most part jurisdictional changes have reinforced its constituency orientation.

Throughout the 1960s, senators' primary objective on Appropriations was to provide funding for programs in their states, with chamber influence and good public policy of secondary interest. No evidence exists to indicate that this has changed in any important way. Appropriations still provides an opportunity for members seeking money for programs in their states to do favors for colleagues, and it thus provides some extra influence and prestige in the Senate. But when more than half of the states are represented on the committee, opportunities to serve noncommittee members are not nearly so numerous as might be assumed. If a change has occurred during the last decade or so, it has been toward a lighter emphasis on chamber influence or prestige. Although personal policy goals seldom have been significant to most Appropriations members, Republicans appointed to the committee since the late 1970s have been much more conservative on fiscal policy matters. Changes in the budgeting environment have shifted the role of all the committees' members

TABLE 3-4   Regional Representation on Selected Senate Committees: 89th/90th, 96th/97th, 99th/100th, and 103d/104th Congresses (Percent from Each Region)

Region	Senate seats per region	Agriculture				Energy and Natural Resources			
		89th/ 90th	96th/ 97th	99th/ 100th	103d/ 104th	89th/ 90th	96th/ 97th	99th/ 100th	103d/ 104th
East	20	12	5	6	7	0	27	11	13
South	22	47	36	29	34	0	18	17	13
Border	8	6	9	12	6	0	9	17	13
Midwest	24	23	40	41	40	17	5	6	10
West	26	12	9	12	12	83	40	50	51

Note: Regions: *East*: Conn., Del., Maine, Mass., N.H., N.Y., Pa., R.I., Vt.; *South*: Ala., Ark., Fla., Ga., La., Miss., N.C., S.C., Tenn., Texas, Va.; *Border*: Ky., Md., Okla., W. Va.; *Midwest*: Ill., Ind., Iowa, Kan., Mich., Minn., Mo., Neb., N.D., Ohio, S.D., Wis.; *West*: Alaska, Ariz., Calif., Colo., Hawaii, Idaho, Mont., Nev., N.M., Ore., Utah, Wash., Wyo.

away from serving as an appeals court for agencies and affected interests that suffered cuts in House action to one of more actively protecting established programs.

Senate Commerce's balance of goals is the opposite of that found on the House Commerce Committee. While Senate Commerce has had a core of strongly policy-oriented members for many years, the majority of senators attracted to the committee have state-related goals. In Senate Commerce, broad jurisdiction over constituency-oriented areas, such as the merchant marine, U.S. Coast Guard, space programs, transportation, and tourism, attracts most members to the panel. Space programs were added to Commerce's jurisdiction when the Aeronautics and Space Sciences Committee was abolished in 1977. That jurisdiction remains under Science and Technology in the House. Senate Commerce also lacks most of the health and energy jurisdiction that attracts policy-oriented members to House Commerce, having lost some energy jurisdiction in the 1977 reforms. The Senate committee, in the view of two former aides, has become somewhat more constituency-oriented as a result of these agenda changes.

Finally, Senate Environment and Public Works has become more constituency-oriented since the early 1970s. In the late 1960s and early 1970s, major legislation for control of air and water pollution was written in the committee under the guidance of senators with personal policy interests in the field. "Since then," one senior aide explained, "the committee has not been as much fun as it was. Those big issues are gone and we don't attract the same kind of member that we once did." In original proposals for jurisdictional reform, Public Works (now Environment and Public Works) was slated to pick up additional jurisdiction over pesticides, ocean policy, coastal management, and other environmental areas that eventually were left under other committees' jurisdictions. Such a change might have boosted the interest of policy-oriented senators in the committee. Its jurisdiction over clean air and clean water legislation does still attract environmentalists but the committee remains primarily attractive to senators for its jurisdiction over rivers and harbors, water projects, highways, and other constituency concerns.

UNREQUESTED COMMITTEES

Many members of both Rules and Administration and Veterans' Affairs indicated that they did not seek assignment to these committees. Rules and Administration primarily is concerned with Senate housekeeping matters, although it does have jurisdiction over election and campaign practices. But no special influence or reelection benefits are gained by membership there. Veterans' Affairs members mention their association with veterans' programs and veterans' groups as electorally useful, but most senators discount its value. The Indian Affairs Committee was not a standing committee when our interviews with members were undertaken. At this time it is a little requested panel. Finally, the Select Ethics Committee is rarely sought by members of the Senate. It has been excluded from Table 3-3 because, unlike its House counterpart, it has no legislative jurisdiction.

JURISDICTIONS, AGENDAS, AND ENVIRONMENTS

We have treated member goals first because they are critical to any understanding of committees and committee behavior. But members' goals do not exist in a vacuum. And committee politics are shaped by more than just these goals. We turn now to committee jurisdictions and the impact they have on the political agendas and environments of the various House and Senate panels. As explained in Chapter 1, the jurisdiction of each committee is formalized in the rules of the respective chambers. But those rules cannot possibly list each and every subject that might fall within the purview of any given committee. Therefore, the formal jurisdictions stated in the rules combine with precedents established by actual bill referrals to form each committee's "real" turf. Because old issues fade and new issues emerge, the actual jurisdiction of most committees is constantly

changing in myriad small ways. Of course, occasionally committee jurisdictions can be altered more substantially. These changes are most dramatic when whole committees are added or subtracted from the roster of
standing committees.[53]

In addition to attracting (or repelling) members, committee jurisdictions determine what sorts of outside groups will make up the political
environment of each panel. A committee's agenda will likewise determine
how much and what kind of media attention it will receive. Members of
Congress often refer to the variety of policy jurisdictions, active political
agendas, and political environments they face when explaining how their
committees differ. And rightly so. Issues and outsiders create both opportunities and constraints for committee members. Popular causes, for
example, provide opportunities for strategically placed committee members to gain publicity back home or even across the nation. The attention
of interest groups, constituents, and others gives committee members an
opportunity to serve them and gain political credits for doing so. But the
same outsiders also can constrain committee members. For example, they
can help define political issues to be considered and limit the range of
politically acceptable options available to a committee or to individual
members. These opportunities and constraints play an important role in
defining the attractiveness of committees to members and shaping their
internal decision-making processes.[54]

Committee environments can be divided into three components,
which vary in character and significance for each panel. First, most committees deal with an *interbranch environment* that includes some part or
parts of the federal establishment: the administration, bureaucracy, and
the courts. For example, some committees—those concerned with tax,
budget, and foreign policy matters—interact primarily with executive
officials representing the viewpoints of the particular administration in
power.[55] Others interact with relatively large numbers of officials from
many agencies, generally focusing on agency activities rather than activities directed by the White House. The appropriations committees are the
best examples of this type, but commerce, science, banking, and public
works (or infrastructure) also fall into this group. Still other committees
normally deal only with officials from a narrow range of agencies; these
include armed services, small business, veterans, agriculture, and
resources. Finally, some committees have little cause for contact with the
executive branch. These include the two rules committees, the ethics
committees, and the House Oversight Committee.

Second, all committees function within an *institutional environment*.
Party leaders, chamber colleagues, and the other chamber make up this
immediate environment. Party leaders come into play for those committees that consider salient national issues on which the parties themselves

have staked out divergent positions. The tax, budget, commerce, energy, judiciary, and labor committees are the most conspicuous in this regard because they routinely deal with issues that divide the parties. Noncommittee colleagues may shape a committee's actions as claimants on committee decisions and as judges of decisions once they reach the floor. An average member's interest in a committee is likely to stem from the relevance of the committee's decisions to the member's own political circumstances. For example, many House and Senate committees regularly receive demands from noncommittee members who are seeking benefits for their constituents. The agriculture, appropriations, armed services, commerce, resources, public works, tax, and veterans' affairs committees of both chambers are in this group. Finally, a handful of committees have environments almost entirely dominated by chamber colleagues: the House and Senate Rules committees, the ethics committees, and the House Oversight Committee.[56]

Third, each committee operates within a *public environment* comprising the general public and representatives of organized interests. A committee's jurisdiction has an immediate impact on the character of this environment. For example, committees with broader jurisdictions are likely to affect a greater number and diversity of organized interests. This not only increases the *external* attention the committee receives but also may increase the pressures or cross-pressures that are placed upon members. In addition to variety, committee jurisdictions determine whether the various panels address high profile, nationally salient issues—taxes, war, civil rights, abortion, or school prayer, for example—or more localized but equally intense interests—loggers, fisherman, tobacco growers, dairy farmers, and whatnot.

Together, the interbranch, institutional, and public environments create a large and complex audience for the activities of most standing committees. But committee environments differ in important ways. It is not possible to treat each committee's environment in detail here. By using summary measures for three important properties, however, we can demonstrate the substantial variation that exists for House and Senate committees. It is to these three properties—fragmentation, salience, and conflict—that we now turn.

FRAGMENTATION

Fragmentation describes the degree to which a committee attracts the attention of outsiders who perceive their interests as unrelated to each other. Fragmentation in a committee's political environment is rooted in the committee's jurisdiction: the larger the number of topics falling under its jurisdiction, the more fragmented its political environment is likely to

TABLE 3-5   Fragmentation among Congressional Committees

Jurisdictional fragmentation	House	Senate

High	Appropriations
	Resources
	Transportation and Infrastructure
	Government Reform
	  and Oversight
	Commerce
	Judiciary
		Appropriations
		Labor and Human Resources
		Environment and Public Works
		Commerce, Science,
		  and Transportation
		Banking, Housing, and
		  Urban Affairs
		Judiciary
		Governmental Affairs

Medium	International Relations Agriculture Banking and Financial Services Education and the Workforce Science Ways and Means National Security	Foreign Relations Energy and Natural Resources Agriculture, Nutrition, and Forestry Finance Armed Services
Low	House Oversight Veterans' Affairs Small Business Select Intelligence Rules Standards of Official Conduct	Veterans' Affairs Indian Affairs Rules and Administration Small Business Select Intelligence

Source: Executive branch reporting arrangements from "House of Representatives Standing Committee Jurisdiction Over Executive Branch Departments" and "Senate Standing Committee Jurisdiction Over Executive Branch Departments," U.S. Congress, Joint Committee on the Organization of Congress, in Background Materials, 103d Cong., 1st sess., S. Prt. 103-55, 511–516.

Note: Fragmentation rankings are a composite measure that combines the number of committees to which executive branch departments report and the number of areas of legislative jurisdiction in the chamber rules. Committees listed in rank order. Budget committees excluded.

be. Major changes in environmental fragmentation are stimulated by changes in a committee's formal jurisdiction and also by changes or fluctuations in the political agenda. But because all possible topics are not always on a committee's active agenda, most changes in environmental fragmentation reflect the number of separate issues under active consideration. Jurisdictional and environmental fragmentation, as we will see in the next chapter, help to structure committees' decision-making processes by defining the political problems presented to them.

For most committees, jurisdictional fragmentation is linked to the fragmentation of their public environments. That is, committees with highly fragmented jurisdictions also have many separate sets of groups and individuals making unrelated demands on committee members. Reformists long have recognized that the breadth, or fragmentation, of committee jurisdictions varies quite widely. And they have argued that revised jurisdictions are desirable to equalize the congressional workload. How widely do committee jurisdictions vary? In Table 3-5 House and Senate committees are grouped according to the average of their rank on two indicators of jurisdictional fragmentation: (1) the number of executive departments that report (in whole or in part) to each committee, and (2) the number of subjects listed in each committee's jurisdiction within its chamber's rules. The resulting rankings yield a fairly accurate view of the spectrum of jurisdictional fragmentation.

Since House and Senate committee structures are roughly parallel, it is not surprising that House committees are ranked similarly to their Senate counterparts. Nonetheless, the slightly larger number of House committees magnifies interchamber differences even when there is relatively little difference between two panels. For example, the Banking committees in the House and the Senate have very similar jurisdictions but rank differently within their respective chambers. Only in a handful of cases do chamber rules establish interchamber differences. Good examples include the House Resources Committee which has a much broader jurisdiction than its nearest Senate counterpart (Energy and Natural Resources) and the Senate Commerce, Science, and Transportation Committee, which is an amalgam of three major House committees. In both chambers the appropriations, government, judiciary, commerce, and transportation/public works committees have highly fragmented jurisdictions.[57]

The House and Senate Appropriations committees attract the attention of myriad groups each year as they consider funding bills for federal programs. These committees have by far the most fragmented public environments. At the other extreme, the House and Senate Veterans' Affairs committees and the Senate Indian Affairs committee regularly face a highly focused, albeit geographically dispersed, set of constituents. In the case of the Veterans' Affairs committees, routine interaction has been established with veterans groups by holding separate hearings on the groups' legislative recommendations each year. No other committees interact with outside groups in this way.

Although one might quibble about the precise placement of any committee as it appears in Table 3-5, the tax committees and the human resources committees deserve special comment. A compelling argument can be made that the two tax committees are "underrated" here. That is, although they focus primarily on one topic (taxes) and one department (Treasury), the tax code is very broad indeed and has discrete affects on a wide variety of groups in American society. These groups do generally carry their messages to the Hill quite independently of one another so the breadth of the committees' jurisdiction does not automatically imply high conflict as well. But the measure used here probably understates the absolute and the relative levels of fragmentation that are present for these two important committees.

The human resources committees (Senate Labor and Human Resources and House Education and the Workforce) have very similar jurisdictions and internal subcommittee structures. But the Senate rule establishing Labor is a bit long winded and the House rule more than usually parsimonious for such a committee. Both committees deal primarily with the Education, Health and Human Services, and Labor departments and with the attendant external constituent groups that benefit from or are regulated by those departments. Thus, the Senate committee's position in this hierarchy is somewhat overstated while the House committee's position is somewhat understated.

SALIENCE

In the abstract, it is possible to conceive of committee jurisdictions comprised of large numbers of politically unimportant items. That is, committees could deal with lots of things people don't care about. By contrast, Congress *could* organize itself so that each committee dealt with at least one very important national issue during the course of a session. Neither is true of course. In reality, committee jurisdictions vary in terms of the importance, or *salience*, of the items within their respective jurisdictions. Salience can be judged in the public at large,[58] as it usually is, within the Congress,[59] or even within particular constituencies.[60] An issue's salience stems at least in part from inherent policy characteristics, such as the pattern of costs and benefits involved in policy alternatives being considered. The greater the number of people affected by a potential policy decision, the greater the issue's salience is likely to be.[61] Not surprisingly, members of Congress are sensitive to the number of people who care about an issue.

When we speak of salience we are generally addressing an issue's importance, priority, or visibility. Given the preeminent status of network television as an information source for the American public, it is reasonable to assume that the amount of time devoted to a topic in network news broadcasts is indicative of public interest in that topic.[62] Table 3-6 shows the amount of television time devoted to topics falling within each committee's legislative jurisdiction, determined from a systematic sample of "CBS Evening News" broadcasts for three time periods—1969–1974, 1975–1980, and 1991–1994.[63]

The data in Table 3-6 demonstrate two major points. First, committee jurisdictions vary dramatically in terms of the national salience of top-

TABLE 3-6   Minutes of "CBS Evening News" Devoted to Topics Falling Within Committee Jurisdictions

	House					Senate		
Committee	1969–1974	1975–1980	1991–1994	Committee	Committee	1969–1974	1975–1980	1991–1994
Foreign Affairs	2,109	4,879	2,526	Foreign Affairs	Foreign Relations	2,109	4,879	2,526
Judiciary	1,216	1,299	2,107[a]	Judiciary	Judiciary	1,518	1,299	2,107[a]
Education and Labor	333	462	862	Education and Labor	Labor	569	808	896
Armed Services	467	524	708	Armed Services	Armed Services	467	623	708
Commerce	823	882	388	Commerce	Commerce, Science, Transp.	698	835	642
Ways and Means	268	347	310	Ways and Means	Finance	268	347	310
Public Works	180	339	280	Public Works	Environment	335	399	240
Science	423	211	177	Science	Energy (Interior)[b]	243	772	163
Resources (Interior)	249	275	135	Resources (Interior)	Agriculture	101	156	125
Agriculture	97	155	125	Agriculture	Banking	280	166	93
Merchant Marine	200	216	99	Merchant Marine	Governmental Affairs	22	90	89
Banking	280	153	93	Banking	Rules and Administration	75	35	55
Government Operations	22	52	58	Government Operations	Veterans' Affairs	42	44	49
Veterans' Affairs	42	44	49	Veterans' Affairs	Small Business	n.a.	10	5
House Administration	54	35	38	House Administration	Abolished in 1977			
Post Office	52	48	17	Post Office	Aeronautics	387	55	n.a.
Rules	10	5	17	Rules	Post Office	52	14	n.a.
District of Columbia	1	6	14	District of Columbia	District of Columbia	1	0	n.a.
Small Business	5	10	5	Small Business				

Source: Vanderbilt Television News Archive, *Television News Index and Abstracts* (Nashville, Tenn.: Joint Universities Libraries, 1969–1980, 1991–1994).

Note: Committees ranked by their 1991–1994 standing. Every other weekday news broadcast used. Cross-cutting issues excluded from the tallies include (1969–1974, 1975–1980) Vietnam/Indochina (2,606, 608) and Energy (343, 614) and (1969–1974, 1975–1980, 1991–1994) Economy (733, 748, 463). For the earlier period, Watergate (1,300) stories also excluded. Appropriations and Budget committees excluded because of duplicate jurisdiction. Select Intelligence, which did not gain legislative jurisdiction until 1992, and Ethics, which has no legislative jurisdiction, also excluded.

[a] Totals include 160 minutes of stories on O. J. Simpson.

[b] Beginning in 1977, energy stories were placed under the Energy and Natural Resources Committee, reflecting the Senate's jurisdictional reforms.

ics within their jurisdictions as measured by nightly news coverage—from thousands of minutes of coverage to virtually no coverage at all. From any given member's point of view, there is nothing automatically attractive or unattractive about this circumstance. For some members the opportunity to appear in the limelight is a powerful attraction; for others, it is something to avoid. Simple exposure is insufficient to guarantee that a high-salience committee will be attractive to members. Matters that fall within the jurisdiction of the two foreign policy committees place them far ahead of other panels in terms of coverage, yet neither committee has been particularly popular during the last decade. Likewise, the highly salient jurisdiction of the judiciary committees is counterbalanced by its highly charged character. Members of this committee must be willing to accept high levels of conflict with high levels of national salience.

Second, although there are some interesting changes, the rank-ordered lists of committees have been remarkably stable. If the salience of committee jurisdictions was more volatile, members would have much greater incentives to transfer from one panel to another. But salience is stable, and members have no particular incentives to shift from one committee to another. The foreign policy and judiciary committees have remained at the top of these lists throughout the time periods covered; the labor, commerce, armed services, environment, public works, and science committees have filled in the middle ground; and the District, veterans', small business, rules, and government committees have consistently brought up the rear. The abolition of the District, Veterans', and Merchant Marine committees in the House in 1995 has had no appreciable impact on committee salience in that chamber.

As with committee fragmentation, interchamber differences do exist because of jurisdictional variation. The Senate Committee on Commerce, Science, and Transportation combines the jurisdictions of three different House committees as well as the former Merchant Marine Committee. In the House, energy jurisdiction—a highly salient issue in the 1970s—was combined with the Commerce Committee's jurisdiction over environmental and health legislation to keep that panel near the top of the list. The revenue, banking, and agriculture committees make up the middle ground in both chambers.

CONFLICT

Conflict refers to the degree to which concerned outsiders see their interests as competing or compatible with each other. This distinction has variously been called the level of controversy, zero-sum versus positive-sum, and competitive versus noncompetitive.[64] Conflict is grounded in a policy decision's perceived distribution of costs and benefits. Conflict among interested outsiders often forces members to pick and choose between competing concerns, favoring some and perhaps alienating others. Thus, the level of conflict in a committee's environment helps to shape the incentives and disincentives for members to participate in various committee activities.

Although salience is closely related to conflict in committee environments, they are analytically distinct.[65] The presence of conflict means that an issue is salient to *someone*. Intense conflict, moreover, may stimulate media and public interest in an issue. But committees with jurisdiction over equally salient subjects often experience quite different levels of conflict in their environments. Members and staff recognize these differences, and they are sensitive to changes in the level of conflict within their committees' environments. One senator characterized this as "pressure." He said of it: "I don't just mean pressure to do something, I mean pressure to choose between two very polarized sides to an issue—that's pressure."

Measuring the level of conflict within and outside committees is difficult. In earlier editions of this book we based our measure on the comments of committee members and staff about the level of conflict within a committee. In recent years, a great deal of theoretical and empirical work has been done on whether committee members differ from their party or chamber colleagues on matters of committee concern. Unfortunately, these measures better demonstrate the relationship between the committee and its parent chamber or party caucus than what is going on within the committees themselves. A more accurate measure of internal committee conflict would be based on committee roll call votes. If most votes within committee are one-sided, or universal, this would be evidence of low committee conflict. If most committee votes were divided, however, we could assume a higher level of committee conflict. Political scientists Joseph K. Unekis and James L. Franke have examined committee-level voting in just this way.[66] Because Senate committee votes are not as readily available, their data are for the House only. In Table 3-7 we have combined the Unekis-Franke data with characterizations of committees in both chambers by members, staff, and the press to estimate committee-level conflict in the House and Senate. Using these sources, we have placed committees into three categories of conflict. The relative salience of each committee's environment and increases or decreased in conflict since the late 1970s and 1980s also are indicated.

If conflict and salience were perfectly correlated, the committees listed in Table 3-7 would run in a perfect diagonal from the top left-hand cell (high conflict, high salience) to the bottom right hand cell (low conflict, low salience). And, generally, this is the pattern we see. Conflict in the public environment is positively related to a committee's jurisdic-

TABLE 3-7   Perceived Conflict and Salience of Committees' Public
Environments

Perceived conflict	Salience		
	High	Medium	Low
High	Appropriations (+)[a]	House Resources (+)	House Administration
	Foreign Policy (+)	Senate Resources	Rules
	Judiciary	Finance	
	Labor	Ways and Means	
	Budget[a]	Government	
	House Commerce	Operations (+)	
Medium	Senate Commerce	Banking	
		Public Works	
		Science (+)	
		Agriculture (+)	
Low	Armed Services		Small Business (+)
			Senate Rules and
			Administration
			Veterans' Affairs
			District of Colulmbia[b]
			Post Office[b]
			Merchant Marine (-)[b]

Source: Conflict measure: Authors' interviews and Joseph K. Unekis and James L. Franke, "Partisanship in Post Reform House Committees" (paper presented at the annual meeting of the Southwestern Political Science Association, San Antonio, March/April 1994). Salience measure from Table 3-6.

Note: Direction of change in conflict during the 1990s noted in parentheses. References are to both House and Senate committees unless otherwise indicated.

[a] Classification based on role in spending and economic policy.

[b] Abolished at the outset of the 104th Congress.

tional salience. Put differently, as issues become more important, or rise near the top of the public agenda, some level of controversy is likely to emerge.

The most obvious exceptions to the link between conflict and salience are the two military committees (Armed Services and National Security) and the Rules and House Administration committees. The latter two feature high levels of conflict—generally of a partisan sort—but receive virtually no public attention. For Rules, this is readily understandable because of its role in setting the floor agenda and the conditions for debating major legislation. House Administration has become the preserve of senior, leadership-appointed members, and is the site of heated debate about the administration of the House's internal bureaucracy.

The armed services committees long have been characterized by a unified, conservative approach to defense policy making. While conflict does crop up, the committees seem little affected by it. By most measures the committees are more conservative than their parent chambers and unified in their outlook toward defense policy.[67] In contrast, the two foreign policy committees also have highly salient jurisdictions but exhibit much more conflict both externally and internally. These two committees are noted for their sharply partisan character and a divisive approach to policy matters within their jurisdictions.[68]

For all other committees, our basic correlation holds true, Those with the most salient jurisdictions—appropriations, budget, judiciary, labor, and the House Commerce Committee—are exposed to and in turn reflect policy conflict. For some members, particularly those with well-established policy positions and safe election districts, this may be an attraction. But it also can be difficult. At the other extreme, the more narrowly based panels—small business, veterans', and the now defunct District, post office, and merchant marine committees—feature low conflict and low salience.

THE COMMITTEE ASSIGNMENT PROCESS

Committee assignments are important to the members who receive them, to the leaders and parties who make them, and to the outside agencies and interests that are impacted by them. For newly elected members, they are the most important decisions to be made, particularly in the House, where representatives are assigned to only one or two standing committees and have limited leverage over the products of other committees. For party leaders, the allocation of committee assignments is an opportunity to influence the composition of committees and reward or punish certain members. Like all members, party leaders are motivated by a mix of political goals. But in their capacity as party leaders, they assume additional responsibilities that originate in the expectations of rank-and-file members. These responsibilities, translated into operational goals, are policy victories and party harmony.[69]

The committee assignment process offers party leaders their first opportunity of each new congress to pursue the goals of policy victories and party harmony. Their involvement occurs in two stages. First, party leaders must establish the size and party balance for each committee. To do so, they must assess the number of vacancies created by retirements, deaths, or defeats; the likely impact of requests for intercommittee transfers; any change in the number of committees; and (in the House) any shift in the balance of Republicans and Democrats. Although size and balance are established in principle at the outset, in practice adjustments occur during the committee assignment process itself.[70] Second, once these matters have been settled, individuals must be assigned to fill the open positions or, more rarely, removed from positions to reflect changes from the previous congress. As the level of change increases, of course, these tasks become substantially more difficult. But the challenges are most acute when turnover is accompanied by a change in the majority party—as occurred in the Senate in 1981 and 1987 and in both the House and the Senate in 1995.

COMMITTEE SIZES AND PARTY RATIOS

Committee sizes and party ratios vary between and within the two chambers. The House, which has more members but nearly the same number of standing committees as the Senate, generally has larger committees. Within both chambers committees with broad jurisdictions (Appropriations and Commerce, for example) are larger than committees with narrow jurisdictions (Small Business and Veterans' Affairs). The size of each Senate committee is established in the standing rules of the chamber (the same rules that establish committee jurisdictions). These rules require at least minor tinkering at the beginning of each new congress to reflect changes in that chamber's composition. House committee sizes are not stipulated in standing rules; instead, they are the product of informal decisions made by the party leaders.

Party ratios on most House and Senate committees are close to the chamber-wide party ratios. For example, at the outset of the 105th Congress Republicans held 55 percent of the Senate seats and established a two-seat advantage on each of the major standing committees—up from a single-seat advantage in the 104th Congress. House Republicans, who lost seats in the 1996 elections, held 52 percent of the seats, but allotted themselves between 54 and 57 percent of the seats on each committee. The only exception to this norm occurs in the House, where the majority party has always maintained an outsized number of seats on the Rules Committee. During the last decade, majority party House Democrats also enlarged their proportion of seats on the Ways and Means and Appropriations committees—a move that was intended to overcome divisions in their own party and ensure control of committee decisions. Although the party balance in the House became much closer in the 104th Congress, majority-party Republicans duplicated the outsized majority only on the Rules Committee—which controls the flow of legislation to the floor—by maintaining there the established 9:4 majority to minority party ratio.[71]

In principle, there is nothing to prevent committees from being either very large or very small. Membership on committees could simply be left open to any interested member—a practice that would greatly enlarge some panels and reduce others. At the other extreme, committees could be kept so small that only a minority of the total membership would even be allowed to serve on one. Although neither of these approaches would be acceptable to members, mentioning them helps place in perspective the choices facing leaders. Should they expand the size of committees and reduce the value of assignments as a leadership resource? If they did this, they might also undercut the efficiency of some committees. Or, should they keep committee sizes small so that chairs can more easily manage their panels, and to serve as precious rewards for the leadership to bestow on friendly colleagues? If they did this, some committee chairs would be quite happy, but membership resentment might grow and members might retaliate by being uncooperative on policy matters.

Faced with these alternatives, it is not surprising that recent leaders have expanded the number of committee seats far more often than they have reduced them. Indeed, the most notable characteristic of decisions regarding committee size in recent decades has been the tendency of the leadership to increase the number of seats available. Although the number of standing committees remained quite stable between 1947 and 1997 (with a net gain of one House committee and three Senate committees), the total number of standing committee seats grew during this period from 482 to 803 in the House and from 201 to 331 in the Senate.[72] This expansion has not been wholly without controversy. Before the beginning of the 100th Congress, for example, House leaders were hard pressed to hold the line on a retrenchment that had occurred during the 99th Congress. At that time, total slots on the so-called "major" committees had been cut from 231 to 214.[73]

In the House, member demand seems to have been the primary cause of committee expansion by Democratic leaders. The first column in Table 3-8 indicates that members' expectations have risen dramatically during the past thirty-five years. Although data are not available for any recent congresses, the pattern established through the 97th Congress is quite clear: the vast majority of new House members seek assignments to more than a single committee. Those who do not typically seek membership on one of the "exclusive" committees and do not wish to provide delegation or party leaders with an excuse for not granting that request. The second column shows the percentage of majority party members actually receiving at least two assignments among those who were eligible (those assigned to exclusive committees are not eligible for two assignments). In the 1950s only about one-third of all House majority party members had

TABLE 3-8   Committee Requests and Seats for House Majority Party
Members, 86th (1959–1960) to 105th (1997–1998) Congresses

Congress	Percentage of freshmen requesting two assignments[a]	Percentage of majority with two assignments[b]	Committee seats per majority member	Total majority committee seats
86th	38	32	1.28	364
87th	58	37	1.34	352
88th	56	43	1.36	352
89th	56	43	1.38	407
90th	54	50	1.44	355
91st	n.a.	55	1.49	361
92d	69	63	1.57	398
93d	89	93	1.72	412
94th	60	83	1.73	503
95th	58	93	1.78	520
96th	88	95	1.78	490
97th	83	96	1.78	432
98th	n.a.	94	1.70	454
99th	n.a.	96	1.73	436
100th	n.a.	97	1.76	455
101st	n.a.	98	1.95	504
102d	n.a.	98	1.98	528
103d	n.a.	99	2.11	545
104th	n.a.	99	1.89	435
105th	n.a.	100	1.96	445

[a] Calculated from written requests to Democratic leaders. Request data for the 86th to 93d Congresses (91st Congress data unavailable) provided by Kenneth Shepsle. Request data for 94th to 97th Congresses collected by the authors. Subsequent years unavailable.

[b] Based upon members eligible for two assignments (not serving on exclusive committees).

two assignments, but that number rose gradually in the 1960s and then shot upward in the early 1970s. These changes also are reflected in the number of seats per member, listed in the third column.[74] The final column in Table 3-8 demonstrates that majority party leaders adjust the number of their own party's committee seats in response to electoral gains and losses. The large Democratic electoral gains in the 89th and 94th Congresses, for example, were accompanied by increases in the party's committee seat allocation, while losses in the 90th and 97th Congresses were accompanied by decreases.

Sentiment to reduce the overall size of House committees and adhere to the two-assignment limitation was very strong among Republican reformers of the 103d Congress. Control of the House during the 104th

Congress afforded Republicans the opportunity to achieve this goal. But theirs has been a mixed success. Because Republican leaders were committed to adhering to the two-committee rule and to reducing the overall size of committees, they substantially reduced the number of seats available to their own, new majority party—from 545 to 435—by eliminating three full committees and achieving modest reductions in their own share of committee seats. Although some Democrats complained bitterly, the Republicans generally allowed Democrats one more seat on each standing committee than Republicans had been given as the minority party during the previous Congress. Eliminating three committees—District of Columbia, Merchant Marine and Fisheries, and Post Office and Civil Service—reduced the number of committee seats by 84, but the only significant gains beyond that point were achieved on the House Oversight Committee (formerly House Administration). More radical cuts, including a request from newly anointed Ways and Means Committee chair Bill Archer (R-Texas) to reduce his panel from 38 to 29 members, were abandoned during negotiations with the new minority party. Said Republican Majority Leader Richard Armey: "We tried to be as responsive as we could. And frankly, we did revise the numbers [to include more seats] out of consideration for the minority's need to be able to fill committee slots."[75] At the outset of the 105th Congress, Archer renewed his request, but was denied once again.

The number of seats on standing committees in the Senate increased by 148 between 1947 and 1997, though during the same period there had been an increase of just four senators and three standing committees. Decisions about Senate committee sizes are constrained by a 1977 limit on the number of assignments senators may hold on committees of various types. But Senate leaders have proven quite willing to seek exemptions to the rule to grant senators' requests for additional committee assignments. In the 101st Congress, for example, thirty senators served on three or more of the twelve major committees for which a two-assignment limit had been set, and numerous others served on more than one minor committee, contrary to the 1977 rule.[76] And at the outset of the 104th Congress at least two senators were exempted from both the major committee limitation and the minor committee limitation: John W. Warner (R-VA.) and Christopher J. Dodd (D-Conn.) each had three major and two minor committee assignments.

COMMITTEE ASSIGNMENTS

Once committee sizes and party ratios have been set, party leaders must make decisions about which members should fill open committee seats. Committee assignments are the responsibility of each party in each cham-

ber, and each has a *steering* committee—also called a committee on committees—to perform this function (see Box 3-3). In both houses, the party
caucus and the full chamber must approve the committee lists prepared
by the steering committees. The two House committees are chaired by
their chief party leaders. House Democrats made the Speaker the chair of
their steering committee in 1973, strengthening that role in 1974 when
the committee-assignment function was stripped from Ways and Means
Democrats and given to the Steering and Policy Committee. Until recently, Senate Democrats also followed the practice of appointing as chair the
chief party leader. In 1988, however, the newly elected majority leader,
George J. Mitchell of Maine, named Daniel K. Inouye (D-Hawaii)—one of
Mitchell's opponents in the leadership race—to the post. The chair of the
Senate Republican Conference names both the members and the chair of
that party's committee. In both chambers, other party leaders also serve
on the committees on committees, providing them with opportunities to
influence committee assignments directly.

The role of party leaders in appointing members to the respective
steering committees gives them some indirect influence on assignment
decisions. In the Senate, for example, the Republican leader is occasionally consulted by the Conference chair—who actually names the Committee on Committee's chair and its members—when it comes time to
make freshman committee assignments.

The Democratic leader in the Senate has the authority to appoint *all*
of the members of the Steering Committee, who in turn feel some obligation to anticipate the leader's desires when seniority is not at stake. During the last couple of decades both parties in the House have strengthened
the role of their leaders on the steering committees. House Democrats
allow their leader to name up to ten members of the committee while the
Republican leader may make two direct appointments and has indirect
influence over several other ex officio members.[77] Most of the members
of the two House steering committees are elected by various caucus constituencies, however, or gain membership by virtue of some other leadership position to which they are elected.

Although there are opportunities to do so, current party leaders do
not exercise special influence on the vast majority of assignment decisions.[78] In general, the steering committees attempt to grant the requests
of members within the constraints of the number of vacancies. Except
under the most unusual circumstances (substantial changes in party
ratios, for example), both parties in both chambers allow members to
retain their assignments as long as they desire—the so-called *property
right* norm.[79] In addition, the parties have adopted formal and informal
rules to help ensure that all members are given reasonably good assignments. House Republicans spread choice seats widely by limiting mem-

Steering Committees

Each party in each chamber has a formally constituted committee charged with making recommendations for committee leaders and committee assignments for their respective members. Although the bulk of their work is done at the beginning of each biennial Congress, they continue to make recommendations whenever vacancies occur for their own party during a given Congress.

In each case the committee's recommendations must be approved by the party caucus or conference and then (in pro forma fashion) by the parent chamber.

- The *Senate Republican Committee on Committees* and its chair are appointed by the conference chair. The committee has eight members (105th Congress).

- The *Senate Democratic Steering and Coordination Committee* and its chair are appointed by the Democratic floor leader. The committee has twenty-five members (105th Congress), as determined by the Democratic Conference.

- The *House Republican Steering Committee* is composed of a leadership group (the Speaker, majority leader, whip, Conference chair, Policy Committee chair, Campaign Committee chair, and two appointees of the Speaker), committee chair group (the senior members of Appropriations, Budget, Rules, and Ways and Means), a regional group (nine regionally elected members plus a representative for small state delegations), and a class group (one sophomore and three freshmen), for a total membership of twenty-six (105th Congress). The Speaker, who chairs the committee, has three votes (or five if he makes no appointments) and the majority leader has two votes.

- The *House Democratic Steering Committee* is composed of the Democratic leader, Caucus chair, Caucus vice chair, whip, Democratic Campaign Committee chair, a co-chair and two vice chairs named by the leader, the four chief deputy whips, twelve regionally elected members, up to ten members appointed by the leader, and the senior Democrats of the Appropriations, Budget, Rules, and Ways and Means committees. The Democratic leader is co-chair of the committee and each member has one vote.

BOX 3-3

bers of Appropriations, Commerce, Rules, and Ways and Means to only one assignment and by limiting other members to two assignments on the remaining, "non-exclusive" committees.[80] House Democrats have very similar rules, with exclusive membership on the top three committees, a single assignment to "major" committees, and an additional assignment (or two if no major committee assignment is awarded) to "non-major" committees. As noted earlier, Senate rules formally limit members to two major committee assignments and one minor committee assignment but then provide for numerous exceptions. To prevent hoarding, each party in the Senate guarantees their members a seat on one of the major committees before any member receives a second top assignment, a rule known as the Johnson Rule after former majority leader and president Lyndon Baines Johnson.[81] Moreover, both chambers require membership rotation on a handful of committees: the Select Intelligence committees and the House Budget Committee are examples.

Currently, the dominant emphasis is on party harmony and accommodation of requests rather than on manipulation of assignments for political advantage. Political scientist Charles O. Jones concludes:

> Such measures as the Johnson Rule, while laudable on other grounds, have made it even more difficult in recent years to employ the committee assignment process for party policy purposes. All Senators are guaranteed major committee assignments regardless of their policy stands.[82]

Nevertheless, party leaders do occasionally make a special effort to place a chosen member on a particular committee. Such efforts are not made more than a few times in any congress, however, as party leaders recognize that frequent demands on the committee on committees would, as one aide put it, "wear thin quickly."

FACTORS SHAPING ASSIGNMENT DECISIONS

The most obvious and important factor affecting a member's chances of success in receiving a desired assignment is the level of competition for appointment to a particular committee. Statistically, no other measurable factor compares with the significance of the impersonal competitive situation in explaining assignment outcomes.[83] In large part, it is simply a matter of luck: the number of vacancies and competitors varies both from committee to committee and over time. Other personal and political factors come into play when there is competition, as there always is for the most important committees. In these situations, leaders and other members of the committee on committees must discriminate among members who actively campaign for support (see Box 3-4). Many members eager for specific assignments write lengthy memos to convince party leaders of

Democratic Freshman Meek . . .

At first everybody told her it couldn't be done. Later, they said if it could be done, it would be the longest of long shots.

But Carrie Meek had a head start and a strong will. Of 63 freshman Democrats [in the 103d Congress (1993–1994)], she was the only one to win a seat on the powerful House Appropriations Committee.

Usually, freshmen never make it into Appropriations. It is an assignment that must be earned by voting with the party, working hard on other committees, and making friends in high places. This year, however, Speaker of the House Thomas S. Foley, D-Wash., said he would make an exception because of the large bloc of new members.

(The leadership actually counts three freshmen among the new members of Appropriations. The other two came to Congress in 1991 in special elections: Ed Pastor, D-Ariz., and John W. Olver, D-Mass.)

Meek's campaign for the seat was under way long before Foley agreed to break the no freshmen rule.

After winning her Florida primary in September and facing no opponent in the general election, Meek went to Washington and began campaigning anew—this time for a seat on the committee that decides how to spend taxpayers' money.

She met the Democratic leadership—the Speaker, the majority leader, the whip, the deputy whips. She met the appropriators. She met the members of the Steering and Policy Committee, who make the committee assignments. She also talked to fellow members of the Congressional Black Caucus and spoke to influential women members.

Even more important, Meek worked through the Florida delegation, which had lost two seats on Appropriations with the retirements of Democrats William Lehman and Lawrence J. Smith. The Florida delegation nominated Meek and Pete Peterson to fill those spots.

"I met them all," Meek said of her search for support. "I went to every office."

BOX 3-4

their personal qualifications or political needs. They also seek support from their state delegations, key interest group figures, and committee chairs. Party leaders and members of the committee on committees may serve as arbitrators between members from the same state, region, or faction who ideally should work together in ensuring group representation through appropriate committees appointments. These campaign activities are often decisive in assignment contests.

. . . *Made All the Right Moves*

Meek also got a boost from the fact that the leadership was looking for diversity among the members, according to one member of the Steering and Policy Committee. Among the 12 new Democrats appointed to Appropriations, three are Hispanic, and three are women, including Meek, who is black.

But while race and gender were a factor in Meek's selection, a much bigger factor seemed to be the way she impressed the members she met.

She told them about herself and her background in politics. A soft-spoken grandmother, Meek, 66, is the child of sharecroppers and the first black elected to Congress from Florida since Reconstruction. She grew up in a poor Tallahassee neighborhood referred to as Block Bottom when segregation was the norm.

Since 1983, she served in the Florida Legislature, where she worked on the Appropriations Committee. She also has worked as a college administrator and teacher.

One point she stressed was her experience as a veteran legislator who did not get elected running against Congress. "I didn't run on coming up here and throwing the bozos out," Meek said.

"She's viewed as somebody who has paid her dues and is a team player and has a lot of potential," said one member of the Steering and Policy Committee.

By the end of the lobbying process, Meek had met every person three to four times. She says she never asked for a commitment, she just tried to make sure the members knew her. When she got back home to Miami from her trip to Capitol Hill, Meek wrote thank-you notes, reminding each person of her desire for a spot on Appropriations.

"It's just like any other campaign," Meek said.

Source: Jill Zuckman, "All the Right Moves," *Congressional Quarterly Weekly Report*, December 12, 1992, 3786.

The range of factors taken into account by members of the committee on committees has changed little during the past twenty-five years. A tally of the comments made by House Democratic Steering and Policy members in nominating members for requested assignments at the beginning of the 97th Congress is reported in Table 3-9. Paralleling findings for the House in the late 1950s, the electoral need of nominees was the most common argument made on their behalf, followed by claims that a par-

TABLE 3-9   Criteria Mentioned by House Democratic Steering and Policy
Committee Members Making Nominations to Standing
Committees (97th Congress)

Criterion	Number of times mentioned
Electoral need of member	19
State committee slot	13
Region committee slot (especially southern)	2
Team player (supports party or leadership)	7
Policy views	6
Seniority	6
Failure to receive another request	6
Responsible legislator	3
Policy expertise	3
General ability and maturity	3
Personal experiences	2
Ideology	2
Endorsements	2
Previous political experience	1
Personal interest	1
Acceptable to committee chair	1
Served on committee as temporary assignee	1

Note: Excludes Steering and Policy consideration of Appropriations and Ways and Means nominees.

ticular state or region "deserved" a seat because it was underrepresented on the committee.[84] A nominee's willingness to support the party and its leadership, his or her policy views, seniority, and other personal characteristics also were mentioned. Interviews with House Republican and Senate Democratic members and leadership aides indicate that similar criteria are important in their steering committees' decisions.

Senate Republicans and Democrats adhere strictly to seniority when it comes to resolving competing demands among nonfreshmen. (See Box 3-1 on p. 70 for an example.) This helps reduce direct personal conflict among senators, but it also reduces the number of opportunities leaders have to influence assignments. Personal factors normally come into play only when senators of equal seniority are competing for the same seat. In the House seniority is important, but not the sole criterion. When seniority differences are a factor, it is often one member's previous effort to get an assignment, rather than seniority per se, that is critical.

The desire to accommodate as many members as possible does not apply equally to all committees. This is especially true in the House, where the opportunities for assignment to the top committees are more limited. During the 95th to 97th Congresses, for example, fewer than half of the House Democratic nominees for prestige committees (including Budget) obtained the assignment, compared with more than 60 percent of policy committee nominees and three-quarters of constituency committee nominees. Freshmen legislators are particularly hard pressed to earn assignments to the top committees. Indeed, in spite of their expansion, only a handful of first-term members has landed a seat on these three important committees—with success coming most frequently on the Appropriations Committee. As we have seen, the appointment of untried freshmen can be disastrous from the leadership's standpoint. It is therefore not surprising that the steering committees look carefully at requests for assignments to these three panels (and to Budget as well) and look more favorably on second or third-term members, about whom they know more.

From the 95th to 97th Congress, Speaker O'Neill provided "leadership support scores" to members of the Steering and Policy Committee for nonfreshmen seeking to transfer from one committee to another, nearly 60 percent of whom were seeking an assignment to Appropriations, Budget, or Ways and Means.[85] In September 1981, former majority leader and then-Speaker Jim Wright made clear the significance of leadership support in September 1981 when he announced to the Democratic Caucus that members of the Appropriations, Budget, Rules, and Ways and Means committees would be held to a higher standard of support than other members.[86] During the organizational meetings for the 104th Congress, Speaker Gingrich was reported to have asked members to sign an pledge of allegiance prior to joining the Appropriations Committee. And, as the 105th Congress organized, Democratic leaders reportedly sought out new members for Ways and Means with appropriate free-trade attitudes before assigning to them one of the limited number of spots available.[87]

In the Senate, an additional factor is often significant for a Democratic member requesting a specific assignment: personal membership on the committee on committees. This is seldom a factor in the House, where the committee on committees is a small proportion of all party members. In contrast, the twenty-five-member Democratic Steering and Coordination Committee (104th Congress) is composed of more than half of all Senate Democrats. Steering Committee members tend to be fairly senior senators who are not seeking new assignments, so few instances of conflict of interest arise. In one reported case, however, a freshman senator had "done all the right things" and had gained the endorsement of a majority of the Steering Committee members. Later, a Steering Committee member decided he wanted an additional appointment—the one the freshman was seeking—and won it "handily" when assignments to that committee came up.

Once the committees have completed their work, the new "line ups" are presented to and ratified by the respective party caucuses and subsequently endorsed by a vote of each chamber. These final steps are rarely subject to much debate and almost never result in any changes. Thus, committee membership is in fact the responsibility of the committees on committees, although their decision is not the formal final step.

THE DISTRIBUTION OF PREFERENCES

If member preferences matter, and we maintain that they do, then once assignments have been made the distribution of these preferences across the various committees becomes of interest. If committees conform to the distributive model introduced in Chapter 1, we would expect to find member preferences unevenly distributed among the various committees. If, however, parties dominate the process—which the procedural changes noted above and in Chapter 2 suggest—then committee preference patterns should exhibit a bimodal pattern, with Democratic contingents reflecting their party's preferences and Republican contingents reflecting theirs. Finally, it is possible that members are purposely dispersed about the committee system in what amounts to a random fashion. That is, each committee could represent a cross-section of members that make it, in effect, a miniature version of its parent chamber.

Comparing the preferences of committee members to those of the larger body of members is difficult, so much so in fact that it has proven to be somewhat controversial among those who study congressional behavior. In our earlier discussion of member goals we saw that some committees attract members disproportionately from certain regions of the country (see Tables 3-2 and 3-4).[88] It is plausible to assume that those members have preferences regarding policy that are somewhat different from members from other regions. It also may be, of course, that members from other regions or types of constituencies are simply indifferent. Either way, to the extent that the positive power of proposing and passing legislation is still invested in committees certain geographic regions will have disproportionate influence over policies that emerge from these panels—the South and Middle West on the agriculture panels and the mountain states on the resources committees, for example. Unfortunately, regional distributions can only imply the possibility of differential preference distributions; they do not readily yield behavioral observations.

Other scholars have measured members' preferences more directly by examining how they vote—primarily on the floor, but more recently also within committee. This approach allows us to observe behavioral differences between committee members, party groups, and the chamber as a whole. But the evidence is somewhat contradictory. Keith Krehbiel, for example, compared committee members and noncommittee members using the ratings that various interest groups have developed to summarize members' voting behavior on issues they feel are important.[89] Krehbiel found that the vast majority of committees in the House—with the possible exception of the National Security Committee—are broadly reflective of the chamber as a whole. This, he concluded, is evidence for the chamber-dominated model of committees.

Several scholars have criticized this approach either because the interest group ratings are unreliable or because the severity of the tests used understates the number of committees that are different from their party or parent chambers.[90] Utilizing larger numbers of floor votes, these studies suggest that more committee delegations behave at variance with the chamber than Krehbiel supposed. The most interesting element of these findings has to do with which committees fall into these categories. Forrest Maltzman found that it is the prestige committee and the policy committee delegations that are most likely to display voting patterns that significantly differ from the parent chambers as a whole.[91] Additionally, he found that a subset of these same committees have Democratic delegations that vote in significantly different directions than their Caucus colleagues. Either way, however, there is agreement that, at best, only a portion of House and Senate committees are significantly enough different to sustain the distributive committees theory. At this point the reasonable student may be tempted to give up trying to make sense of all this! But in fact some sense can be made.

First, there is general agreement that a handful of committees tends to be more conservative than the parent chamber as a whole. These include the Agriculture, Armed Services, and Commerce committees in the Senate and the Agriculture, Armed Services, Science, and Veterans' committees in the House. At the other end of the political spectrum, several committees attract members whose preferences, as displayed in their floor voting, are more liberal than the chamber as a whole. These include the Education and Labor, Foreign Affairs, and, at times, Judiciary committees in the House and the Labor and Foreign Relations committees in the Senate. Put another way, although statistically significant differences between floor voting and committee delegations do not always exist, there certainly is noticeable variation across the range of committees in each chamber and over time.

This latter point is illustrated by the data summarized in Figures 3-1 and 3-2. These figures use a common measure of conservatism to place committee delegations on a liberal/conservative spectrum. Committees with delegations that vote in a more conservative fashion are closer to the top, and committees with delegations that vote in a more liberal fashion

FIGURE 3-1   House Committee Support of the Conservative Coalition, 1959, 1977, and 1995

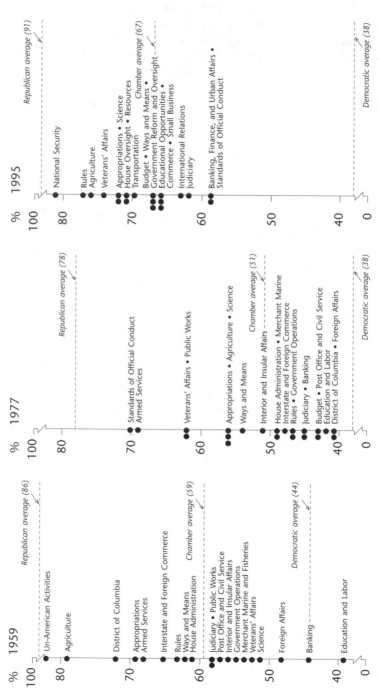

Source: Norman J. Ornstein, Thomas E. Mann, and Michael J. Malbin, Vital Statistics on Congress, 1995–1996 (Washington, D.C.: Congressional Quarterly, 1996), 218; updated by the authors.

Note: Percentage of conservative coalition votes on which members voted in agreement with the position of the conservative coalition. Conservative coalition votes are those on which a majority of northern Democrats voted against a majority of southern Democrats and Republicans—the conservative coalition.

are nearer to the bottom. The House and Senate average on this scale—that is, their political center of gravity—also is indicated. These data make it clear that there is variation among the committees. But they are not static. In some years the committees are packed more closely together, they move toward the center. In others, they are spread more widely across the political spectrum. It also is clear that the chambers' centers fluctuate from year to year. In the midst of all this variation, however, the committees do stay in roughly the same positions relative to one another over time. With very few exceptions—the now-defunct District of Columbia Committee in the House being the most dramatic—committees near the top or bottom of the scale in 1959 remained in roughly the same position in 1993. We have already noted that committee jurisdictions and members' motivations have remained fairly stable over time. Here is additional evidence that members attracted to these panels have behaved in relatively similar fashion as well.

Second, agendas make a difference. If the agenda changes, members are presented with a larger or a smaller number of items on which they may differ with their party colleagues. Put differently, the agenda may contain a larger or smaller number of items on which liberals and conservatives disagree in some years than in others and these differences may affect where committees fall on scales intended to measure ideology. Political agendas also can affect electoral outcomes. In the late 1950s and early 1960s conservative southern Democrats made up a large portion of the Democratic majority. They often voted in concert with Republicans—which is the definition of the conservative coalition measure plotted in Figures 3-1 and 3-2. By the late 1970s, northern Democrats made up a much larger proportion of the party, and the political center of gravity moved in a more liberal direction in both chambers. The early 1990s saw it swing back once again. Agendas, therefore, affect the distribution of preferences directly by presenting members with certain voting decisions and indirectly by altering the collection of members present in either chamber at a given point in time.

Third, several of the most important committees—Appropriations, Ways and Means, and Budget—tend to stay anchored at the middle of the scale. We can say of these committees that they reflect fairly well the distribution of preferences within their party caucuses and, as a result, within their chambers. As noted earlier, these so-called "control" committees serve important party-wide functions within the House and Senate. Their legislative products—budget resolutions, tax bills, and appropriations—touch upon a wide variety of government policy areas and functions. It is not surprising, then (and on this the scholarly literature is pretty unified), that the parties take special care in making appointments to these panels.

FIGURE 3-2   Senate Committee Support of the Conservative Coalition, 1959, 1977, and 1995

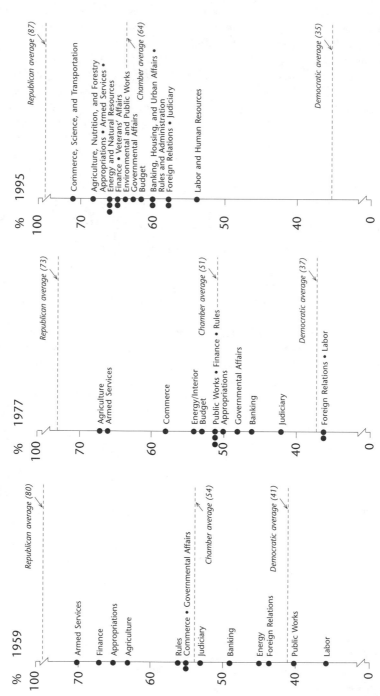

Source: Norman J. Ornstein, Thomas E. Mann, and Michael J. Malbin, *Vital Statistics on Congress, 1995–1996* (Washington, D.C.: Congressional Quarterly, 1996), 223; updated by the authors.

Note: Percentage of conservative coalition votes on which members voted in agreement with the position of the conservative coalition. Conservative coalition votes are those on which a majority of northern Democrats voted against a majority of southern Democrats and Republicans—the conservative coalition.

In sum, we believe that committees are differentially attractive and that members have a variety of motivations for seeking specific assignments. But party leaders also have a stake in the assignment process, and their decisions on these matters, along with various rules, constrain the freedom members have to pursue those motivations. Once assignments are made the distribution of preferences—ideological, partisan, substantive, regional, or whatever—is not uniform. We also believe that no single model can account for the behavior of committees or committee members. As agendas change, the level of interest that a party caucus has in a given committee may also change, as will the level of interest members display in joining a particular panel. Notice, for example, in Figure 3-1 the movement of the House Rules Committee from a conservative position in the 1950s to a liberal position in the 1970s, then back toward the conservative pole in the 1990s in concert with the majority as it moved to reflect the party position. The Rules Committee of the 1950s was, by all accounts, a roadblock to liberal agenda items dominated by southern Democratic chairs and unanswerable to the majority party. Expansion of the committee and alterations in the assignment process put an end to that. Majority party Democrats had a stake in the matter, and they did something about it. By contrast, the parties in both chambers tolerated moderates and liberals on the labor panels and conservatives on the armed services panels throughout the period.

Agendas, environments, and members' goals are central to our understanding of committee politics. Whether reelection, good public policy, power, partisanship, some other motivation, or some mix of motivations conditions any given members' activities, virtually all observers agree that they are key to explaining patterns of committee activity. In other words, agendas, environments, and member goals are what make committees different from one another and also what make the committee systems of the House and Senate different from one another. From this, several expectations emerge.

First, we have seen that preference patterns are "cleaner" for House committees than for Senate committees. Thus, the internal elements of committee politics—leaders, subcommittees, and staff allocation and use—are likely to be more distinct in the House than in the Senate. Second, on committees where policy motivations predominate, we expect to find more competition for resources and greater emphasis on shared decision-making authority. In effect, these committees will have increased the autonomy of subcommittees during the postreform period and will have shared their resources (staff) more widely. Third, constituency committees will display a more or less opposite pattern. Staff structures should be more centralized, decision making patterns will emphasize cooperative strategies of legislative development, and leaders who promote collective decisions will be valued by committee members. And fourth, party and agenda change will continue to shape patterns of committee decision making. But these effects should be more pronounced in the House—where majorities rule—than in the Senate—where supermajorities are needed to reach most important decisions. In other words, increased partisanship will have a more pronounced impact on the internal operation of House committees, particularly House policy and prestige committees, than on Senate committees. Evidence bearing on these subjects is presented in the next chapter.

NOTES

1. Gramm's switch was not entirely without cost. Although Republicans credited him with the seniority he had accrued while he was a Democrat just the one term they could not simply give back to him all three of the committee assignments that he held as a Democrat. Thus, although he returned to the Budget Committee and to the Veterans' Affairs Committee, he lost his seat on the Energy and Commerce Committee. Energy and Commerce is treated by House Republicans as an exclusive committee assignment. Membership there precludes any other assignments. As a majority-party Democrat, Gramm could serve on all three; but as a minority-party Republican he could not. There were, no doubt, many reasons for Gramm's subsequent shift to the Senate, but this certainly must have contributed to his decision.
2. English is quoted by Richard E. Cohen in "The Means Test," *National Journal*, April 22, 1995, 972.
3. Jill Zuckman, "Freshmen Go a-Courtin' To Land Coveted Seats," *Congressional Quarterly Weekly Report*, December 4, 1992, 3748.
4. Jonathan Fuerbringer, "Desperately Seeking the Right Committees," *New York Times*, November 11, 1986.
5. Richard F. Fenno, *Congressmen in Committees* (Boston: Little, Brown, 1973). The implication of Fenno's work is that members of committees differ from noncommittee members not only in their motivation for membership on congressional committees but also in their policy preferences. We do not suggest that legislative outcomes or even committee outputs reflect these differences in every case. Anticipated responses by committee members, lack of positive power, and sheer indifference at the floor stage may mute those differences—at least as measured by committee and floor voting. Also, some committees are arguably "representative" of chamber majorities. Nonetheless, we do feel that differences go to substance as well as to motivation and, indeed, that the two are closely linked. For a somewhat different view, at least regarding preference outliers, see Keith Krehbiel, "Are Committees Composed of Preference Outliers?" *American Political Science Review* 84 (March 1990): 149–163.
6. Charles S. Bullock III, "Motivations for U.S. Congressional Committee Preferences: Freshmen of the 92d Congress," *Legislative Studies Quarterly* 1 (May 1976): 201–212.
7. Bullock used this question in his study of the 92d Congress House freshmen. We used the same question during interviews with freshmen of the 97th Congress and again during interviews conducted with new members of the

100th/101st Congresses. We combined two classes in the latter case because of very small class sizes. New interviews were not conducted for this edition for two reasons. First, the underlying motives first discovered by Fenno had proven stable as had the character of the committees. And second, changes in committees adopted at the outset of the 104th Congress were made so close to the assignment process itself that new members would have had no time to digest the significance of the changes relative to their goals. It is likely that a subsequent round of interviews will be undertaken for a future edition. Additional discussion of the original interviews can be found in Steven S. Smith and Christopher J. Deering, "Changing Motives for Committee Preferences of New Members of the U.S. House," *Legislative Studies Quarterly* 8 (May 1983): 271–281.

8. This written record is not quite so useful because it often represents a senator's attempt to sell himself or herself to party leaders as a candidate for a particular committee assignment, instead of reflecting his or her genuine personal motivation for interest in a committee. The correspondence also excludes committee preferences expressed orally to party leaders and preferences that did not lead to a formal request for assignment. Charles S. Bullock III, "U.S. Senate Committee Preferences and Motivations" (Paper at the annual meeting of the American Political Science Association, Denver, September 2–5, 1982).

9. Two additional motivations—predecessor cues and a delegate-model philosophy—were mentioned by members. Nine House freshmen in the 97th Congress indicated that they listed a committee because their predecessor was on the committee. In some cases, the predecessor's cue was tied directly to the reelection goal because freshmen saw the predecessor's assignments as an indicator of which committees would be useful at home. In most instances, though, the predecessor's assignments served merely to direct members who believed that someone from their district or state ought to serve on a certain committee to represent its constituency properly. These members made no mention of reelection needs. These variations in constituency-oriented motivations may stem from the focus of these data on preference motivations rather than on goals pursued after assignment. The predecessor version can lead merely to assignment to a certain committee (dictating no particular behavior in pursuit of district interests after appointment to the committee). Indeed, it is difficult to distinguish delegate-motivated from reelection-motivated behavior in committee activities, despite the fact that the two goals are clearly separable in members' responses about committee preferences. This interpretation is similar to the discovery by Herbert Weisberg and his colleagues that Ohio state legislators often distinguish between service to their constituents and reelection as goals for their activity. See Herbert S. Weisberg, Thomas Boyd, Marshall Goodman, and Debra Gross, "Reelection and Constituency Service as State Legislator Goals: It's Just Part of the Job" (paper presented at the annual meeting of the American Political Science Association, Denver, September 2–5, 1982).

10. Eighty-five percent of our House respondents mentioned constituency concerns in interviews for the 100th/101st Congresses down from 87 percent in the 97th. The Senate figures for constituency mentions are 85 percent (101st) and 100 percent (97th). Policy mentions for the House were 74 percent (101st), down from 80 percent (97th); for the Senate, 85 percent (101st), down from 89 percent (97th). Power/prestige mentions for the House were

17 percent (101st), down from 34 percent (97th); for the Senate, 15 percent (101st and 97th). These changes reflect a higher proportion of respondents mentioning only a single motivation during interviews.

11. Republicans also designate Commerce an exclusive committee.

12. Rules reported from the Rules Committee are in the form of simple resolutions that are passed by a majority vote on the House floor before a bill's consideration in the Committee of the Whole. The resolution stipulates in detail the conditions for debate on a piece of legislation.

13. Few Democrats actively consider Rules because the Speaker has virtual control over appointments; also, few freshmen mention it as a committee preference.

14. Bruce I. Oppenheimer, "The Rules Committee: New Arm of Leadership in a Decentralized House," in *Congress Reconsidered*, ed. Lawrence C. Dodd and Bruce I. Oppenheimer (New York: Praeger, 1977).

15. Barbara Sinclair, *Legislators, Leaders, and Lawmaking: The U.S. House of Representatives in the Postreform Era* (Baltimore: Johns Hopkins University Press, 1995), 138.

16. Oppenheimer, "The Rules Committee," in *Congress Reconsidered*, ed. Dodd and Oppenheimer, 103–105.

17. On the evolving use of rules, see Stanley Bach and Steven S. Smith, *Managing Uncertainty in the House of Representatives: Adaptation and Innovation in Special Rules* (Washington, D.C.: Brookings Institution, 1988); and Sinclair, *Legislators, Leaders, and Lawmaking*, 136–162.

18. James G. Gimpel, *Fulfilling the Contract: The First 100 Days* (Boston: Allyn and Bacon, 1996), 115–117.

19. Quoted in Diane Granat, "House Appropriations Panel Doles Out Cold Federal Cash, Chafes at Budget Procedures," *Congressional Quarterly Weekly Report*, June 18, 1983, 1209.

20. See Fenno, *Congressmen*, 3–4.

21. Hook, "The Influential Committees: Money and Issues," *Congressional Quarterly Weekly Report*, January 3, 1987, 22.

22. Fenno, *Congressmen*, 4.

23. Kiewiet and McCubbins report that up until the mid-1980s Republican appointments to the committee were more liberal than the caucus norm. But they take note of the emerging schism among Republicans. See D. Roderick Kiewiet and Mathew D. McCubbins, *The Logic of Delegation: Congressional Parties and the Appropriations Process* (Chicago: University of Chicago Press, 1991). This schism also was widely reported in the press. For an example, see Janet Hook, "Bitterness Lingers From GOP Assignments," *Congressional Quarterly Weekly Report*, May 16, 1987, 961.

24. Jeff Shear, "Force Majeure?" *National Journal*, March 11, 1995, 601.

25. Neumann's quote, and other details of these events, can be found in Jeffrey Goldberg, "Adventures of a Republican Revolutionary," *New York Times Magazine*, November 6, 1996.

26. See Malcolm E. Jewell and Chu Chi-Hung, "Membership Movement and Committee Attractiveness in the U.S. House of Representatives, 1963–1971," *American Journal of Political Science* 18 (May 1974): 433–441.

27. See John F. Manley, *The Politics of Finance* (Boston: Little, Brown, 1970), chap. 4.

28. For member reactions to this change, see Catherine E. Rudder, "Committee Reform and the Revenue Process," in *Congress Reconsidered*, ed. Dodd and

Oppenheimer, 128–130; and Randall Strahan, *New Ways and Means: Reform and Change in a Congressional Committee* (Chapel Hill: University of North Carolina Press, 1990): 56–60.

29. On the earlier period, see Fenno, *Congressmen*, 4–5; for an extended assessment of the committee and members' goals, see Strahan, *New Ways and Means*, chap. 4.

30. For examples of constituency interests, see David S. Cloud, "A Dozen Special Tax Breaks Have a Life of Their Own," *Congressional Quarterly Weekly Report*, May 23, 1992, 1425–1430; and John R. Cranford, "House Tax Writers Go To Work On Long List of Small Favors," *Congressional Quarterly Weekly Report*, July 11, 1992, 2034–2035. On PAC contributions, see Steven Pressman, "PAC Money, Honoraria Flow to Tax Writers," *Congressional Quarterly Weekly Report*, September 14, 1985, 1806.

31. Stephen Gettinger, "Newest Budget Panel Members Confront Jargon, Turf Battles and a Looming Deficit," *Congressional Quarterly Weekly Report*, January 31, 1989, 188–189.

32. Allen Schick, *Congress and Money: Budgeting, Spending and Taxing* (Washington, D.C.: Urban Institute, 1980), 100.

33. Ibid., 110.

34. The House Budget Committee rejected strong reconciliation orders to other House committees in 1980, in contrast to its Senate counterpart.

35. Schick, *Congress and Money*, chap. 8.

36. LeLoup, *Fiscal Congress*, 53–61. Also see John W. Ellwood and James A. Thurber, "The Politics of the Congressional Budget Process Re-examined," in *Congress Reconsidered*, 2d ed., ed. Lawrence C. Dodd and Bruce I. Oppenheimer (Washington, D.C.: Congressional Quarterly, 1981) 254.

37. Schick, *Congress and Money*, 118, 129.

38. For a treatment of recent changes in the budget process and its implications for power distributions within Congress, see James A. Thurber, "Congressional-Presidential Battles to Balance the Budget," in James A. Thurber, ed., *Rivals for Power: Presidential-Congressional Relations*, ed. James A. Thurber (Washington, DC: CQ Press, 1996): 191–213.

39. Controversy is not entirely without electoral benefits. Members of the Energy and Commerce Committee, for example, enjoyed a welcome rise in donations from PACs interested in the fate of the Clean Air Act in 1990. See Chuck Alston, "As Clean-Air Bill Took Off, So Did PAC Donations," *Congressional Quarterly Weekly Report*, March 17, 1990, 811–817.

40. For example, at the outset of the 100th Congress the three new Democratic members of the Energy and Commerce Committee all came from coal-producing districts that would be adversely affected by acid rain legislation within the committee's jurisdiction. Janet Hook, "House Leaders Make Committee Assignments," *Congressional Quarterly Weekly Report*, January 10, 1987, 86.

41. For an in-depth treatment of the committee and its leaders, see Andree E. Reeves, *Congressional Committee Chairmen: Three Who Made an Evolution* (Lexington: University of Kentucky Press, 1993).

42. Careful readers may note that we have dropped Education and Labor's (ambiguous) double listing, which appeared in the first edition of this book. There is some consensus that the committee had become fairly dormant, at least as far as labor was concerned. It also frequently lost its legislative battles on the floor. For more see Richard E. Cohen, "Labor Comes Alive,"

National Journal, July 16, 1988, and Jill Zuckman, "Will Clinton Restore Good Will To Education and Labor?" *Congressional Quarterly Weekly Report*, November 21, 1992, 3671–3675.

43. Alan Fram, "A Member's Menu for Airport Pork," *Washington Post*, May 14, 1987.

44. This observation is consistent with Fenno's findings. See Fenno, *Congressmen*, 148.

45. During the 104th Congress, for example, Sen. Robert C. Byrd (D-W. Va.) served on both Appropriations and Armed Services a circumstance not atypical for someone of his vintage in the Senate—and Sen. Chuck Robb (D-Va.) served on Armed Services and the less-coveted Foreign Relations. During the 104th Congress there was a total of 87 seats on the four committees; thus, 85 of the 100 members have seats on one of these panels.

46. Norman J. Ornstein, Thomas E. Mann, and Michael J. Malbin, *Vital Statistics on Congress, 1989–90* (Washington, D.C.: CQ Press, 1990), 120. See also Barbara Sinclair, "The Distribution of Committee Positions in the U.S. Senate: Explaining Institutional Change," *American Journal of Political Science* 32 (May 1988): 277–301.

47. In mid-1983, Republican Senate majority leader Howard Baker of Tennessee announced that he would no longer feel compelled to honor "holds" on legislation. Holds had become so commonplace that Baker found it very difficult to set the schedule for the floor. Nonetheless, his attempts, and those of his successors, failed. See Walter J. Oleszek, "Legislative Procedures and Congressional Policymaking: A Bicameral Perspective," in *Congressional Politics*, ed. Christopher J. Deering (Chicago: Dorsey, 1989), 186–188; and Barbara Sinclair, *The Transformation of the U.S. Senate* (Baltimore: Johns Hopkins University Press, 1989), 125–138; and Sarah Binder and Steven S. Smith, *Politics or Principle?: Filibustering in the U.S. Senate* (Washington, D.C.: Brookings Institution, 1997).

48. For a treatment of the Senate Foreign Relations Committee see James M. McCormick, "Decision Making in the Foreign Affairs and Foreign Relations Committees," in *Congress Resurgent: Foreign and Defense Policy on Capitol Hill*, ed. Randall B. Ripley and James M. Lindsay (Ann Arbor: University of Michigan Press, 1993), 115–153.

49. Schick, *Congress and Money*, 95, 99.

50. Moseley-Braun is quoted by Nan Robertson, in "The Sorority," *Modern Maturity* (September/October 1996): 37.

51. For a treatment of the Senate and House Armed Services Committees, see Christopher J. Deering, "Decision Making in the Armed Services Committees," in *Congress Resurgent*, ed. Ripley and Lindsay, 155–182.

52. The five senators were Alan Cranston (D-Calif.), Dennis DeConcini (D-Ariz.), John Glenn (D-Ohio), John McCain (R-Ariz.), Don Riegle (D-Mich.). The Ethics panel ultimately criticized all five senators but formally reprimanded only Cranston. For a summary of the case, see Phil Kunz, "Cranston Case Ends on Floor With a Murky Plea Bargain," *Congressional Quarterly Weekly Report*, November 23, 1991, 3433–3438.

53. For discussions of the problems of jurisdictional alignments, see U.S. Congress, Senate, Temporary Select Committee to Study the Senate Committee System, *The Senate Committee System*, 94th Cong., 2d sess., 151–187; U.S. Congress, Senate, The Commission on the Operation of the Senate, *Policy Analysis on Major Issues*, 94th Cong., 2d sess., 4–24; U.S. Congress, House,

Select Committee on Committees, *Monographs on the Committees of the House of Representatives*, 93d Cong., 2d sess.; and U.S. Congress, Joint Committee on the Organization of Congress, *Background Materials*, 103d Cong., 1st sess. S. Prt. 103–55, 496–607.

54. The claim that agendas and interested outsiders differ in important ways among committees would not be disputed by any observer of Congress, and yet identifying a useful set of properties to characterize committees' agendas and environments is a difficult task. One possible approach is to focus on the subject matter or policy decision per se, that is, to identify properties inherent to the policy issue itself. Properties such as the pattern of costs and benefits, complexity, divisibility, volume, and novelty have been noted. See, for example, John Ferejohn, *Pork Barrel Politics* (Stanford, Calif.: Stanford University Press, 1974), 5; James Q. Wilson, *Political Organizations* (New York: Basic Books, 1973), 330; Theodore J. Lowi, "American Business, Public Policy, Case Studies and Political Theory," *World Politics* 16 (July 1964): 677–715; and John F. Manley, *The Politics of Finance* (Boston: Little, Brown, 1970), 92–95. Committees' agendas may differ on each of these properties and may become more or less alike over time.

Policy properties, unfortunately, have proven difficult to use for empirical research. Consequently, most scholars attempt to establish the empirical import of their concepts only by example or else shift away from direct measures and rely instead on decision makers' perceptions of issues they face. The latter approach usually is justified further on the grounds that it is the participants' perceptions that are significant anyway, although it is often implied that perceptions are closely related to the objective characteristics of issues. When dealing with the multifaceted jurisdictions of congressional committees, however, even perceptual measures are difficult to employ rigorously.

Policy properties, in turn, usually are assumed to have a strong causal connection to the nature of committees' political environments. James Q. Wilson, for example, argues that a policy with very concentrated benefits for a small segment of society, but with widely dispersed costs, will engender less interest and opposition than a policy with concentrated benefits and costs. See Wilson, *Political Organizations*, 327–337. From a committee member's point of view, it is often the political alignments stimulated by an issue, rather than the characteristics of the issue itself, that are significant.

55. Evidence for these observations may be found in the appendix, Tables A4 and A5, of the first edition of this book.

56. For an extended treatment of the various forces at play in committee environments, see Forrest Maltzman, *Competing Principals: Committees, Parties, and the Organization of Congress* (Ann Arbor: University of Michigan Press, 1997).

57. The Budget committees have not been included in the ranking because, strictly speaking, they do not have direct jurisdiction over specific agencies or programs, except for the area of budget policy.

58. David E. Price, *Policymaking in Congressional Committees* (Tucson: University of Arizona Press, 1979), 564; and E. E. Schattschneider, *The Semisovereign People* (Hinsdale, Ill.: Dryden Press, 1975), chap. 2.

59. Barbara Hinckley, "Policy Content, Committee Membership, and Behavior," *American Journal of Political Science* 19 (August 1975): 543–557.

60. For an example of this approach, see Richard L. Hall and Frank W. Waymon, "Buying Time: Moneyed Interests and the Mobilization of Bias in Congres-

sional Committees," *American Political Science Review* 84 (September 1990): 797–820. See also Lester M. Salamon and John J. Siegfried, "Economic Power and Political Influence: The Impact of Industry Structure on Public Policy," *American Political Science Review* 71 (September 1977): 1026–1044.

61. V. O. Key, Jr., characterizes issue salience in just this way in *Public Opinion and American Democracy* (New York: Knopf, 1963), 172–175.

62. There are other examples of using news coverage to measure agendas and salience at the national level. Frank R. Baumgartner and Bryan D. Jones use newspaper coverage in their study of agenda change in American politics. See Baumgartner and Jones, *Agendas and Instability in American Politics* (Chicago: University of Chicago Press, 1993). Shanto Iyengar and Donald R. Kinder use network news stories to measure the salience of particular subjects at the national level. See Iyengar and Kinder, *News That Matters: Television and American Opinion* (Chicago: University of Chicago Press, 1987), chap. 3.

We use the number of minutes of news as our indicator of national salience. A parallel, and more direct, measure has been constructed by Stephen Hess. Hess has exploited the files of the Senate's press gallery staff to determine the number of cameras in committee hearings and meetings (from February 1979 to June 1985) that represented national and local media outlets. He then summarizes these using our grouping of Senate committees. The results are fairly dramatic. For that period, 61.8 percent of the national cameras appeared at the seven policy committees, 15 percent at the three mixed policy/constituency committees, 19.7 percent at the constituency committees, and 3.4 percent at the two housekeeping panels (Rules and Ethics). By contrast, 49.4 percent of the local crews appeared at the policy committees, 15.7 percent at the mixed panels, 31.7 percent at the constituency panels, and 3.2 percent at the two housekeeping committees. Thus, Hess's findings provide additional support for our views on the national and local appeal of Senate committees. It should be noted that Hess's rank ordering of Senate committees by salience for the late 1970s and early 1980s is very similar to our own. Regrettably, no similar data are available for the House. See Stephen Hess, *Live From Capitol Hill: Studies of Congress and the Media* (Washington, D.C.: Brookings Institution, 1991), Tables B-3 and B-4, 187–188. See also Stephen Hess, *The Ultimate Insiders: U.S. Senators in the National Media* (Washington, D.C.: Brookings Institution, 1986).

63. Data in Table 3-6 were collected from the Vanderbilt Television News Archive, which provides a synopsis of each story and a running time count of each broadcast. Stories involving events that fell under no committee's jurisdiction, such as those on presidential election campaigns, obituaries, sporting events, and other human interest coverage were excluded, as were features such as the daily stock market report.

This approach has two limitations. First, it provides a measure of national salience only. We have no comparable measure for salience within particular constituencies. Second, restricting the study to each committee's legislative jurisdiction means that topics a committee explores as part of its wider oversight jurisdiction are neglected. This restriction, which is necessary for reducing coding ambiguities, should not affect the relative standing of committees, with the exception of the House Government Operations and Senate Governmental Affairs committees.

Three sets of news stories present special coding difficulties because they fall within the legislative jurisdictions of two or more committees. These sets are listed at the bottom of Table 3-6. The tallies for the affected committees do not include the time allocated to these stories and thus understate the media's attention to matters falling under their jurisdictions. In the case of the war in Indochina, the foreign policy and armed services committees shared common interests. No standing committee has explicit jurisdiction over the state of the economy, although committee with jurisdiction over fiscal and monetary policy, especially the appropriations, tax, and banking committees, have directly related jurisdictions. Finally, as noted in Chapter 2, several committees with jurisdiction over energy, especially the House Commerce Committee, have higher relative standing than their ranking indicates.

64. Hinckley, "Policy Content"; Lowi, "American Business"; and Price, *Policymaking*.
65. Price, *Policymaking*, 46.
66. See, in particular, Joseph K. Unekis and James L. Franke, "Partisanship in Post Reform House Committees" (paper presented at the annual meeting of the Southwestern Political Science Association, San Antonio, March/April 1994).
67. See Krehbiel, "Are Committees Composed of Preference Outliers?", 149–163; and Christopher J. Deering, "Decision-Making in the Armed Services Committees," in *Congress Resurgent : Foreign and Defense Policy on Capitol Hill*, ed. Ripley and Lindsay, 155–182.
68. For a treatment of the two foreign policy committees, see James M. McCormick, "Decision-Making in the Foreign Affairs and Foreign Relations Committees," in *Congress Resurgent*, ed. Ripley and Lindsay, 115–154.
69. Barbara Sinclair, *Majority Party Leadership in the U.S. House of Representatives* (Baltimore: Johns Hopkins University Press, 1983), chap. 1.
70. Prior to the 104th Congress, for example, Republicans established committee sizes and party ratios and then endorsed the slate of committee chairs proposed by party leaders. A few days later, however, a number of additional assignments were made to accommodate requests from minority party leaders for additional Democratic committee slots. The addition of Republicans offset the larger Democratic contingent and preserved the party ratios desired by Republican leaders. The additions are reported by Jonathan D. Salant, "New Chairmen Swing to Right; Freshmen Get Choice Posts," *Congressional Quarterly Weekly Report*, December 10, 1994, 3493.
71. On Appropriations none of the subcommittees has less than a 6:4 ratio of Republicans to Democrats, with some as high as 7:3.
72. The House total for the 104th Congress was down slightly from 1989, when 812 seats were allotted to House Democrats and Republicans.
73. *Congressional Quarterly Weekly Report*, November 22, 1986, 2935.
74. In the early 1970s, with the help of Speaker Carl Albert (D-Okla.), reformers successfully pushed for Democratic Caucus rules guaranteeing all Democrats two assignments (except for members of the three exclusive committees). This helps to explain the sudden jump between the 92d and the 93d Congresses in the percentage of members with two assignments and the number of seats per member.
75. Guy Gugliotta, "Democrats Protest as Republicans Shrink Hill Committees," *Washington Post*, December 10, 1994, A1.
76. The Senate's limits are spelled out in Senate Rule XXV, as are the artful exceptions, which must be worded without naming the senators to whom they apply. See Judy Schneider, "Senate Rules and Practices on Committee,

Subcommittee, and Chairmanship Assignment Limitations, as of April 20, 1982," Congressional Research Service, May 18, 1982. Senators also exceed limits on the number of subcommittees to which they may belong. And, when aggregated with full committee assignments, the totals can be staggering. For example, during the 102d Congress, ten Senators had 15 or more committee and subcommittee assignments and one of these individuals had accumulated memberships on 22 committees and subcommittees. Data reported in U.S. Congress, Joint Committee on Congress, *Background Materials*, 485.

77. In 1989 the Republicans strengthened the leader's position somewhat by raising the number of votes cast by the floor leader from 1 to 12 and by the whip from 1 to 6. Nonetheless, this amounted to only 18 votes out of a total of 195 possible in the committee's weighted voting scheme at that time. Background on the dispute that led to this change may be found in Janet Hook, "Bitterness Lingers from GOP Assignments," *Congressional Quarterly Weekly Report*, May 16, 1987, 961. Further changes in the Republican Steering Committee have brought it much closer to the approach used by House Democrats—a mixture of regional representation and senior committee and party leaders now comprise a much smaller committee. During the transition from Democratic to Republican control of the House, documentation through formal rules often lagged behind actual practice. Thus, the January 1995 editions of the House Republican Conference rules provided no description of the formation or procedures of the Republican Steering Committee. A Speaker's Office document, "Structure Establishing the Republican Steering Committee," provides a description of the committee's formation while another document, "Republican Steering Committee Procedural Guidelines: 104th Congress," sketches out its operations.

78. On the House, see Sidney Waldman, "Majority Party Leadership in the House of Representatives," *Political Science Quarterly* 95 (Fall 1980): 373–393. On the Senate, see Robert L. Peabody, *Leadership in Congress* (Boston: Little, Brown, 1976): 349–350. During his brief tenure as Speaker, Jim Wright used committee assignments more aggressively than most recent occupants of that office. For examples, see John M. Berry, *The Ambition and the Power* (New York: Viking, 1989), 82–83, 467, 542, 568.

79. For discussion of this norm, see (for the House) Kenneth A. Shepsle, *The Giant Jigsaw Puzzle : Democratic Committee Assignments in the Modern House*, (Chicago: University of Chicago Press, 1978), 29; and (for the Senate) Donald R. Matthews, *U.S. Senators and Their World* (New York: Vintage, 1960), 127. More recently, work on committee assignments simply assumes that members will continue their memberships on existing committees. See, for example, Gary W. Cox and Mathew D. McCubbins, *Legislative Leviathan: Party Government in the House* (Berkeley: University of California Press, 1993), chap. 1.

80. The House Oversight, Select Intelligence, and Standards of Official Conduct committees are exempt from these limitations. Also, Republican rules permit the Steering Committee to recommend waivers when "circumstances warrant such recommendations."

81. Robert L. Peabody, "Senate Party Leadership: From the 1950s to the 1980s," in *Understanding Congressional Leadership*, ed. Frank H. Mackaman (Washington, D.C.: CQ Press, 1981), 82; and Sinclair, *The Transformation of the U.S. Senate*, chaps. 1 and 2.

82. Charles O. Jones, "Senate Party Leadership in Public Policy, " in U.S. Senate, Commission on the Operation of the Senate, *Policymaking Role of Leadership in the Senate*, 94th Cong., 2d sess., 26.

83. Shepsle, *The Giant Jigsaw Puzzle*, chap. 9; Steven S. Smith and Bruce A. Ray, "The Impact of Congressional Reform: House Democratic Committee Assignments," *Congress & the Presidency* 10 (Autumn 1983): 219–240.

84. The standard work on House committee assignments in the 1950s is Nicholas A. Masters, "Committee Assignments in the House of Representatives," *American Political Science Review* 55 (June 1961): 345–357; parallel comments on Senate committee assignments may be found in Matthews, *U.S. Senators*. Findings on state or regional representation can be found in Charles S. Bullock III and David England, "Prescriptive Committee Seats in Congress," unpublished manuscript, March 17, 1989, 1–42.

85. See Table 8-5 of the first edition.

86. Wright's action was precipitated by the defection of Phil Gramm and other conservative supporters of the Reagan administration's budget and tax cuts of 1981 reported back at the beginning of this chapter. Although Wright had erred in using his influence to get Gramm on the Budget Committee, his announcement, which helped to prevent immediate disciplinary action against Gramm, merely made explicit what generally had been the leadership's attitude about the top committees. For an account of these events and Wright's four-point plan for dealing with defecting Democrats see Barbara Sinclair, *Majority Party Leadership in the U.S. House* (Baltimore: Johns Hopkins, 1983): 91–92.

87. The "letter of fidelity" was reported in *Newsweek*, April 10, 1995, 27. The "free-trade test" was reported by Alissa J. Rubin, "Consensus May Have Its Day At Turbulent Ways and Means," *Congressional Quarterly Weekly Report*, December 7, 1996, 3338–3339.

88. Using a standard measure of significance, the chi-square, we can say that the observed distributions that appear in Tables 3-2 and 3-4 are sufficiently different from the expected distributions to be unlikely to have occurred by chance. That is, the distributions are statistically significant.

89. Keith Krehbiel, *Information and Legislative Organization* (Ann Arbor: University of Michigan Press, 1991).

90. The debate can be found in the following: Richard L. Hall and Bernard Grofman, "The Committee Assignment Process and the Conditional Nature of Committee Bias," *American Political Science Review* 84 (1990): 1149–1166; James M. Snyder, "Artificial Extremism in Interest Group Ratings," *Legislative Studies Quarterly* 17 (1992): 319–345; Keith Krehbiel, "Deference, Extremism, and Interest Group Ratings," *Legislative Studies Quarterly* 19 (February 1994): 61–77; and John Londregan and James M. Snyder, "Comparing Committee and Floor Preferences," *Legislative Studies Quarterly* 19 (May 1994): 233–266.

91. Forrest Maltzman, "Meeting Competing Demands: Committee Performance in the Postreform House," *American Journal of Political Science* 39 (August 1995): 653–182.

CHAPTER 4

Inside Committees: Leaders, Subcommittees, and Staff

Shortly after the start of the 102d Congress, in the winter of 1991, freshman representative Maxine Waters, D.-Calif., arrived late to her first meeting of the Veterans' Affairs Committee. The committee was in the midst of a discussion to which Waters expressed a dissenting opinion. Rep. G. V. "Sonny" Montgomery, the longtime Democratic chair of the committee and a stickler for punctuality, responded to Waters with a rebuke: "By the way, Maxine, this committee starts on time." In the fall of 1994, Mark W. Neumann arrived in Washington from Janesville, Wisconsin, and found out what it was like to join the National Security subcommittee of the House Appropriations Committee: "I'm brand new at this point. I'm sitting at this little added-on table at the end of the big table—like a kid's table." Like Waters, Neumann too had the audacity to question the committee's consensus: "They looked at me like I was from another planet," he recalled.[1] As new members join longstanding committees, they discover that the panels have ingrained moods, habits, and personalities that generally go unquestioned by the more senior members. New members face a choice, much as Waters and Neumann did. They can join the club, or they can resist. Unlike Waters and Neumann, most members follow the old adage: "In order to get along, you've got to go along."

Each congressional committee is a world of its own. Most members will serve on a committee for many years, even decades, before attaining a top leadership post. In the process, enduring friendships develop and longstanding rivalries emerge. Each committee has its own clown, bully, curmudgeon, and compromiser, and each develops its own traditions and standard operating procedures. But as we saw in the previous chapter, a consistent mix of policy problems, political demands, and personal goals yields substantial continuity in how most committees conduct their internal affairs. Committees are a conservative force in House and Senate politics. Left to their own devices they will settle into decision-making patterns that reinforce their political goals.

But committees are rarely left to their own devices, and the tendency toward continuity does not go unchallenged. Incremental shifts in procedures, structures, and resources—a nearly constant feature of congressional politics—have impacts within committees. More importantly, agendas change; leaders come and go; membership turnover transforms the character of committees; and the strength of party coalitions alternately increases and decreases.

In this chapter we look at continuity and change within congressional committees. In particular, we examine committee and subcommittee leaders, the role of subcommittees in shaping legislation, and the distribution and role of staff resources. The central questions here concern the apparent ebb and flow of power within committees. Are committees centralized or decentralized? Do they delegate authority and autonomy to their subcommittees? Are committee staff "unelected representatives" or simply an extension of committee leaders' power? Has the Republican takeover of Congress affected the internal distribution of committee power? Has that power been recentralized within the hands of the full committee chairs?

COMMITTEE LEADERS

The impact of full committee chairs is one of the most important barometers of committee power in the House and the Senate. To place this in perspective, contrast the following two scenarios. First, assume that full committee chairs attain their posts solely on the basis of seniority—a circumstance not far from the truth, as we will shortly see. Further assume that the rules permit those chairs virtually complete control over their panels' budgets, agendas, staff, subcommittee structure and memberships, and all other elements of committee activity. Now, just to top this off, assume that committee legislation nearly always succeeds on the floor—with few amendments and rare defeats. Obviously, this describes a circumstance of considerable power for committees and their chairs.

By contrast, imagine a committee system where advancement comes not from seniority but rather adherence to the party line, or perhaps even some mechanical rotation procedure involving the subcommittee chairs. Then take away internal control over committee structure and activities. Finally, assume that committee bills in this environment are frequently amended or routinely defeated on the floor. Just as obviously, these circumstances describe committee chairs with substantially less power—beholden in the one case to party leaders and in the other to the subcommittee chairs or committee rank-and-file. To accurately gauge the power of committees, we must be able to understand the role of the committee and subcommittee chairs and know where they fit along this spectrum of relative power.

SELECTING COMMITTEE LEADERS

Throughout this century, both parties in both chambers have adhered to the seniority principle. This simple rule—actually an unwritten custom so widely recognized that it is called a rule—provides that the member of each party with the longest continuous service on a committee serves as the chair or ranking minority member of that panel. Seniority has its advantages. It reduces intracommittee conflict by routinizing advancement to leadership positions. For most committees, it ensures that experienced legislators will advance to positions of authority. But seniority also insulates committee leaders from party leaders and rank-and-file committee members, increases committee autonomy, and, it must be admitted, allows some members who are well past their prime to become committee chairs.

Although formal procedures for selecting party leaders have existed for decades their effect has been simply to reinforce the overriding and inviolate rule of seniority. Over the past twenty-five years, however, numerous challenges to seniority have emerged in both chambers. Rules changes, particularly in the House, have diminished the rigidity of seniority. There are three important elements to the process of selecting committee and subcommittee chairs. First, there are formal procedures for naming or nominating leaders that limit the extent to which challenges to the seniority rule are tolerated. Second, there are limits that may be placed upon members regarding how many leadership positions they may occupy. And third, the presence of term limits may force rotation. As we shall see, each party in each chamber has used these elements to limit the power of committee and subcommittee leaders.

The standing rules of the Senate and House each require that committees and their chairs be appointed by action of the chamber. In practice, this means that a simple resolution embodying these actions must be passed. Senate rules actually permit separate votes on any chair at the request of a single senator, but deference to seniority makes such votes unheard of. House rules make clear that committee memberships and the election of committee chairs emanate from the respective party caucuses. In both chambers, therefore, this floor action simply endorses decisions made separately by the two party caucuses.[2]

When it comes time to appoint party members to committee leadership positions, the two party caucuses decide in effect whether there is any good reason to violate seniority. Without a compelling reason to do otherwise, the parties simply appoint or reappoint their most senior member on the committee. In the Senate, where multiple committee assignments allow some members to be near the top on several panels, this can sometimes result in a curious game of musical chairs. For example, in 1984 Sen. Jesse Helms (R-N.C.) exercised his seniority by claiming the chair of the Senate Foreign Relations Committee; he had been chairing the Agriculture Committee. His claim bumped Sen. Richard Lugar (R-Ind.) from that position—one he had held since 1981. Personal factors were sufficiently important in this case to allow Lugar to bring the matter to a vote in the Republican Conference, but Helms's seniority claim prevailed. Even senators who personally preferred Lugar did not wish to undercut this tradition. "It was simply the seniority system. You're either for it or you're agin it," said assistant minority leader Alan K. Simpson of Wyoming.[3] In another case, Sen. Fred Thompson, R.-Tenn., became the chair on Senate Governmental Affairs at the outset of the 105th Congress—just two years after joining the Senate. His extraordinarily rapid ascent was caused by a large number of retirements in 1996 and many subsequent switches by Thompson's more senior colleagues. In all, there were nine new Senate chairs in the 105th Congress.

In the House, the ironclad nature of the seniority rule established early in this century was broken by the mid-1970s. New party rules stated explicitly that seniority could not be the sole criteria for advancement. More importantly, both parties adopted procedures for the secret-ballot election of full committee chairs and ranking minority members. House Democrats took the additional step of requiring separate elections for the subcommittee chairs of the Appropriations Committee. And both parties moved to increase the influence of their principal leaders in the committee assignment process. Taken together, these changes had the effect of placing committee leaders on a shorter leash. Moreover, a small but steady series of defeats by sitting chairs or heirs apparent served as object lessons for others who might be threatened.

In the Senate, neither party altered its stance toward strict compliance with seniority until 1995, when Senate Republicans adopted a new procedure requiring secret-ballot votes on all chairs (or ranking members should the party be in the minority). The mere presence of this rule led to a raft of speculation on the fate of those moderates in line to become full committee chairs. According to one rumor, Sen. John H. Chafee, a moderate Republican from Rhode Island, would be challenged for the chair of Environment and Public Works. In a much more widely discussed case, there was talk on Capitol Hill that Indiana senator Dan Coats would challenge Sen. James M. Jeffords, a moderate Republican from Vermont, for the chair of the Labor and Human Resources Committee. Neither challenge actually materialized when the Republicans gathered to organize for the 105th Congress—in part, it was said, because Senate

Congressional Seniority . . .

Tired of congressional seniority and the perks of office? Want to trade in your clutch of back-slappers, glad-handers, pork-barrelers, and influence peddlers for a new bunch of dedicated public servants?

So go cold turkey. Move to Kansas.

Here's a six-member delegation that today boasts the Senate majority leader, three committee chairs, and 75 years' worth of seniority. This is serious clout, enough so that a "small" state like Kansas (pop. 2.5 million) can thumb its nose at California's 54-member delegation. It's not the votes, baby, it's the people casting them.

Next year, however, in a laudable bow to self-imposed term limits, Kansas's seniority will drop to 2½ years, or perhaps even zero. The presumptive dean (pending reelection) will be Rep. Todd Tiahrt (R), a father of three currently tied with several dozen freshmen colleagues for seventh to last in seniority out of the 435 House members. He will replace Sen. Robert J. Dole, the presumptive GOP presidential nominee who is abandoning Congress to run for president and taking his 27½ years of seniority with him.

Tiahrt, a 44-year-old conservative, believes in slowing the growth of federal spending to a crawl, and recently trimmed his mustache "to show people what a real cut is." Actually, congressman, a real cut is losing 72½ years of seniority, as Kansas soon will discover.

Eight months ago Tiahrt was sweating bullets. The Wichita press was giving him a hard time, big labor was airing $100,000 worth of ads portraying him as the enemy of working America, and the Democrats had voted him "most vulnerable" among Kansas's all-Republican delegation.

Then weird things began to happen. On Nov. 20 [1995], Sen. Nancy Landon Kassebaum (R), chair of the Senate Committee on Labor and Human Resources, announced she would not run for a fourth term. She has 17½ years of seniority. Eight days later, Rep. Jan Meyers (R), chair of the House Committee on Small Business, announced her own retirement, opening a safe seat for a race in November. Meyers has 11½ years of seniority.

On Jan. 18, [1996] Rep. Pat Roberts (R) announced he would run for Kassebaum's Senate seat, abandoning his own safe district and the chair-

BOX 4-1

Majority Leader Trent Lott, R.-Miss., discouraged such challenges. Regardless, the new procedure will have the effect of binding Republican senators more closely to the will of their party. Even more dramatically, like House Republicans, GOP senators now limit their members to six years as a full committee chair and six years as a ranking minority mem-

. . . It's Not in Kansas Anymore

manship of the House Agriculture Committee. He has 15½ years of seniority in the House, which is worth zippo at the other end of the Capitol.

Then came the earthquake. On May 15, Dole announced his resignation from the Senate. . . . Two days later, Rep. Sam Brownbeck (R), Tiahrt's fellow House freshman, decided to abandon a third safe district to run for the Dole seat.

So here's Tiahrt, who admits, "I'm still trying to get the hang of this job," playing Lone Ranger. Shortly he will be joined by Kansas Lt. Gov. Sheila Frahm (R), who will take Dole's seat on an interim basis in hopes she can defeat Brownback in the primary and a Democrat in November. If she wins, she will add six months of seniority to Tiahrt's two years.

All this has cheered Tiahrt, not because he had designs on the deanship, but because the enemy now has fatter targets than him to shoot at. Maybe Kansas voters are smiling, too, especially those who believe that incumbency is a disease. But maybe not. If seniority is what brings color to their cheeks, recent events cannot have brought joy.

States that have majority leaders or committee chairs can expect sweets in many bills making their way through Congress. States with backbenchers carrying the mail get bupkes.

Dole has an office on the second floor of the Capitol where Thomas Jefferson was sworn in as president. Guys like Tiahrt are stuffed in the bowels of the Longworth House Office Building next to the elevator shaft.

Dole gets on C-SPAN all the time, and moves huge pieces of legislation with his name on them. Tiahrt is proud to have gotten two high-schoolers from his district accepted as House pages. Dole makes speeches at $5,000-a-plate fund-raisers. Tiahrt orders out for pizza and does telephone interviews with Wichita radio stations.

"I have a vision for a strong delegation," Tiahrt said, trying Dole-ful solemnity on for size. "Of course," he added with a grin, "I hope I'm around long enough."

Source: Guy Gugliotta, "Seniority—Soon It's Not in Kansas Anymore," *Washington Post*, June 4, 1996, A15. © *Washington Post*. Reprinted with permission.

ber. Senate Democrats have no similar rules adhering strictly to seniority. (For an example of the vagaries of seniority, see Box 4-1.)

Accruing seniority toward leadership posts is one reason why members are reluctant to transfer between committees, where they must start at the bottom of the seniority ladder. For members, seniority provides a measure of predictability to committee careers. So long as they continue to be reelected, they stand an excellent chance of gaining positions of power on their respective committees. Subcommittee chairs traditionally were appointed by the full committee chair of each committee, giving full committee chairs the opportunity to manipulate subcommittee activity. This procedure was transformed into a more egalitarian one in the 1970s. Now, appointments to subcommittee chairs and ranking minority posts are handled in much the same way as appointment to full chairs, except they are accomplished within committee rather than on the floor.

House Republican Rules state that procedures for selecting subcommittee chairs shall be left to the chair of the full committee. This allows some leeway for party and committee leaders to make adjustments without being constrained by routine procedures. At the outset of the 104th Congress, Republican leaders did intervene in this process and, in a few cases, seniority was ignored. For example, representatives Tom Davis (R-Va.) and David McIntosh (R-Ind.) were appointed subcommittee chairs on the Government Affairs and Oversight Committee even though they were freshmen. However, Republicans in general adhere to seniority when selecting their subcommittee chairs or ranking members.

House Democrats allow each committee member to "bid," in order of seniority, for the available subcommittee chairs (or ranking member slots). These bids may be rejected by a secret ballot of Democratic committee members. While seniority generally is observed, this procedure gives party members on the committee the right to reject a subcommittee chair and elect an alternative. This has happened more than a dozen times since the mid-1970s. For Democrats, but not Republicans, subcommittee seniority rather than full committee seniority is used in the selection of chairs or ranking positions on the House Appropriations subcommittees. In the Senate, both parties also allow committee members to select their subcommittee chairs or ranking positions in order of seniority.

To limit the power of senior members and more evenly distribute committee leadership posts, both chambers moved in the 1970s to limit the number and type of chairs any one member can hold. These rules have been tinkered with ever since. At present, House Republican rules limit members to a single committee or subcommittee chair. In addition, the highest ranking members of the leadership team are prohibited from holding a full committee chair.[4] Democratic Caucus rules are filled with limits and exceptions, but in general state that members may be chair or ranking member of only one full committee or one subcommittee with legislative jurisdiction. Senators, in contrast, are limited to one subcommittee chair on each of the committees on which they serve (normally three), with the exception of full committee chairs, who are limited to chairing two subcommittees (one major and one minor) in most cases.

The most dramatic, but as of this writing least certain, of the rules changes modifying seniority is the implementation of term limits. In the House, term limits were part of the reforms proposed in the Contract With America and implemented on the first day of the 104th Congress. These limits, which force members to give up committee or subcommittee chairs after six years, have been written into the standing rules of the House. Thus, unless revoked, they will apply to the Democrats if they regain power in the House.[5] In the Senate, this limitation, which applies only to full committee chairs since subcommittee chairs are so widely held anyway, has been written into the Republican Conference rules. If these limitations remain in force they will have a dramatic impact on committee and subcommittee leadership. Although there is almost constant turnover in leadership positions the limits will force a much more rapid exchange. Members will no longer be allowed to serve in a long and uninterrupted fashion as a committee leader.

FULL COMMITTEE CHAIRS IN THE HOUSE AND SENATE

The full committee chair is the most powerful member on the vast majority of committees. He or she benefits from years of experience in dealing with the policy problems and constituencies of the committee, exercises considerable control over its agenda, schedules meetings and hearings, influences the scheduling of subcommittee meetings and hearings, normally names conferees, controls the committee budget, supervises a sizable staff, and often serves as a spokesperson for the committee and party on issues that fall within the committee's jurisdiction. Consequently, the support of the full committee chair can be critical to bill sponsors. This is as true today as it was thirty and forty years ago.

Generally speaking, the negative or blocking power of committee chairs is stronger than their positive power to get legislation passed. The chairs' blocking power stems primarily from the ability to delay consideration of legislation, even when a majority of committee members favors it and a subcommittee has endorsed it. In both the House and Senate there are rules that provide ways to circumvent an uncooperative chair. In practice, however, these rules are seldom, if ever, employed. The mere presence of the rules means that no contemporary chair would refuse to hold committee meetings.

The negative power of chairs is stronger in the House than in the Senate. In the House, the most obvious way of circumventing an obstructionist chair—offering a bill as a floor amendment to another bill—rarely is possible because of a strict germaneness rule requiring amendments to be directly relevant to the bill or portion of the bill to which they are attached. The Senate lacks such a rule, which allows senators to sponsor floor amendments that embody legislation being blocked in committee but unrelated to the measure being debated on the floor. However, chairs of Senate committees can do favors for their colleagues, such as expediting the consideration of another bill or agreeing to hold a hearing on an issue, that give them something to trade for support in their efforts to block legislation. Thus, even in the Senate chairs have substantial advantages over rank-and-file members and can deter routine circumvention of standard committee practices.

Full committee chairs vary in the manner and degree to which they exploit parliamentary procedure to influence committee decisions. This variation is to some extent a function of personality, but it also flows from the political context in which chairs operate. Chairs who frequently are at odds with committee colleagues and outsiders on highly controversial legislation cannot afford to take the same approach as chairs who normally find consensus on major legislation within their committees. Broadly speaking, chairs of prestige and policy committees are more likely to find themselves in a political struggle with committee colleagues and therefore are more likely to exploit the full range of their parliamentary tools to pursue their policy objectives.

Threats to the power of committee chairs may come from above— that is, from chamber majorities and leaders—or from below—that is, from committee rank and file or subcommittee leaders. In recent years the Senate, which long has been more floor-oriented and slavish to seniority, has seen a larger number of challenges to committee leaders from below—particularly in circumstances where chairs were perceived as ineffective. In 1991, for example, Democrats on the Senate Foreign Relations Committee convinced chair Claiborne Pell (D-R.I.) to decentralize the committee by allowing subcommittees greater control of their agendas, the authority to mark up (draft) legislation, and the staff resources to pursue those activities.[6] And in 1995, Republican subcommittee chairs on the Armed Services Committee received much more leeway to schedule hearings and control the agendas of their panels after a move to depose committee chair Strom Thurmond (R-S.C.) was reported in the press. (See Box 4-2.) In contrast, the House, which had already moved sharply toward subcommittee power in the 1970s, has seen more of a reigning-in from above during the past decade. This trend was particularly pronounced during the 104th Congress.

Compared with their predecessors of the 1950s and 1960s, committee chairs now are more constrained and accountable and face more effective competitors for control of the policy recommendations of their committees. This is due in part to changes in the formal rules limiting chairs' discretion on a variety of procedural matters, particularly in the House, and in part to the acquisition of resources by other members who may not share the policy views of chairs. In the House, new Republican rules admonish committee chairs that "early and ongoing cooperation" (Rule 2) with the leadership is required on matters designated as "Leadership Issues." They further instruct committee chairs to ensure that bills on which the Republican Conference has taken a position be "managed in accordance with such position on the Floor of the House of Representatives" (Rule 14). In the 1970s, both the House and the House Democratic Caucus adopted rules to reduce the influence of full committee chairs by democratizing committee procedures and requiring more formal powers for subcommittees (see Chapter 2 for details).

The Senate lacks chamber rules that directly limit the role of committee chairs in organizing their committees. Like the House, however, the Senate also adopted rules in the 1970s that provide guidelines for the conduct of committee meetings, hearings, and voting, and require committees to publish additional rules governing committee procedures. But, unlike the House, Senate chamber and party rules do not specify internal committee organization in any detail and are silent on the functions of subcommittees. Compared with the rules of House committees, most Senate committees' rules are very brief and usually do not even mention the structure, jurisdictions, or functions of subcommittees. In most cases, the full committee chair is assumed to have great discretion, although even that is left unstated. The referral of legislation to subcommittees, the discharge of legislation from subcommittees, and the distribution of power between the full committee and subcommittees remain under the formal control of nearly all the Senate's full committee chairs. Nonetheless, most committees follow the practice of allowing each senator to choose a subcommittee assignment before anyone receives a second choice. On the whole, Senate chairs are granted more discretion in designing the internal decision-making processes of their committees than House chairs, and Senate subcommittee chairs enjoy less autonomy than their House counterparts.

In the House, during the period of Democratic rule, committee chairs had to be responsive to the demands of the Democratic Caucus or risk losing their positions. They also had to tolerate independent subcommittees with professional staffs. Their ability to control committee decisions by procedural means, even the ability to keep issues off the agenda, was undermined by the empowerment of subcommittees. The Republican takeover halted the trend toward subcommittee power and reinforced the move to centralization as the Speaker and other members of the leadership team closely monitor committee progress on top agenda items. During the 104th Congress, Republican leaders frequently went far beyond simply monitoring committee progress. On several occasions they intervened aggressively on bills central to the Republican program and all members seemed to understand that they had to support key elements of

Low-Key Revolt May Spur Thurmond . . .

Senate Armed Services Chairman Strom Thurmond, R-S.C., has survived what he calls a "power play" by other Republicans on the committee, but he may end up giving his restive colleagues much of what they wanted—more power over the committee's agenda.

Despite reports that some senior Republicans are worried that the 92-year-old Thurmond is not up to the job of leading the committee, a budding effort to ease him out of the chair quietly died the week of Feb. 6 [1995].

But Thurmond moved to address festering issues that some senators said inspired the failed putsch. Some Republicans have complained that the committee was too slow out of the legislative starting gate and that Thurmond has hoarded too much power.

Ending weeks of delay, Thurmond Feb. 9 set up the panel's six new subcommittees. He gave the green light to subcommittee chairmen to begin hearings and, in a Feb. 6 memo, gave them wide latitude to set their own agendas. And he began asking other Republicans to help preside at full committee hearings. That could herald a significant power shift within the committee, where control over the agenda was highly centralized under former chairman Sam Nunn, D-Ga. Thurmond took over as chairman after the GOP won control of Congress in November [1994].

"As long as the subcommittee chairmen have some flexibility to deal with the issues they want, this controversy goes away," said committee member Sen. Rick Santorum, R-Pa.

"I'm optimistic the subcommittees are going to be strengthened," said Sen. John W. Warner of Virginia, the panel's No. 2 Republican.

Tensions among Armed Services Republicans date to 1993, when Thurmond reclaimed his right to be ranking Republican, bumping Warner from the post and putting Thurmond in line to become chairman if the Republicans took over the Senate. Thurmond had previously ceded the No. 1 GOP slot in order to be ranking Judiciary Committee Republican. When Thurmond maneuvered to return to Armed Services as ranking Republican, conservative committee members cheered him on. They believed Warner had been too cozy with Nunn.

BOX 4-2

the program. The chairs would deliver, as Republican chief deputy whip, Dennis Hastert (R-Ill.) put it, or "they won't be chairmen of their committees." [7]

Resources acquired by other members also reduced the power of full committee chairs. We noted in Chapter 2 the guarantee of staff for sub-

... *To Give Colleagues Freer Hand*

Born in 1902, Thurmond has worked hard to maintain an image of physical vigor, but he has slowed in recent years and . . . [s]ome senators worry that he lacks the stamina to lead the committee effectively. . . .

Warner and Senate Majority Whip Trent Lott, R-Miss., agreed to meet to talk about Thurmond. But before that could happen, the sensitive issue made its way into print. *Newsweek* magazine reported that Lott [who also serves on Armed Services] and Warner tried to persuade Majority Leader Bob Dole, R-Kan., to urge Thurmond to step aside. Lott told reporters Feb. 7 that he and Warner met with Dole only after the report surfaced, and he denied that their aim was to replace Thurmond.

"He will stay as chairman of the committee," Lott said. Thurmond dismissed the episode as a "power play."

Thurmond's hold on the Chairmanship was never actually in doubt. In the deferential, seniority obsessed Senate, it has been extremely rare for chairmen to be forced out, even when they've been in more fragile condition than Thurmond.

The jockeying in Thurmond's case reflected GOP frustration with his stewardship. Armed Services was the last committee to organize its subcommittees. Early hearings all were handled by Thurmond in full committee.

"There were some concerns that Strom was running this pretty close to the vest," said Santorum.

That is how the panel ran under Nunn, who set the committee's agenda. But now Republicans, some of whom are subcommittee chairmen for the first time in their careers, are less willing to accept a centralized power structure.

"It's a new experience for a lot of us," Lott said. "Other members are anxious to get going.

Thurmond is moving to appease restless subcommittee chairmen. "I want to provide you the maximum flexibility in the formulation of your hearings," he told them. . . .

Source: Janet Hook and Donna Cassata, "Low-key Revolt May Spur Thurmond To Give Colleagues a Freer Hand," *Congressional Quarterly Weekly Report*, February 11, 1995, 466.

committees and the minority party contingents. In addition, rank-and-file members of both chambers gained larger personal staffs to support their legislative activity. In the House, a limit on the number of people a member could hire for a personal staff increased from just eight employees in the 1950s to eighteen full-time and four part-time employees today. In the Senate, no such limits exist; rather, senators are limited by a budget, which is set according to state size. Although they have been pared back recently, these budgets are much more generous than they were several decades ago. The effect has been to increase the average senator's personal staff from around ten in the early 1960s to more than forty in the 1980s.

Rank-and-file members have benefited from other developments as well. As organized groups have proliferated in Washington, rank-and-file members have found additional sources of expertise, bill-drafting assistance, and support for building coalitions. Innovations in information technology have increased the ability of nonleaders to gather information that challenges the assertions of committee chairs. And, in spite of recent cutbacks, the expansion of congressional support agencies (such as the Congressional Budget Office, Congressional Research Service, and General Accounting Office)[8] in the last two decades has multiplied the number of experts members can summon for assistance. A consequence of larger subcommittee and personal staffs and improved political resources is that more members have the capacity to participate in committee decision making in a meaningful and timely way. Committee chairs no longer monopolize access to policy and political expertise, they are less likely to win by default because potential opponents could not draft timely amendments, and they can count on their competition to appeal important decisions to the floor and to the other chamber. In short, the context of committee chairs has become substantially more complex, less predictable, and more competitive.

COMMITTEE TYPES AND CHAIRS

Although formal rules impose constraints common to every committee in a chamber, the role of the full committee chairs varies as it is shaped by committee-specific characteristics.[9] Systematic analysis of this phenomenon is virtually nonexistent, but a few informed observations can be offered. Most obviously, the character of committees' agendas directly conditions the role of full committee chairs. In general, chairs of committees handling highly fragmented, nationally salient, divisive agendas confront the greatest challenges. Chairs of the prestige and policy committees (see Chapter 3 for details on these categories) have responded by building large committee staffs. But the sheer size of their agendas compels full committee chairs to set their own priorities carefully, becoming actively involved in writing legislation on only a few of the most important issues. Formerly, this was achieved by chairing one of the key subcommittees as well as the full committee. In the House this is no longer possible, however, as both parties now prohibit their committee chairs (or ranking minority members) from leading a subcommittee of the committee they head.

Chairs on prestige and policy committees also have personal policy goals that often put them in conflict with committee colleagues. To succeed they must become policy combatants, drawing upon both formal and personal resources to further their cause. These chairs seek support on important issues where consensus is difficult to achieve. Successful chairs of prestige and policy committees are generally very assertive and aggressive in promoting particular issues and policy positions. Recent examples include John Kasich (R-Ohio) of the House Budget Committee, Robert Livingston (R-La.) of House Appropriations, Bill Archer (R-Tex.) of Ways and Means, former chair and now ranking minority member John Dingell (D-Mich.) of House Commerce, and, in the Senate Bob Dole (R-Kan.) of Senate Finance, former chair and current ranking minority member Edward M. Kennedy (D-Mass.) of Senate Labor and Human Resources, and Orrin G. Hatch (R-Utah) of Senate Judiciary.[10]

In the House during the 104th Congress, the new Republican chairs of prestige and policy committees were chosen, in several cases without regard for seniority, for their loyalty to the party program and the energy that they would bring to their jobs. Thus, the less-aggressive Carlos Moorhead of California, the senior Republican on both the Commerce and Judiciary committees, was passed over in favor of Thomas J. Bliley, Jr., (Va.) and Henry Hyde (Ill.), respectively, as the chairs of these two important panels. Livingston was nominated and elected chair of the Appropriations committee over Joseph McDade of Pennsylvania, who was under an indictment, and two other more senior members. And, although McDade was acquitted, Speaker Gingrich retained the aggressively partisan Livingston as chair at the outset of the 105th Congress.

The most senior Republican members on the constituency-oriented panels, however, did ascend to those chairs, even though in several instances they were measurably more moderate than the Republican Conference as a whole.[11] Not surprisingly, it was these chairs, along with those of Budget, Government Oversight, and Ways and Means, who heard most frequently from party leaders during the first 100 days of the 104th Congress. Thus, while Democratic committee chairs on these committees frequently had faced challenges from within their panels, the new Republican leaders found their greatest challenges from without.

Constituency committee members appear to have more clearly defined expectations about committee leadership than do policy committee members. Unlike policy committee members, whose definition of a "good" leader varies from issue to issue, constituency committee members seek a dependable, generally bipartisan, consensus-oriented leader committed to providing or preserving benefits for fairly stable, predictable, and bounded constituencies. Logrolling, comity, and specialization are stronger on constituency committees than elsewhere, and leaders are expected to reinforce these norms. Constituency committee members who want to compliment their chairs describe them as "consensus builders," "pragmatists," and "permissive" leaders, rather than as aggressive friends or foes. Maintaining a longstanding coalition in support of constituency benefits is normally the first priority for constituency committee chairs. (See Box 4-3 for a particularly colorful example.) As we noted, these panels were relatively undisturbed in the House during the transition to Republican rule. But even here, it appears, increasing partisanship may have repercussions for committee leaders.[12]

SUBCOMMITTEE CHAIRS IN THE HOUSE AND SENATE

Subcommittee chairs form the second tier of leadership positions in the House and the Senate. For most members, the acquisition of subcommittee chairs, which are rare enough to be of value but plentiful enough to be gained early in one's legislative career, represents an opportunity to enter a middle management position. The influence and perquisites of holding a subcommittee chair vary tremendously within and between the two chambers, and they have changed over time. But they remain an important barometer for the distribution of power within these two legislative chambers. If subcommittee chairs gain power at the expense of full committee chairs, the center of gravity within the House or Senate shifts toward the rank and file. If they lose power, the opposite occurs. But whether powerful or not, members of the House and Senate long to acquire these positions, if for no other reason than as proof of their advancement on Capitol Hill.

Although neither the chambers nor the parties formalized rules on the matter until the early 1970s, subcommittee chairs have been widely spread among the members on the basis of seniority since passage of the Legislative Reorganization Act of 1946. In some cases these positions were worth little in terms of legislative power. In the Senate, for example, the powerful Democratic chair of the Senate Finance Committee (1966–1980), Russell Long of Louisiana, generally assured that there were enough subcommittees of the full committee so that each of his majority colleagues could be a subcommittee chair. By the 96th Congress (1979–1980) the committee boasted eleven subcommittees—including one on Tourism and Sugar specifically designed for Sen. Spark Matsunaga of Hawaii.[13] This multitude of subcommittees in no way diminished the influence Long had on tax policy, and it made his colleagues happy. At the other extreme, subcommittee chairs on the powerful Appropriations Committee are tantamount to, and treated like, full committee chairs in the House.

Shuster: A Veteran Road Warrior

Time was when Rep. Bud Shuster, R.-Pa., faced criticism and even ridicule for his single-minded pursuit of hometown road projects. A long-time member of the House GOP minority, Shuster broke with Republican presidents Ronald Reagan and George Bush in order to get millions of dollars to build up his rural, rugged south-central Pennsylvania district, which includes Altoona and the legendary highway rest-stop town of Breezewood.

Though his hometown of Everett honored the congressman with a stretch of road named the "Bud Shuster By-Way," there was much grumbling about Shuster's "pork barrel" politics. Humorist Dave Barry lampooned an automated pedestrian sidewalk that Shuster sought for Altoona.

But times have changed, and Shuster now is chairman of the Transportation and Infrastructure Committee. And the omnibus transportation bill he will manage next year [1997] may authorize as much as $180 billion for transportation projects across the country.

He dismisses potential opposition from House Budget Committee Chairman John R. Kasich, R- Ohio, who wants to cut spending. "You don't persuade Kasich," Shuster said. "You beat Kasich."

And he talks with pride about having the biggest committee in the House, with 66 members. He says that will enable him to solicit many viewpoints when writing legislation, and give him more clout in the House. "When we go to the floor, I've got 66 votes to start with," he said.

Shuster seems curiously out-of-step with the goals of the GOP Congress; many Republicans came to power pledging to curb spending. But the lure of pumping funds into their districts may prove more politically powerful than a fiscally conservative philosophy. Dozens of lawmakers of both parties revealed their hands-on interest in transportation funding by asking to join Shuster's committee following the November elections. Even Kasich has toned down his opposition. He sidestepped questions last month about Shuster's proposals to boost transportation spending, stressing instead that his home state should receive a greater share of road-building funds.

Outside Congress, deficit hawks continue to pummel Shuster proposals such as using funds in deficit-reduction accounts to build up infrastructure. "This is just ludicrous," said Carol Cox Wait, president of the watchdog group Committee for a Responsible Federal Budget. But Shuster insists that the more money the government pumps into transportation, the better it will be for the nation. "I hope they put on my tombstone, 40 years from now: 'He helped build America,' " the chairman said.

Source: David Hosansky, "Shuster: A Veteran Road Warrior," *Congressional Quarterly Weekly Report,* December 14, 1996, 3395.

BOX 4-3

TABLE 4-1   Number of Committee or Subcommittee Chairmanships and Percentage of Majority Party Holding Chairmanships, Selected Congresses (1955–1998)

Congress		Number of committee and subcommittee chairmanships[a]	Percentage of majority party holding chairmanships
House			
84th	(1955–1956)	102	27.2
90th	(1967–1968)	153	44.9
94th	(1975–1976)	173	49.1
98th	(1983–1984)	152	46.4
100th	(1987–1988)	162[b]	49.6
103d	(1993–1994)	135	43.4
104th	(1995–1996)	106	40.3
105th	(1997–1998)	104	44.1
Senate			
84th	(1955–1956)	103	87.5
90th	(1967–1968)	115	85.9
94th	(1975–1976)	168	91.9
98th	(1983–1984)	119	96.3
100th	(1987–1988)	101	87.0
103d	(1993–1994)	102	82.4
104th	(1995–1996)	86	81.5
105th	(1997–1998)	86	90.9

Source: Norman J. Ornstein, Thomas E. Mann, and Michael J. Malbin, Vital Statistics on Congress, 1987–1988 (Washington, D.C.: Congressional Quarterly, 1987), 128–129, 131–132; updated by the authors.

[a] Standing committee and subcommittee chairs only.
[b] Includes formal task forces when committee has no other subcommittees.

In 1955 about 25 percent of House majority party and nearly 90 percent of Senate majority party members held a committee or subcommittee chair. By the early 1970s little had changed in the Senate, but a Democratic Caucus rule change limiting its members to a single subcommittee chair, coupled with rapid expansion in the number of subcommittees, nearly doubled that proportion in the House. As the data in Table 4-1 indicate, the distribution of chairmanships peaked in the mid-1980s and receded until the 105th Congress. The decline was largely an artifact of reductions in the number of subcommittees and the fact that full committee chairs also served as subcommittee chairs. Rules changes implemented by House and Senate Republicans have placed new restrictions on full committee chairs. Thus, the distribution rebounded sharply at the outset of the 105th Congress—to 44.1 percent in the House and to 90.9 percent in the Senate.

Expansion of the number of House subcommittee chairs increased the speed with which majority party members could expect to obtain a formal committee leadership position. But it also reduced the level of experience and expertise in these sometimes important legislative positions. In the 1960s, for example, the average House Democrat had to wait in excess of nine years—almost five terms—before gaining a subcommittee chair. By the end of the following decade, the average new subcommittee chair had served only five years in the House, a significant reduction. Yet there is substantial variation among the committees. Subcommittee chairs on the prestige committees waited nearly six terms, even after the rules changes, to gain their posts while chairs on policy and constituency committees waited about four and less than three terms, respectively, to gain theirs.[14] As the number of subcommittees declined and turnover decreased through the 1980s this trend also reversed.

In addition to ensuring wider distribution of subcommittee chairs, House Democrats in the 1970s passed the "subcommittee bill of rights" (described in Chapter 2) that provided subcommittee chairs with the resources and procedural guarantees necessary to expand their leaders' power. In the House, subcommittee chairs became potentially more powerful and, as a result, even more highly desirable. House Democrats had greater incentive to compete for these positions and to create more of them. Between the mid-1970s and mid-1980s, more than a dozen subcommittee chairs and heirs apparent were challenged, and several of them were rejected by committee colleagues in favor of less senior competitors.[15] Significantly, virtually no serious challenges to incumbent subcommittee chairs or heirs apparent have occurred in recent years in the Senate. Subcommittee leadership positions are not worth fighting over on most Senate committees, as subcommittees do not have a role in writing legislation, and on nearly all Senate committees the work of subcommittees on important legislation is shown little deference by the full committee.

How important has the expansion in the number of subcommittee chairs been? Is it possible for full committee chairs to continue to manage legislation, dictate strategy, and control policy within their committees? After all, subcommittee recommendations must be approved by the full committee. Unfortunately, it is very difficult to determine with any precision the extent to which genuine legislative leadership responsibilities have shifted from full committee chairs to subcommittee chairs.

More systematic evidence on the importance of subcommittee chairs is being gathered. Two scholars, C. Lawrence Evans and Richard L. Hall, have measured the roles of members in the internal deliberations of a few House and Senate committees. By asking informed committee staff about the influence of committee members on specific bills and tracking the level of participation in committee markups, Evans and Hall were able to rank committee members by their contributions to the legislative product. Evans's study of four Senate committees found that full committee and subcommittee chairs and ranking minority members are the most active and influential members, with other members of the relevant subcommittees following in importance.[16] Senate subcommittee leaders were more active participants in shaping the content of legislation than full committee leaders, Evans found, although the tendency was more pronounced on two of the committees studied, Judiciary and Labor and Human Resources, than on the other two, Commerce, Science, and Transportation and Environment and Public Works. When it came to using procedural tools to slow or speed committee consideration of legislation, however, full committee chairs were somewhat more active than subcommittee chairs.[17] Similarly, Evans and Hall found House subcommittee chairs and ranking minority party members the most active participants in shaping the content of legislation on Energy and Commerce, Agriculture, and Education and Labor, followed in roughly descending order by full committee chairs, full committee ranking minority members, and other members of the reporting subcommittee.[18] Evans's and Hall's findings support the now accepted view that subcommittee leaders are central players in most legislative battles.

In the absence of detailed analysis of the sort developed by Evans and Hall for several congresses, we must rely on a less refined indicator to assess change in the role of subcommittee chairs over time. One such measure is the frequency with which subcommittee chairs manage legislation on behalf of their committees when the legislation reaches the chamber floors.[19] Each bill coming to the House or Senate floor is "managed" by a member who assumes the leading role in debate, defends the bill against unfriendly amendments, and normally controls time for the majority party when the time for general debate is restricted. Sometimes the skills of the bill manager—knowledge of parliamentary procedure, sensitivity to shifting policy preferences, and good personal relations with colleagues—are crucial to preserving committee recommendations.[20] At other times lack of controversy on the floor makes bill management a routine matter. But even then, bill management can have symbolic importance because it indicates who represents the committee on that matter before the chamber.

Since 1971, the Democratic Caucus of the House has directed committee chairs to allow subcommittee chairs to manage bills whenever possible. As Table 4-2 indicates, subcommittee chairs quickly acquired the responsibility for managing most of the bills that reached the House floor. Full committee chairs still managed legislation out of proportion to their numbers, and they managed some of the most important legislation. The farm bill and the annual defense authorization bill, for example, which

TABLE 4-2   Institutional Position of Bill Managers, Selected Congresses (1959–1994), in Percentages

	Congress								
Institutional position	86th (1959–1960)	89th (1965–1966)	91st (1969–1970)	92d (1971–1972)	93d (1973–1974)	94th (1975–1976)	95th (1977–1978)	99th (1985–1986)	103d (1993–1994)
House									
Full committee chair	54.1%	48.3%	40.0%	39.4%	35.7%	30.8%	28.2%	25.2%	41.3%
Subcommittee chair	30.3	41.8	49.0	49.4	53.1	63.3	66.9	70.6	53.1
Other	15.6	10.0	11.1	11.2	11.1	5.9	4.9	4.2	5.6
Total	100.0	100.1	100.1	100.0	99.9	100.0	100.0	100.0	100.0
Senate									
Full committee chair	15.3		14.3				13.6	12.2	10.7
Subcommittee chair	30.6		26.8				21.9	11.2	5.8
Majority leader/whip	12.7		23.2				45.2	59.0	56.2
Other	41.4		35.7				19.4	17.6	27.3
Total	100.0		100.0				100.1	100.0	100.1

Source: These data were collected from the *Congressional Record* for the respective congresses.

Note: Commemorative legislation is excluded.

are composites based upon the work of a series of subcommittees, continued to be managed by the chair of the full committee. But the basic pattern for the House in the 1970s and 1980s was for subcommittee chairs to manage legislation that originated in their subcommittees. In some cases, particularly for the Banking, Energy and Commerce, Judiciary, and Ways and Means committees, the central role of subcommittee chairs as bill managers represented a sharp break with the practice of the pre-1970s period.[21]

As the data in Table 4-2 indicate, however, this trend also has been reversed. On several House committees, chairs either continued to manage virtually all committee products or they have regained this prerogative. During the 103d Congress, for example, Democratic chairs E. "Kika" de la Garza (Texas) of Agriculture, Jack Brooks (Texas) of Judiciary, Gerry Studds (Mass.) of Merchant Marine and Fisheries, and G. V. "Sonny" Montgomery (Miss.) of Veterans' Affairs managed all or virtually all of the legislation that came from their committees. The move toward omnibus legislation is a partial cause of this trend, as is the move toward fewer bills overall. The fact is most committees are producing less legislation and the legislation that is produced may be the product of several subcommittees of the full committee.

There has been no need for a rule on bill management in the Senate, where bill sponsors long have managed their own legislation on the floor. In many cases, it is the full committee or subcommittee chair with jurisdiction who serves as both sponsor and bill manager. In recent decades, however, most of the bill management duties in the Senate have been assumed by the majority leader and now by the majority whip (see Table 4-2).

Since the early 1970s, majority leaders have sought ways to streamline floor consideration of minor, noncontroversial bills. By managing such bills themselves, floor leaders minimize the speechmaking by bill sponsors and often save sponsors the trouble of having to go to the floor for the consideration and passage of their bills. Democratic majority leader Robert Byrd (in the 96th Congress), Republican majority leader Robert Dole (99th Congress), and Democratic majority leader George Mitchell (103d Congress) all assumed personal responsibility for shepherding bills through the final stages of the legislative process.[22]

The reliance on bill sponsors and the majority leaders to manage bills has meant that Senate committee and subcommittee chairs manage a very small, and declining, proportion of bills compared with their House counterparts. As in the House, however, some of the most important bills that emerge from Senate committees continue to be managed by the full committee chair. Overall, these data emphasize the limited impact of Senate subcommittees generally.

Party Support among Committee and Subcommittee Chairs

In Chapter 1 we noted that the distribution of policy preferences has important consequences for the balance of committee power. When party coalitions are cohesive and salient agenda items excite party conflict, committees are more likely to be dominated by the party caucuses. If party coalitions are weak, however, the link between party and committee leaders also will be weak and committees may experience greater autonomy. If there is a mismatch between the two—party leaders or committee leaders who are out of synch with one another—internal pressures will build up and reforms can be expected. Mapping out the distribution of preferences among leadership groups helps us to understand the dynamics of politics within the chambers and the ebb and flow of power within and among committees.

In the 1950s, 1960s, and early 1970s, the Democratic majorities in both chambers were substantially more liberal in ideological outlook than many full committee chairs. As we noted in Chapter 2, this mismatch of committee leaders and their party caucus was a byproduct of the seniority system and the defeat of many northern, more liberal Democrats in the 1946 and 1952 elections when the Republicans gained majorities in both chambers. Southern conservatives continued to gain seniority on their committees and eventually acquired a disproportionate share of the chairs. The reforms of the 1970s were in part a reaction to their power. Remaining conservative chairs moderated their policy positions, particularly in the House, where they faced election by the Democratic Caucus every two years. In terms of voting behavior on partisan issues, chairs in both chambers increased their support for positions propounded by a majority of their party (see Table 4-3). The trends in each chamber are worth a look.

In the House, the support trend among committee chairs is quite remarkable when compared with that of all Democrats. In the 92d Congress (1971–1972), full committee chairs were far less supportive of party positions than the average Democrat; indeed, the average party support score for full committee chairs was nearly identical to the average score for southern Democrats. Party reforms to make chairs more accountable, combined with retirements, yielded higher levels of party support among chairs. Since the mid-1970s, when the reforms were instituted, full committee chairs have been at least as supportive of party positions as the average Democrat, and usually have been nearly as supportive as northern Democrats. Subcommittee chairs, whose accountability runs to committee colleagues rather than to the party caucus, actually have been somewhat less supportive of party positions, on average, than the typical Democrat, although they have been substantially more supportive than southern Democrats.[23]

TABLE 4-3 Percent Support for Party Positions among Full Committee Chairs, Subcommittee Chairs, and Party Groups, 1971–1996

	Congress												
Group	92d (1971–1972)	93d (1973–1974)	94th (1975–1976)	95th (1977–1978)	96th (1979–1980)	97th (1981–1982)	98th (1983–1984)	99th (1985–1986)	100th (1987–1988)	101st (1989–1990)	102d (1991–1992)	103d (1993–1994)	104th (1995–1996)
House													
Leaders[a]	78.3	85.3	87.0	80.0	82.6	73.5	74.5	84.8	87.3	91.5	84.2	92.6	95.2
Committee chairs	47.2	56.1	62.8	69.1	71.3	70.5	76.3	79.6	82.8	82.0	79.8	82.4	89.1
Subcommittee chairs	53.6	65.5	64.1	64.2	68.1	68.9	75.5	78.8	79.7	76.7	76.4	82.2	87.7
Majority party[b]	65.6	57.7	67.7	65.4	68.6	70.5	75.0	79.3	80.5	81.0	80.0	84.0	89.0
Northern Democrats	74.9	71.2	77.2	72.8	74.6	77.5	80.8	83.1	84.0	83.5	83.5	86.5	—
Southern Democrats	47.5	37.5	46.6	48.4	56.3	54.3	60.7	69.3	72.5	73.0	73.0	78.5	—
Senate													
Leaders[a]	70.0	74.0	72.0	78.5	82.5	86.5	82.1	91.3	89.0	90.8	80.5	90.5	97.5
Committee chairs	47.6	55.1	60.7	64.7	63.0	76.3	74.3	73.2	83.7	81.9	74.2	86.9	86.0
Majority party[b, c]	60.0	66.0	65.0	64.5	66.0	78.5	75.5	75.8	80.0	81.0	80.0	84.0	89.0
Northern Democrats	69.5	76.0	74.0	73.5	71.5	—	—	—	81.8	82.9	83.9	89.4	—
Southern Democrats	43.0	39.5	42.0	44.5	55.0	—	—	—	76.0	72.2	69.6	76.3	—

Source: Calculated from party support scores published annually in *Congressional Quarterly Weekly Report.*

[a] House leaders include majority leader, whip, and chief deputy whip, except for the 92d Congress, when leaders include majority leader, whip, and the two deputy whips and the 103d Congress when leaders include four chief deputy whips. Senate leaders include majority leader and whip.

[b] The Senate majority was Democratic in the 92d–96th and the 100th–103d Congresses and Republican in the 97th–99th Congresses. The House majority was Republican in the 104th Congress.

[c] Majority party scores are equivalent to subcommittee chair scores, as nearly all majority party members hold a subcommittee chair.

In the Senate, separate scores for subcommittee chairs are not necessary because nearly all majority party members hold such a position. Like their House counterparts, Senate full committee chairs were substantially less supportive of their party's positions than the average majority party member in the early 1970s. During the 1970s, when Democrats maintained majority control of the Senate, the chairs became more supportive of the party position, though not to the same degree as their House counterparts. After the Republicans gained majority control in the 97th Congress (1981–1982), the new full committee chairs proved more supportive of their party's positions than their Democratic predecessors. In both chambers, then, chairs of the 1980s demonstrated greater policy congruence with their parent parties than had been seen in the preceding decades. With one important exception in each chamber, there have been no serious challenges to the reelection of full committee chairs based on partisan issues, and what few constraints on their behavior have been imposed.[24] What action there is has been at the subcommittee level, where members in line for chairs by virtue of their seniority have been challenged by committee colleagues. These challenges sometimes have reflected important policy differences, although not always on issues of partisan concern.

The Senate exception arose from a floor vote on a proposed constitutional amendment requiring a balanced budget. On the vote, which took place on March 2, 1995, only a single Republican, Sen. Mark O. Hatfield of Oregon, voted in opposition to the amendment. As it turned out, the amendment failed on the floor by a single vote. Hatfield, who chaired the Appropriations Committee, was a senior, moderate Republican. Although votes on constitutional amendments traditionally have been considered "conscience" votes, a number of less senior, generally more conservative Senate Republicans, many of whom had previously served in the House, sought to punish Hatfield by replacing him as chair of the committee. When it became clear that their efforts would fail, no vote on the issue was taken in the Republican Conference. But majority leader Bob Dole did appoint a task force to study ways of strengthening party discipline in the Senate. As recounted in Chapter 2, that task force, which was chaired by Sen. Connie Mack of Florida, proposed a series of rules changes to the Republican Conference. Three of those that were adopted—six-year term limits for chairs, secret ballot election of chairs, and a GOP agenda-setting process that takes place prior to those secret ballots—greatly increased the prospects for future Senate challenges.[25]

On four occasions during recent congresses, House Democrats have moved to relieve aging, full committee chairs of their duties in favor of younger, more vigorous leaders. In two cases—the replacement of Transportation Committee chair Glenn Anderson (D-Calif.) by Robert Roe (D-

N.J.) and the replacement of Appropriations Committee chair Jamie Whitten (D-Miss.) by William Natcher (D-Ky.)—these duties simply devolved to the next most senior member. In a third case, again involving the Appropriations Committee, a violation of seniority did occur when two members—Neal Smith of Iowa and David Obey of Wisconsin—jockeyed for position to replace Natcher. When Natcher died, the Caucus chose Obey to replace him.

The fourth case led to one of the important exceptions noted above. It involved House Armed Services, a committee with members having views on defense matters that are much more conservative than House Democrats and somewhat more conservative than the House as a whole. In 1985, Les Aspin (D-Wis.) successfully challenged Melvin Price (D-Ill.), the incumbent chair of the committee. Price's failing health and lack of energy were the primary causes for his replacement—although he did have a track record of support for the Republican administration's defense policies. Aspin, then the seventh-ranking Democrat on the committee, offered more vigorous leadership and promised more active opposition to administration policies. Two years later Aspin himself ran afoul of his partisan colleagues on critical issues—new strategic missiles, procurement reform, chemical weapons, aid to the Nicaraguan contras, and defense spending generally.[26] On an up-or-down decision on his reappointment, Aspin was rejected. A few days later, however, he prevailed in a three-way vote against committee colleagues who sought to replace him.

Although Aspin retained his seat, the experience became an object-lesson lesson for his colleagues and for the operation of the seniority system in the House. First, Aspin's 1985 challenge to Price demonstrated that, under the right circumstances, House Democrats were willing to ignore seniority. Second, Aspin's close call in being reelected reflected the fairly high standard of conformity to party preferences expected of chairs managing legislation that House Democrats considered vital to their party interests. It is a message that other chairs must have registered. Third, Aspin's ultimate reelection indicates how difficult it is to find a satisfactory alternative to an incumbent chair. It is one thing to express displeasure with the performance of an incumbent chair, but quite another to find an alternative candidate a majority will support. Reliance on seniority, resolves the question of choosing between the alternatives, and minimizing internal party strife.

COMMITTEE LEADERS IN THE POSTREFORM ERA

Full committee chairs in both the House and Senate lost power as a result of reforms in the 1970s. In the House, subcommittee chairs were the beneficiaries of these reforms, which produced changes in structure, procedure, and resources that enhanced their role in the legislative process. In the Senate, a more subtle shift in power occurred that can be traced to a change in the norms of the institution that benefited rank-and-file members.[27] But as early as the 1980s, several developments emerged that halted and, in the case of some committees, even reversed this trend. Roger H. Davidson has called this postreform period an era of "cutback politics."[28]

One such development was the move toward *omnibus bills*, large, multipurpose packages of disparate legislation, particularly for budget-related concerns, such as reconciliation bills and continuing appropriations resolutions.[29] Committees found it useful in the 1980s to add miscellaneous provisions, even the texts of whole bills, to necessary or priority measures to ensure that their legislation was considered on the floor and by the other chamber. Full committee chairs play a central role in coordinating the packaging of such measures and then representing the committee before the Rules Committee, on the floor, and in conference.

Beginning in 1980, Congress adopted budget resolutions that required various committees to report legislation, known as *reconciliation bills*, that saved money or enhanced revenues for the federal government. The introduction of tough "reconciliation instructions" also enlarged the role of full committee chairs.[30] Chairs have assumed a major role in representing their committees in discussions with the budget committees and party leaders about reconciliation instructions and bills, and they normally serve as the chief negotiators in conference. The partisanship of the issues involved in budget and reconciliation measures also thrusts full committee chairs to the fore as spokespersons for their party. Of course, other committee members, particularly subcommittee chairs, also play a major role in crafting omnibus and reconciliation measures. Full committee chairs do not perform these functions in isolation. But these developments and adaptations have increased both the importance of coherent, effective strategy for committees and the prominence of the most obvious source of such strategy, the full committee chair.

Budget constraints in the 1980s also limited the role of subcommittees by reducing the number of new policy initiatives that could be pursued. Some previously active subcommittees turned to oversight hearings and investigations to fill the void; other subcommittees became dormant. And with fewer pieces of legislation flowing from subcommittee to full committee, subcommittee legislation was afforded closer scrutiny by the full committee. The sheer volume of legislation passing through full committee no longer served to preserve the autonomy of subcommittees as it had in the 1970s. The workload and agenda changes placed full committee chairs and other committee members in a better position to question subcommittee recommendations.

Full committee chairs adapted in other ways as well. Many chose to chair an important subcommittee dominating policy making within its jurisdiction, often to the dismay of committee colleagues.[31] Others chose to shift their attention to oversight hearings and investigations. House Energy and Commerce chair John D. Dingell (D-Mich.), as chair of his committee's oversight subcommittee, stole the political limelight by using his subcommittee's broad oversight jurisdiction to conduct investigations in areas falling under the legislative jurisdiction of other subcommittees. House Banking Committee chair Henry B. Gonzalez (D-Texas) reserved for the full committee widely publicized hearings on the supervision of the savings and loan industry during the Reagan administration—hearings that just as easily could have been held by the subcommittees for financial institutions or general oversight.[32] In both cases, the full committee chairs' quick action and control over a substantial staff allowed them to become the central players on important issues. In addition, by most accounts, rank-and-file members, especially but not exclusively in the House, became convinced that decentralization had gone too far and had created inefficiencies. Greater tolerance for stronger committee leadership naturally followed.

So while full committee chairs clearly were not as autocratic as they once had been, aggressive chairmen such as Sen. Barry Goldwater (R-Ariz.) and Sen. Sam Nunn (D-Ga.) of the Armed Services Committee, Sen. Orrin Hatch (R-Utah) of the Labor and Human Resources Committee, Rep. Jack Brooks (D-Texas) of the House Judiciary Committee, as well as Dingell and Gonzalez, were more willingly tolerated than they might have been even a few years earlier. There were limits, of course, as Aspin learned. But full committee chairs retained important advantages and in most cases continued to be the most powerful members of their committees. This remains true today.

SUBCOMMITTEES

During the 1970s, as the evidence on bill management suggests, subcommittees became increasingly important and occasionally quite independent in House decision making but retained a more varied and sometimes ambiguous role in the Senate. Written jurisdictions, guaranteed staff, and required bill referral grant House subcommittees a degree of independence from full committee chairs that is not found on most Senate committees. The patterns in the House in the late 1970s led some observers to label House decision making *subcommittee government*. Powerful subcommittees can have a decentralizing effect on the institution, and they can weaken the full committees chairs. Weaker subcommittees allow for a more centralized legislative process, more powerful full committee chairs, and potentially closer linkages to party leaders and party programs. In the next chapter we will demonstrate how important it is to view the broader institutional context before accepting generalizations about committees and subcommittees. We seek now to answer several questions specific to the subcommittee environment. First, what sort of variation is there in the number and structure of subcommittees? Second, how has the subcommittee assignment process altered the power structure within House and Senate committees? Third, to what degree is subcommittee government a fair characterization of how committees operate internally? And, finally, assuming subcommittee government was (or is) present, is the postreform literature correct in suggesting that the trend has been reversed?[33]

VARIATION IN SUBCOMMITTEE STRUCTURE

Subcommittees became more important after the Legislative Reorganization Act of 1946 consolidated committee jurisdictions and reduced the number of standing committees in both chambers. Growth in the number of subcommittees commenced after World War II and peaked in both chambers during the 94th Congress (1975–1976) as individual committees responded to changes in the policy problems they faced and to members' demands for their own subcommittees. Subcommittees in the Senate dropped sharply during the 96th Congress (1979–1980) and again at the outset of the 104th Congress (1995–1996). In the House, the number of subcommittees moderated after the 94th Congress, but saw no sharp decline until the 103d and the 104th Congresses. Today, of the panels with authority to report legislation, six in the Senate and three in the House have no standing subcommittees.

In the 1970s, some House full committee chairs resisted efforts to create legislative subcommittees. Their resistance was eventually overcome by the 1974 House rule that required "each standing committee. . . , except the Committee on the Budget, that has more than twenty members [to] establish at least four subcommittees." Later, problems associated with growth in the number of House subcommittees—jurisdictional squabbles between subcommittees, scheduling difficulties, the burden of subcommittee hearings on executive officials—led the Democratic Caucus to limit most full committees to eight subcommittees.[34] As pressures mounted to reduce the size and cost of Congress and its bureaucracy, further limits were placed on the number of subcommittees: first a 103d Congress Democratic limit of six subcommittees for most committees, and then, a 104th Congress Republican limit of five subcommittees for most committees.[35]

Neither the Senate nor the Senate parties have a formal rule on the number of subcommittees, but limits on the number of subcommittee assignments that individual senators may hold effectively constrain the number of subcommittees that can be created. The stricter enforcement of limits on subcommittee assignments in 1985 led five committees to eliminate one or more subcommittees after a few senators were forced to give up one of their subcommittee chairs. On other committees, enforcement of the rule meant there were not enough members able and willing to take subcommittee assignments. That year, a total of ten Senate committees were compelled to eliminate at least one subcommittee.

Committees of all types—large and small, policy oriented and constituency oriented, more active and less active—have been prompted to create subcommittees. The size and diversity of a committee's jurisdiction influences the number of subcommittees established.[36] This is most obvious at the extremes. The appropriations committees have the most comprehensive jurisdictions, the most complex agendas and political environments, and the most subcommittees—thirteen. In the House, committees that are low in jurisdictional fragmentation have few subcommittees. The Rules Committee has two subcommittees, Small Business has four, Veterans' Affairs has three, and Oversight has none. The Senate counterparts to these committees have no subcommittees. Not surprisingly, policy committees average better than one subcommittee more than constituency committees in both chambers.

In addition to their standing subcommittees, committees occasionally create other subunits. Most but not all committees allow the chair to create an ad hoc subcommittee to handle a matter that falls in the jurisdiction of more than one subcommittee. The use of task forces, special panels, and units with similar names has gone beyond isolated efforts to handle issues cutting across subcommittee jurisdictions, particularly in the House. In the 1970s, the House Committee on Education and Labor maintained a task force on pension issues, which created an additional chair and allowed committee members to exceed their subcommittee assignment limit.[37] House Ways and Means used a set of task forces to devise parts of the massive tax reform package enacted in 1986. In the 1970s and 1980s, House Budget employed a fairly permanent set of task forces to study parts of the budget and budget process in lieu of standing subcommittees with authority to write legislation. In the 1980s, House Armed Services added "panels" on defense policy, weapons acquisitions policy, and other topics. These went so far as to permit noncommittee members to join. At present, the House National Security Committee is authorized to maintain a special oversight panel in excess of the otherwise strict limit on subcommittees. House rules now prohibit all but a few committees from exceeding the five-subcommittee limit. And those same rules carefully limit "subcommittees" by whatever name. Any subunit of a full committee that lasts longer than six months counts against the limit.

SUBCOMMITTEE ASSIGNMENTS

Much of the independence of present-day subcommittees derives from the process by which their members are appointed. Before the 1970s, full committee chairs created subcommittees, set their jurisdictions, and appointed subcommittees and their chairs. The democratization of committee procedure in the 1970s made the subcommittee assignment process a matter of self-selection. In the House, chamber rules are silent on subcommittee assignment procedures, so party rules and practices govern the allocation of subcommittee assignments. House Republicans leave the process to the committee chair (or ranking member) of each full committee, but most of their leaders have adopted a *bidding* approach that allows members to select their subcommittees in order of seniority and ensures that each round of selections is complete before second or third choices are made.[38] House Democrats' rules formally provide for a process of self-selection in order of seniority, whereby every member is allowed a choice before second choices are permitted. In the Senate, committee rules often mandate a process guaranteeing members a first (or second) subcommittee choice before any other member receives a second (or third) choice, and all party contingents operate that way even in the absence of a formal rule. Consequently, committee members are no longer dependent on the full committee chair for desirable subcommittee assignments and generally may act without fear of putting subcommittee assignments in jeopardy.

Members gained more subcommittee assignments in the 1960s and early 1970s. As rank-and-file members demanded assignments to subcommittees that served their political goals, the number and size of subcommittees gradually increased, and the typical member gained more subcommittee seats. In the House, the average number of assignments per member grew from 2.5 in the 88th Congress (1963–1964) to 4.0 in the 94th (1975–1976)—a level that was maintained until the 103d and 104th Congresses cut back the number of subcommittees. More assignments meant more meetings to attend, which created scheduling conflicts that in turn caused difficulties in obtaining quorums for meetings. In the 1970s, the Democratic Caucus limited each of its members to five subcommittee assignments, although it since has granted numerous exemptions to allow members additional assignments. The exemptions sometimes were granted so that members could serve on subcommittees handling problems vital to their constituencies, or to retain expertise or a necessary ideological balance on particular subcommittees.[39] While in the minority, House Republicans had no formal limit but were constrained by the number of subcommittee seats allocated to them by the majority party Democrats. At the outset of the 104th Congress, however, Republicans changed the standing rules of the House to include a limit of four subcommittees for all members.[40] Today, the average number of subcommittee assignments per member has declined to about three per member.

Subcommittee assignments have expanded in the Senate as well. Between the mid-1960s and mid-1970s, the number of subcommittee assignments held by the average senator increased from 6.6 to 11 per member. In 1977, the Senate adopted limits on the number of subcommittee assignments a senator could hold (eight for most senators), which brought the average back to 6.6.[41] This forced a contraction in the number of subcommittees because some committees found that there were not enough eligible senators to serve. However, when the Republicans gained control of the Senate in 1981, they added several new subcommittees and began to grant exemptions to the limits on subcommittee assignments. By 1983, the number of senators serving on more than eight subcommittees was thirty-two, roughly one-third of the Senate, and the average had risen to 7.5. As we have noted, restraint was exercised in the following congresses, so the average senator has held about seven subcommittee assignments in recent congresses. At the beginning of the 104th Congress, of course, the number of subcommittees was dramatically reduced. Indeed, not one of the committees listed as minor in Senate rules currently has any subcommittees.

THE PATH OF LEGISLATION

The presence of numerous subcommittees and subcommittee assignments, even when bolstered by rules that grant subcommittees some independence from parent committees and their chairs, does not guarantee a decision-making pattern that is properly labeled "subcommittee government." Independence in activity does not necessarily provide autonomy in decision making, although it is probably a necessary condition for autonomy. Even active, seemingly independent subcommittees remain the creatures of parent committees that may ignore or amend their recommendations and alter their jurisdictions and duties. (For a humorous example of the various contending forces that may come into play at the subcommittee level, see Box 4-4.)

Committees have developed a variety of roles for their subcommittees, which makes it inappropriate simply to characterize committees as centralized or decentralized. One way to examine the functions of subcommittees is to trace the path taken by individual measures. Virtually all

Tardy Pooper

Rep. James V. Hansen (R-Utah) appears to have come up with a nifty way of dealing with those bothersome Democrats on the House Resources subcommittee on national parks, forests, and lands, which he chairs.

Hansen set a vote last week on seven bills and was told the Democrats were going to raise substantive and procedural objections. Hansen, who's a stickler for promptness, was upset that some Democrats were missing and other members were milling about in the anteroom. Hansen and a few GOP members were present when Hansen banged the gavel.

"I ask unanimous consent that all the bills on the list be passed as they are marked up," Hansen said. "Is there objection? Hearing none, so ordered. The committee is adjourned." He banged the gavel again and was smiling broadly as he walked past Rep. Bill Richardson (D-N.M.), the ranking minority member. "Bill, it's over, don't come in," Hansen said.

Richardson, who was standing just outside the hearing room, thought Hansen was joking, and was stunned to find out the 9-second hearing had ended. "The North Koreans have walked out of negotiations," Richardson said yesterday, "but at least they don't have negotiations among themselves. This is an all time low."

Next thing you know, Rep. George Miller (D-Calif.), ranking member on the full committee, fired off an angry letter to Chairman Don Young (R-Alaska), calling the move "an affront to the minority," an "outrageous abuse of authority" and a "direct insult to the integrity of this committee."

Talk about sour grapes. As the great Melvin A. Steinberg, former president of the Maryland Senate, once said: "You either run the gavel or the gavel runs you."

It turns out, however, that the parliamentarians, having reviewed the tape of the micro-hearing, concluded that Hansen didn't say the magic words in quite the right way.

Miller's request that the subcommittee do it over [was] going to be granted. "Nothing really happened," a Republican source said. Hansen was just trying to make his point."

Source: Al Kamen, "Tardy Pooper," *Washington Post,* May 31, 1996, A21. © Washington Post. Reprinted with permission.

BOX 4-4

legislation passed by Congress is first referred to or considered by a committee, where hearings may be held, legislative language is drafted and modified, and a vote is take to report it to the floor. As subcommittees have gained greater independence, a similar process increasingly has been

TABLE 4-4   Percentage of Measures Referred to and Percentage of
Measures Reported from Committees that Were Referred to
Subcommittee or Subject to a Subcommittee Hearing,
Selected Congresses (1969–1994)

	Congress			
Action taken	91st (1969–1970)	96th (1979–1980)	100th (1987–1988)	103d (1993–1994)[a]
House				
Referred	35.7	79.8	84.6	81.4
Reported	75.4	80.0	79.7	81.2
Senate				
Referred	41.5	41.1	42.3	31.2
Reported	40.0	44.8	46.3	43.5

Source: Calculated from information provided in the *Final Calendar* for each committee for the respective congresses.

Note: Excludes House and Senate appropriations committees because they do not produce committee calendars comparable to those of the other committees. Matters related to nominations and commemorative legislation are excluded from the data.

[a] Totals include data derived from calendars from earlier congresses for three committees because calendars for the 103d Congress were unavailable. These are House Judiciary (101st Congress), Senate Governmental Affairs (102d Congress), and Senate Energy and Natural Resources (102d Congress).

carried out at the subcommittee level before full committee action. That is, in many cases, subcommittees assume the initial responsibility for discussing and designing legislation, thereby setting the agenda for subsequent stages in the legislative process. The extent to which these responsibilities have shifted to subcommittees can be seen in the number of measures referred to or reported from subcommittees (see Table 4-4).

Consider the House first. The percentage of legislation referred to House subcommittees more than doubled between the 91st Congress (1969–1970) and the 96th Congress (1979–1980), a level that was maintained in the 100th (1987–1988) and 103d (1993–1994) Congress. Until the 1970s, many full committee chairs maintained key measures and measures unlikely to be acted upon by the committee at the full committee level. This meant, of course, that full committee chairs retained control of legislation they opposed. But since 1975, when the 1973 Subcommittee Bill of Rights was implemented in most House committees, subcommittees have become the dungeons where most legislation dies.

There is much less change in the path taken by legislation eventually reported to the House floor. Even in the late 1960s, most legislation brought to the floor had been referred to subcommittee at some point in committee deliberations, if only for a hearing. It is obvious that subcommittees had become quite important by that time. Not all reported legislation has been referred to subcommittee, however. Since the reforms in the mid-1970s, several House committees have adopted rules to keep certain types of legislation at the full committee, as they are free to do under House and Democratic Caucus rules. The Ways and Means Committee keeps legislation amending the income tax sections of the Internal Revenue Code at the full committee; Resources retains matters pertaining to native American Indians for the full committee; and International Relations requires that the markup of foreign assistance and Peace Corps authorization be conducted by the full committee. In addition, many House committees routinely hold Senate bills sent to the House at the full committee, particularly late in a session when there is little chance of further action or when similar legislation already has been reported to the floor.

In contrast to the House, the Senate's pattern of referral shows little change. A majority of both referred and reported legislation remains at the full committee, and most Senate committees do not routinely refer legislation to subcommittee. Rather, legislation remains on the docket of the full committee, even when a subcommittee chooses to hold a hearing and write legislation on the subject.

Within the aggregate pattern of the Senate there is tremendous variation, far more than in the House. Because the Senate and the Senate parties do not have rules governing the referral of legislation to subcommittees, Senate committees have adopted a wide range of rules and practices to govern subcommittee referral. Most Senate committees have no formal rule on the subject, leaving referral to the chair's discretion or established practice.

Two Senate committees have adopted rules that are quite specific. The Judiciary Committee, for example, makes the requirement that "except for matters retained at the full committee, matters shall be referred to the appropriate subcommittee or subcommittees, except as agreed by a majority vote of the Committee or by the agreement of the Chairman and the Ranking Minority Member."[42] In contrast, the Finance Committee's rule states that "all legislation shall be kept on the full committee calendar unless a majority of the members present and voting agree to refer specific legislation to an appropriate subcommittee."[43] A third committee, Agriculture, authorizes the full committee chair to withdraw measures from a subcommittee if it should "fail to report back to the full Committee . . . within a reasonable time."[44] But there is no guarantee within those same rules that subcommittees will receive measures from the full committee.

SUBCOMMITTEE MEETINGS AND HEARINGS

An additional measure of the importance of subcommittees is the frequency of full committee and subcommittee meetings and hearings. Most formal meetings of committees and subcommittees are *markups*, sessions at which legislation is considered in detail and perhaps reported to the full committee or the floor. The relative frequency of full committee and subcommittee markups indicates the degree of reliance on subcommittees for drafting the details of legislation. *Hearings* are sessions in which committees or subcommittees receive testimony from witnesses—administration officials, interest group representatives, independent experts, and constituents. Hearings often assist committees in gathering information about policy problems and solutions, but they can also serve as platforms to publicize a cause. Thus, while hearings have less direct impact on the content of legislation, they can be important tools in building majority coalitions for or against legislation.

The pattern of meetings and hearings (Table 4-5) confirms the chamber differences that we noted above. The percentage of House meetings and hearings held by subcommittees increased greatly during the 1970s and has held steady since. All House committees with legislative subcommittees now have a rule that authorizes the subcommittees to meet, hold hearings, conduct investigations, and report legislation to the full committee on matters within their jurisdictions.[45] In fact, nearly all House committees reserve the conduct of hearings for their subcommittees. Throughout the 1980s, even full committee chairs pursued most of their own interests through hearings of the subcommittees they chaired rather than by using the full committee. This arrangement allowed a division of labor within committees and the pursuit of simultaneous hearings on a range of subjects. No committee members are excluded by this process because they are allowed to sit with any subcommittee during hearings and to question witnesses.

The key change in the House concerns the frequency of subcommittee meetings or markups. During the 1970s, enough committees were compelled to change their decision-making practices to shift the percentage of meetings held by subcommittees from just under 50 percent to just over that amount, a level that was maintained through the 1980s before falling in the 1990s. Full committees still meet frequently, of course, because they must approve legislation recommended by subcommittees. As a result of the changes of the 1970s, the typical decision-making pattern in House committees has three stages: subcommittee hearings, subcommittee markup, and full committee markup. The degree to which the full committee rejects or modifies subcommittee recommendations cannot be discerned from these data, but the pattern of meetings suggests

TABLE 4-5   Percentage of Committee Meetings and Hearings Held by
Subcommittees, Selected Congresses (1959–1994)

	Congress				
	86th (1959–1960)	91st (1969–1970)	96th (1979–1980)	100th (1978–1988)	103d (1993–1994)
House					
Meetings	45.6	47.9	56.1	52.0	44.5
Hearings	72.3	77.0	90.7	95.1	86.9
Senate					
Meetings	27.1	30.6	19.1	18.6	15.6
Hearings	77.7	79.6	65.2	64.4	59.4

Source: Data are calculated from information provided in the "Daily Digest" of the Congressional Record of the respective congresses.

Note: House Appropriations Committee excluded because it did not report its meetings in the "Daily Digest" in the 86th, 91st, 96th, and 100th Congresses. Meetings and hearings on nominations are excluded.

that full committees meet nearly as often as subcommittees to consider legislation.

Although the overall pattern of committee and subcommittee behavior remains the same there have been some changes in the 1990s. First, both House parties now prohibit the chair or ranking member of a full committee from also holding that position on a subcommittee. Thus, full committee chairs cannot use a "personal" subcommittee the way committee leaders could in the 1980s. Second, the level of meetings held by the subcommittees has returned to its pre-reform level. In part, this simply reflects the reduced number of subcommittees. But it also seems likely that it is related to the legislative trends of the era—fewer, larger, and more multiply referred bills. Full committee chairs are now more likely to hold a few important items for "original" consideration by the full committee.

In contrast, a longstanding, two-stage process remains typical in Senate committees: subcommittee hearings and full committee markup. Most Senate committees, but not all, operate on the assumption that subcommittee markups are an inefficient use of senators' scarce time when full committee markup follows anyway. In fact, the percentage of meetings held in subcommittee in recent congresses remains lower than the House percentage of more than thirty years ago. Fewer than one in five Senate committee meetings is a subcommittee meeting.

The view of subcommittees in the Senate is so different that its Rules and Administration Committee seriously suggested in 1988 that the Senate adopt a rule barring subcommittee markups. Although this did not happen, the recommendation reflects widespread concern among senators that there are too many demands on their time to tolerate subcommittee markups. Attendance at subcommittee markups has proven to be a serious problem, and many committees have independently eliminated subcommittee markups of their own accord.[46]

SUBCOMMITTEES IN CONFERENCE

In addition to a greater role in initiating legislation within committees and managing legislation on the floor, House subcommittee members gained a more significant role in conference committees during the 1970s. Participation in conference is critical if subcommittee members are to have power. Conferences normally are the last stage at which the details of major legislation are modified before the legislation is finally approved and sent to the president. When subcommittee members are confident that they will be appointed to the conference, they can gauge strategy in committee and on the floor with the knowledge that they will be responsible for negotiating with the other chamber and thus may have the opportunity to reshape the legislation before it is finally enacted.

The role of subcommittees in conference is a product of their role within the full committees. The initiators of much legislation, House subcommittee chairs and members are natural choices for conference delegations. Their importance was enhanced further by a 1977 rule requiring the Speaker to name conferees "who are primarily responsible for the legislation" and, "to the fullest extent possible, include the principal proponents of the major provisions of the bill as it passed the House."[47] Although these instructions leave the Speaker with substantial discretion and reliant upon the recommendations of the full committee chair in most cases, subcommittee members with appropriate jurisdiction usually meet these conditions and are appointed to conferences.[48]

The net result of the changes in intracommittee decision-making patterns during the 1970s was a substantial increase in the number of House conference delegations dominated by members of the *sub*committee of appropriate jurisdiction. Table 4-6 indicates that prior to the 1970s the number of House conference delegations dominated by subcommittee members was about equal to the number of delegations appointed without regard to subcommittee membership. These latter delegations generally included a handful of the most senior members of the full committee. It is important to note here that subcommittee membership was an organizing principle for about half of the House delegations even before reforms imposed a more decentralized decision-making process on most House committees.

TABLE 4-6   Number of Conference Delegations Structured by Full
Committee and Subcommittee Membership, Selected
Congresses (1965–1994)

	Congress			
Chamber	89th (1965– 1966)	96th (1979– 1980)	99th (1985– 1986)	103d (1993– 1994)
House				
Subcommittee delegations	72	109	50	73
Full committee delegations	60	33	76	30
Deliberately mixed delegations	8	21	21	15
Ambiguous cases	1	1	0	1
Total	141	164	147	118
Senate				
Subcommittee delegations	74	77	21	44
Full committee delegations	55	59	27	36
Deliberately mixed delegations	1	17	5	4
Ambiguous cases	8	4	0	0
Total	138	157	53	88

Source: Calculated from information contained in the Calendars of the United States House of Representatives and History of Legislation (final editions) for the respective congresses.

By the late 1970s, the democratization of decision-making practices within committees was transparent in the composition of conference delegations. Three-fourths of the House delegations were either the nearly exclusive province of subcommittee members or combined a set of subcommittee members with other committee members. Among the full committee delegations, seniority was less consistently observed. The proportion of subcommittee-oriented delegations fell during the 1980s, however, as the total number of delegations declined precipitously, but rebounded by the 103d Congress.

The Senate and its committees lack formal rules instructing the Senate's presiding officer or committee chairs on who should be appointed to conferences, although the presiding officer is directed by a largely unenforceable rule that conferees should be supportive of the Senate position. As in the House, lists provided by full committee chairs usually guide the presiding officer. Members from the relevant subcommittee tend to take greater interest in the issue and to take the lead in full committee consideration on the bill. Furthermore, unlike the House, where it is virtually impossible to challenge the Speaker's choices, the Senate formally votes on its conferees, which enables a senator to object to or even filibuster the appointment of conferees. Subcommittee members who are principal authors of bills or important provisions are seldom excluded from the Senate conference delegation when they seek appointment.

Several features of the Senate pattern of change in the composition of conferences are notable. Like House delegations, Senate delegations frequently were organized by subcommittee membership in the mid-1960s. Surprisingly, Senate delegations were somewhat more likely than House delegations to exhibit a subcommittee orientation at that time. But by the late 1970s, while the House became far more subcommittee-oriented, the Senate showed virtually no change and, on balance, was therefore less subcommittee-oriented than the House. In the 1980s, the same forces operating in the House appear to have operated in the Senate, making its delegations less subcommittee-oriented than they had been in the 1970s, before returning in the 103d Congress to the levels of the previous decade.

The record of subcommittee representation in conference delegations cautions against simplistic interpretations of the role of subcommittees. Even in the House, where subcommittees' independence is more firmly established, subcommittee membership does not structure conference appointments in many situations. Subcommittees are not autonomous creatures in the legislative process.

COMMITTEE STAFF

Committee staff both reflect and condition power in committees. Well-educated professionals bring polish and expertise to their jobs. They are among the top policy specialists in their fields, in or out of government. Beyond the administrative tasks of arranging meetings and hearings and managing the paperwork associated with legislating, committee staff influence the agenda-setting decisions of chairs, advocate or even champion legislative proposals, conduct investigations, negotiate on behalf of committees and their chairs, and work to build coalitions in committee, on the floor, and in conference. The assistance of quality staff can give a committee or subcommittee chair a substantial advantage over competitors in legislative politics.[49]

For over a century, the various types of staff support have been prized objects in the House and Senate. Committee staff also have been controversial. Proponents contend that expanded committee staff help members cope with burgeoning workloads. Committee staffs, along with personal staff and support agencies, help Congress to compete with the expertise of the executive branch and scrutinize the claims of special interests. Critics suggest they damage committee operations, overload committees with make-work, make possible endless hearings that take administration officials away from their duties, insulate members from each other, and enable committees and subcommittees to pursue topics beyond their legitimate jurisdictions. Most important, critics contend, committee staff wield too much power in negotiating and making innumerable decisions about the details of legislation on behalf of their bosses. The popular press has characterized committee staff as "the new power elite," "the new Senate barons," "governors on the Hill," and "shadow government."[50] Former Rules Committee chair Richard Bolling (D-Mo.) put it this way: "Some staffing is disastrous, but the key is whether they do useful work. You can have a staff where 50 percent are stirring the pot and they're not putting anything in the pot. They're just stirring. On the other hand, you can have a staff that makes a committee function."[51]

TYPES OF COMMITTEE STAFF

The advent of modern congressional committee staffing can be traced to the Legislative Reorganization Act of 1946, which provided committees with ten full-time staff members. These ten committee staff members were divided into two categories: four members were to be "professionals" and six were to be "clerks." Professional staff were intended to provide committees with substantive expertise relevant to the subject matter of each committee while the clerks were to provide nonpolicy-oriented administrative and secretarial help. Since then, committee staff, under a variety of different names (investigative staff, associate staff, and temporary staff, for example) have been added to aid committee members. In very broad form, the original distinction between professional staff and clerks remains today—with associate, investigative, and temporary staff all forms of the professional cadre.

The actual size of committee staff varied somewhat during the two and half decades following the 1946 act, although the guarantee of ten-member staffs remained the same. In 1970, the second Legislative Reorganization Act increased the statutory staff support of each committee to six professional assistants. The act established a procedure whereby each committee could make annual requests for staff assistance beyond the statutory amount, which opened the door to large staff increases. These assistants came to be called investigative staff. Since then, each chamber has made alterations in its committee staffing arrangements pretty much independently.

In 1974, for example, the House increased the number of statutory positions for each committee to thirty—eighteen professional and twelve clerks. Today, House rules guarantee each standing committee at least thirty professional staff. (The exceptions are Appropriations and Budget, which may set their own staffing levels.) At the request of the minority party, up to ten of these professionals may be assigned to the minority party group within each committee.[52] This rule, too, can be traced to the Reorganization Act of 1970. During the 1980s the smallest House committee staffs numbered in the thirties or forties (District of Columbia and Veterans' Affairs) while the largest had more than 100 (Appropriations, Education and Labor, and Energy and Commerce). By 1990, only one House standing committee had fewer than forty assistants while six exceeded 100. One committee, Appropriations, had over 200 staff assistants.[53] Thus, most House committee staff, and virtually all subcommittee staff, fall into the investigative category. That is, they are funded pursuant to the annual requests of the House committees.

In 1975 the House strengthened the independence of subcommittees by guaranteeing that both the chair and ranking minority member of each standing subcommittee could appoint at least one staff member. Unless authorization for additional staff is obtained from the House, through the annual request for investigative assistants, subcommittee staff come out of the allocation guaranteed to the full committee, which directly reduces the number under the control of the full committee chairs and ranking minority members. This rule dramatically altered staffing patterns in House committees. Both the size and independence of subcommittees had peaked by the early 1990s. With fiscal pressures on the rise and heightened criticisms of excessive decentralization, the House moved to reduce the level of staffing—a shift most heavily felt by subcommittees. Furthermore, new Republican rules, adopted at the outset of the 104th Congress and sustained in the 105th, ensure that subcommittee staff will be controlled by the full committee chair. The rule merely requires the chair to "ensure that sufficient staff is made available to each subcommittee to carry out its responsibilities under the rules of the committee."[54]

Senate committees also used the 1970s' procedures to hire investigative staff, which also grew quite large. In 1981, however, the Senate abolished the distinction between statutory and investigative staff and moved to biennial funding resolutions for staff support.[55] Senate rules make no specific allotment of staff support to the minority party. But since 1977 they do permit the minority party caucus of any committee to request at least one-third of the funds available for the appointment of staff of their choice.[56]

Another type of staff, *associate staff*, represent a cross between committee staff and members' personal office staff. Associate staff usually work out of members' personal offices and often are difficult to distin-

FIGURE 4-1   Staff of Members and of Committees in Congress, 1891–1996

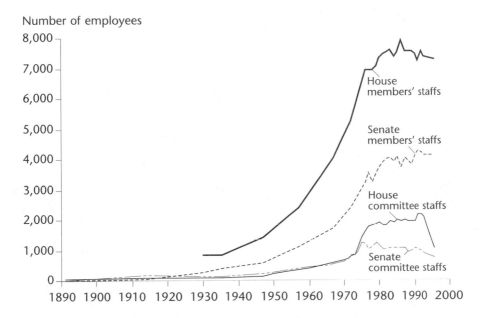

Source: Norman J. Ornstein, Thomas E. Mann, and Michael J. Malbin, *Vital Statistics on Congress, 1995–1996* (Washington, D.C.: Congressional Quarterly, 1996), 134; updated by the authors.

guish from the legislative assistants that appear on members' personal office budgets. The Senate initiated the practice on a large scale in 1975 when it authorized each senator to hire up to three people to assist him or her on committee business. Emulating the Senate, the House authorized each member of three prestige committees—Appropriations, Budget, and Rules—to hire staff assistants at committee expense to assist her or him with committee duties. Appropriations committee members were allowed to hire two associates while Budget and Rules members could each hire one. In the 102d Congress members of a fourth House committee, Ways and Means, received an $11,000 supplement to their office accounts to help pay a personal aide who would be responsible for that committee's issues. Associate staff in the House were reduced but not eliminated by cuts implemented at the outset of the 104th Congress. Appropriations members were reduced to a single associate, Rules members retained their single associate, and continuing members of the Budget Committee were allowed to keep their associate staff assistants though funding for assistants was withheld from new members of the committee.

GROWTH AND DISTRIBUTION OF COMMITTEE STAFF

The growth of committee staff is shown in Figure 4-1. Gradual expansion in the 1950s and 1960s turned into an explosion in the 1970s before leveling off in the 1980s and then declining in the early 1990s. This growth was the product of several factors. Committees requested and received more staff to manage larger legislative and investigative workloads. Congress sought to bolster its capacity to compete with the executive branch and its store of expertise. Individual chairs viewed larger staffs as an important resource for expanding the number of issues they could address, the number of hearings they could organize, and the number of bills they could write, all of which enhanced their personal influence and political careers. Finally, and most important, the expansion stemmed creating staff for subcommittees and the minority party.

The surge in committee staff size during the 1970s was much greater in the House than in the Senate. While the total number of House committee staff more than tripled between 1969 and 1979, Senate committee staff grew by only 80 percent or so (see Table 4-7). The different rates of increase are due primarily to the tremendous expansion of subcommittee staff in the House. Senate committees retained far more centralized staffing arrangements. House subcommittee staff grew by a total of nearly 650 percent, thanks to a new Democratic Caucus rule; Senate subcommittee staff grew by less than 50 percent. In 1979, just two Senate committees, Judiciary and Government Affairs, employed nearly three-fourths of the subcommittee staff of the Senate.

Changes in the House were quite remarkable. In 1970, twelve House committees had no separate subcommittee staff. Of the seven committees with staff designated as subcommittee staff, only Appropriations and Government Operations had clearly decentralized forms of staff organization in which some staff members worked nearly exclusively for a single subcommittee chair. By 1979, only three House committees with subcommittees (Armed Services, District of Columbia, and Veterans' Affairs) had not created separate subcommittee staffs. By the 1980s, House committees, operating under requirements that committee staff be shared with subcommittees and the minority, had very similar distributions of staff between the full committee and subcommittees. The share of staff allocated to subcommittees peaked in the 99th Congress. The Republican takeover in 1995 brought with it increased variation in the size and balance of committee and subcommittee staff. For example, the Commerce Committee and the Economic and Educational Opportunities Committee identified no separate subcommittee staffs in the 104th Congress.

Senate committees, because they are not constrained by chamber or party rules requiring separate subcommittee staff, varied widely in the

TABLE 4-7   Percentage of Committee Staff Allocated to Subcommittees, 1969–1996

Congress		Subcommittee staff allocation			
		House		Senate	
91st	(1969–1970)	23.2	(461)	42.1	(504)
92d	(1971–1972)	27.7	(575)	44.6	(635)
93d	(1973–1974)	36.4	(664)	40.5	(775)
94th	(1975–1976)	32.8	(1,083)	32.1	(859)
95th	(1977–1978)	38.8	(1,250)	27.7	(869)
96th	(1979–1980)	43.0	(1,608)	34.5	(902)
97th	(1981–1982)	39.8	(1,507)	32.5	(906)
98th	(1983–1984)	44.2	(1,479)	40.8	(922)
99th	(1985–1986)	45.8	(1,566)	41.4	(863)
100th	(1987–1988)	45.8	(1,545)	37.3	(790)
101st	(1989–1990)	45.2	(1,600)	38.7	(834)
102d	(1991–1992)	44.7	(1,833)	34.7	(1,069)
103d	(1993–1994)	40.5	(1,719)	31.2	(985)
104th	(1995–1996)	38.0	(1,090)	26.1	(777)

Source: Charles B. Brownson and Ann L. Brownson, eds., *Congressional Staff Directory* (Mt. Vernon, Va.: Staff Directories Ltd.), respective years.

Note: Total number of committee and subcommittee staff in parentheses.

manner in which they staffed subcommittee activities in the 1980s. Some, such as Governmental Affairs, Judiciary, and Labor, were much like House committees in allowing subcommittee leaders to appoint their own staff. Others, such as Armed Services and Banking, did not appoint separate subcommittee staffs but assigned certain subcommittee responsibilities to full committee staff assistants. In such cases, the staff assistant had two bosses—the full committee chair and the subcommittee chair. In some committees, such as Agriculture, there was little meaningful differentiation among committee staff and usually little separate subcommittee activity, particularly with respect to drafting legislation.

Within the constraints set by statute, chamber, and caucus rules, the character of committee jurisdictions and agendas shape decisions about how to organize and utilize staff. The most obvious influences are the size and diversity of a committee's jurisdiction. Large, diverse jurisdictions are associated with large committee staffs. The appropriations, commerce, judiciary, and labor committees of the two chambers have very large staffs, even at the full committee level, reflecting the workload of these committees. The rules, small business, and veterans' committees have very small staffs. Overall, the rank-order correlation between jurisdictional fragmentation and staff size was .75 in the House and .85 in the Senate (on a 0-to-1 scale) in 1996.[57] In general, the prestige and policy committees have larger, more diverse jurisdictions and therefore require more staff assistance.

Members' personal goals reinforce these differences. The activism found on policy committees leads subcommittee chairs to demand large staffs of their own. The greater emphasis on common interests on constituency committees allows their subcommittee chairs to rely on smaller and more centralized staffs. Political scientist David E. Price, who would later become a member of the House, described two primary roles for committee staff.[58] Staff *professionals* view their roles as supportive of corporate committee goals, so they are geared toward serving the entire membership. Turnover in the membership or in chairs may not have implications for their jobs. *Entrepreneurs* tend to be linked to a single member and that member's legislative goals. When their boss changes position, say from one subcommittee chair to another, they nearly always move, too. The evidence suggests that *professionals* are found disproportionately on constituency committees. The clarity and homogeneity of the legislative goals of constituency committees make it possible for staff aides to develop a professional relationship with most members, which in turn helps staff members survive as committee and subcommittee chairs come and go. In contrast, staff activists who constantly survey the political landscape for new issues and eagerly pursue extensive hearings and investigations are well suited to policy-oriented members.

PATTERNS OF SUBCOMMITTEE ORIENTATION

Movement toward an increased reliance on subcommittees was one of the most striking features of the postreform House. The absence of any real reliance on subcommittees in the Senate stood in stark contrast. Although the reforms of the 1970s have become more distant, this distinction between the House's use of subcommittees and the Senate's use of subcommittees remains today. To summarize these differences and trace longitudinal change during the last several decades, we have constructed a composite measure of subcommittee orientation for each standing committee. This measure is the mean of the following indicators: (1) the percentage of measures considered on the floor that were managed by a subcommittee chair, (2) the percentage of measures reported to the floor that were referred to a subcommittee or on which a subcommittee hearing was held, (3) the percentage of meetings (primarily markups) that were subcommittee meetings, and (4) the percentage of staff specifically allocated to subcommittees.

The composite measure of subcommittee orientation highlights the differences between the House and the Senate (see Tables 4-8 and 4-9). It also demonstrates that both chambers have continued to move away from the use of subcommittees during the postreform period. House committees, which had an average subcommittee orientation of 47 percent in the 91st Congress (1969–1970), 59 percent in the 96th Congress (1979–1980), and 57 percent in the 100th Congress (1987–1988), declined to 50 percent by the 103d Congress (1993–1994). In contrast, Senate committees' reliance on subcommittees declined throughout this entire period: from 31 percent, to 25 percent, to 19 percent, and finally to 20 percent during the 103d Congress. Moreover, as a result of changes implemented at the outset of the 104th Congress—reductions in staff, elimination of committees and subcommittees, and stricter control over the congressional agenda—it is nearly certain that the subcommittee index will dip even further.

Unlike the immediate postreform period, the index of subcommittee orientation declined for most committees between the 96th (1979–1980) and 99th (1985–1986) Congresses. In most cases, this was due to a decline in the proportion of meetings held by subcommittees and in the proportion of reported measures receiving subcommittee referral or hearings. This pattern appears to be associated with the move to more omnibus bills, particularly reconciliation bills. Because of time constraints and political considerations, committees often incorporated legislation in their reconciliation packages without following the usual procedure of conducting subcommittee hearings and markups before full committee action. Legislating in this fashion undercut the role of subcommittees during that period.[59]

During the most recent period, however, the shift in subcommittee orientation is attributable to reductions in bill management by subcommittee chairs and a reduction in the number of staff allocated to subcommittees. By most indicators, and with a few notable exceptions, chairs in the 1990s have simply been more aggressive than they were during the 1980s. The Republicans who took control of these same panels were no more shy than their Democratic predecessors—indeed, energy and activism were stated criteria for appointment to a committee chair at the outset of the 104th Congress.

The variation in subcommittee orientation also is related to the goals of committee members, at least in the House. In the 91st Congress (1969–1970), House policy and constituency committees had nearly identical scores on the subcommittee orientation index—48.5 and 47.5, respectively. But by the 96th Congress (1979–1980), after the period of reform, policy committees had become decidedly more subcommittee-oriented than constituency committees—70.3 and 59.3, respectively. Sub-

TABLE 4-8   Subcommittee Orientation of House Committees, Selected Congresses (1969–1994)

Committee type	Congress			
	91st (1969–1970)	96th (1979–1980)	100th (1987–1988)	103d (1993–1994)
Prestige committees				
Appropriations	n.a.	n.a.	n.a.	n.a.
Budget	—	0	0	0
Rules	n.a.	n.a.	n.a.	n.a.
Ways and Means	0	44	33	35
Policy committees				
Banking, Finance, and Urban Affairs	30	78	69	49
Education and Labor	41	65	56	61
Energy and Commerce	42	79	71	75
Foreign Affairs	39	52	50	46
Judiciary	62	78	70	50
Government Operations	77	70	64	68
Constituency committees				
Agriculture	51	57	55	44
Armed Services	60	58	46	45
Natural Resources	53	63	63	73
Merchant Marine and Fisheries	59	62	52	51
Public Works and Transportation	37	75	58	77
Science, Space, and Technology	50	68	71	70
Small Business	—	48	35	10
Veterans' Affairs	33	38	44	44
Others				
District of Columbia	57	51	46	41
House Administration	66	63	75	46
Post Office and Civil Service	37	65	72	67
Select Intelligence	—	n.a.	n.a.	32
Average	47	59	54	50

Note: Figures are the mean of the percentage of measures managed by subcommittee chairs, percentage of reported measures subject to subcommittee referral or hearings, percentage of meetings held in subcommittee, and percentage of staff allocated to subcommittees. Committee scores are based on data summarized in Tables 4-2, 4-4, 4-5, and 4-7. Committee names reflect usage in the 103d Congress. Committees without subcommittees are included in the summary calculations.

committee orientation index scores for both sets of committees receded somewhat during the next four congresses, but the difference between the two types remained about the same. It is fair to say that, in aggregate, this distinction still remains. However, it is much reduced, and the variation among committees in both groups is greater than it was two decades ago. Overall, change in the subcommittee orientation of House committees was greater among policy committees—both the increase and the decrease—than among constituency committees. It was on policy committees that activist, policy-oriented members found independent subcommittees most useful; but it was also on these committees that decentralization had its most jarring effect, undermining efforts to craft bills that would find sufficient support on the House floor to succeed.

No similar differences between committee types appear in the Senate. Senators, who have more committee assignments and parliamentary prerogatives on the floor, are less dependent on subcommittees for achieving personal political goals. As Table 4-9 indicates, there is tremendous variation among committees of each mix of member goals.[60]

THE RISE AND DECLINE OF SUBCOMMITTEE GOVERNMENT

Committees occasionally have been called "little legislatures." The evidence provided in this chapter suggests that the characterization is apt in many ways. Committees have leaders selected by the respective parties; committees have jurisdictions that define the policy turf of their various subcommittees; committees have rules and procedures that establish constraints and encourage relatively orderly decision-making processes; and committees have a variety of resources, most particularly in the form of staff aides, that allow them to do their work. In each of these ways, the internal world of committees reflects critical elements of the parent chambers that created them. But we also have shown that committees differ within and between the two chambers.

Characteristics of committee jurisdictions, the nature of committees' policy environments, and members' personal political goals shape the distribution of power within, and the decision-making processes of, House and Senate committees. Since House members' goals are more sharply etched than those of their Senate counterparts, it is not surprising to find House committees falling into slightly more distinct sets of decision-making patterns. Thus, the internal development patterns of House and Senate committees during the postreform period share some similarities but diverge in important ways as well.

During the immediate postreform period "subcommittee government" was a more appropriate description of the internal decision-mak-

TABLE 4-9   Subcommittee Orientation of Senate Committees, Selected Congresses (1969–1994)

Committee type	Congress			
	91st (1969–1970)	96th (1979–1980)	100th (1987–1988)	103d (1993–1994)
Policy committees				
Budget	—	0	0	0
Foreign Relations	9	10	1	24
Governmental Affairs	46	43	34	27
Judiciary	51	37	40	38
Labor and Human Resources	60	50	32	17
Mixed policy/constituency committees				
Armed Services	29	34	21	18
Banking, Housing, and Urban Affairs	32	20	27	29
Finance	3	9	6	20
Constituency committees				
Agriculture, Nutrition, and Forestry	25	43	20	32
Appropriations	n.a.	n.a.	n.a.	n.a.
Commerce, Science, and Transportation	38	32	39	38
Energy and Natural Resources	45	36	32	39
Environment and Public Works	19	31	33	17
Other				
Rules and Administration	16	0	0	0
Select Intelligence	—	n.a.	0	0
Small Business	—	—	13	14
Veterans' Affairs	—	0	0	0
Average	31	25	19	20

Note: Figures are the mean of the percentage of measures managed by subcommittee chairs, percentage of reported measures subject to subcommittee referral or hearings, percentage of meetings held in subcommittee, and percentage of staff allocated to subcommittees. Committee scores are based on data summarized in Tables 4-2, 4-4, 4-5, and 4-7. Budget, Select Intelligence, and Veterans' Affairs do not have subcommittees and the Rules and Administration Committee had none in the 96th, 100th, and 103d Congresses. Mean scores for each congress are calculated including committees with and without subcommittees.

ing processes of House committees than Senate committees. House sub-committees developed a more formally institutionalized role—one that was codified in the standing rules of the House and of the two parties. It is important to appreciate that this institutionalized role served the interests of individual representatives, at least as they perceived them at the time. Within this system of rules seniority was weakened but not abandoned. Representatives with sufficient seniority were, after all, in line to benefit from the acquisition of subcommittee chairs. And these chairs gave them additional staff, control over hearings on matters under their subcommittee's jurisdiction, and the power to initiate or block legislation in the absence of actions by the full committee.

By contrast, during this period nearly all of the majority party senators already chaired at least one subcommittee, with many chairing a second and some even a third. Thus the typical senator was less dependent on any one subcommittee or subcommittee chair for his or her legislative livelihood than the typical representative. The tremendous demands on senators' time made them less likely to insist that their subcommittees be active, effective, decision-making units. Most did have a strong incentive to control the agenda and resources necessary for hearings before their subcommittees—a demand that could and did place them at odds with the more aggressive full committee chairs. As a result, the importance of Senate subcommittees was and is more variable. On several Senate committees, subcommittees play no formal role in writing legislation. And over the last decade or so reliance on subcommittees has declined on some Senate committees. Rather than developing an entrenched role in committee decision-making processes, Senate subcommittees have proven to be a component of just one very individualistic decision-making process.

The independence acquired by House subcommittees and their chairs during the reform period had negative consequences, as well. These consequences affected rank-and-file members, full committee chairs, party leaders, and the policy process itself.[61] And they provided the seeds for the backlash that occurred during the late 1980s and the 1990s. The number of meetings and hearings House members were expected to attend increased greatly, approaching senators' workloads. There was a widespread feeling among representatives that they lacked control over their own legislative lives. They lost control over their legislative priorities and found it difficult to specialize in a discrete subject matter as they had in past years. They had become more dependent on committee and personal staffs, and somewhat less dependent on close working relationships with their colleagues.

Subcommittee independence also developed at the expense of the full committee chairs' power. On most House committees, full committee chairs could do very little to block a determined subcommittee chair's effort to hold hearings, recommend legislation, and place the legislation on the full committee's agenda. They lacked firm control over the flow of legislation to subcommittees, over committee staff, and over the agenda that many Senate chairs retained. House chairs became and remain more dependent on personal skills to lead their committees than on their formal powers; accommodation and responsiveness became more characteristic of their actions.

For majority party leaders in the House, the rise of independent subcommittees was a mixed blessing. No longer confronted with committee chairs who held dictatorial control over their committees, party leaders enjoyed easier access to committee members and greater influence on committee decisions. But a more open and democratic process also meant more demands on party leaders. Not surprisingly, party leaders came to look back fondly on the era when a like-minded coalition of party and committee leaders could accomplish a great deal in the House. When conflicts did arise between chairs and their more junior colleagues, the leaders typically sided with the chairs. This was especially true when it came to challenging the application of seniority in the naming of committee chairs.

The undesirable consequences of independent subcommittees should be kept in perspective. Today, they are more serious in the House than in the Senate, and even in the House the substantive role of subcommittees varies. Clientelism and parochialism may be magnified by independent subcommittees, but many interests that were locked out by autocratic full committee chairs now have several avenues of access to committees. It is important to recognize that subcommittee chairs cannot dominate committee decision making the way some full committee chairs once did. On controversial issues, subcommittee chairs cannot guarantee party leaders that legislation will be reported to the floor in a particular form at a particular time. The allocation of subcommittee assignments by self-selection means that subcommittee chairs have no more control than full committee chairs over the composition of their subcommittees—far less control than most full committee chairs enjoyed before the reforms of the 1970s. Subcommittee chairs are not assured of control of their own subcommittees' policy decisions. Hence, the independence of subcommittee chairs does not guarantee subcommittee autonomy. Subcommittee chairs are dependent on the support of a majority of the full committee, which often is difficult to obtain.[62]

On balance, therefore, most rank-and-file members, committee leaders, and party leaders had good reasons to be happy with the retrenchment that occurred in the House during the early 1990s. Fewer subcommittees, smaller staffs, greater agenda control, and better policy coordination at the party level helped to reduce some of the strains the rapid move to sub-committees had caused. Moreover, as both parties moved toward increasingly hostile trench warfare, a divide-and-conquer strategy became too easy for the more centralized party. During the 1980s, that party was the Republicans. Thus, Democrats in the House were more tolerant of a move back toward leadership control.

Although full committee chairs in the House have regained some of the ground they lost during the 1970s, and characterizations of "subcommittee government" appear now to be overstatements, it would be an error to suggest that we have turned the clock back to the 1950s and 1960s. Committees are no longer the personal fiefdoms of their chairs. Full committee chairs remain powerful players, but they now are more accountable and responsive to their committee colleagues, party caucuses, and parent chambers. These changes are more conspicuous in the House, where they were forced through by more deliberate and sweeping reform efforts. But in the Senate, too, chairs now seldom wield the autocratic authority that at least a few chairs did forty years ago.

NOTES

1. Details of Waters' experience can be found in Kitty Dumas, "Waters Stirs Up a Tempest, Challenging Montgomery," *Congressional Quarterly Weekly Report*, November 23, 1991, 3460–3462. Neumann's recollections appear in Jeffrey Goldberg, "Adventures of a Republican Revolutionary," *New York Times Magazine*, November 3, 1996.
2. Technically, the parent chambers elect heads of full committees (and other committee members), but they rely on the majority party to nominate a member for each chair. House Rule X(6) provides that "one of the members of each standing committee shall be elected by the House, from nominations submitted by the majority party caucus, at the commencement of each Congress, as chairman thereof." Senate Rule XXIV requires that "the Senate, unless otherwise ordered, shall by resolution appoint the chairman of each [standing] committee and the other members thereof. On demand of any senator, a separate vote shall be had on the appointment of the chairman of any such committee and on the appointment of the other members thereof."
3. John Felton, "In Victory for Seniority System, Helms Wrests Post from Lugar," *Congressional Quarterly Weekly Report*, January 24, 1987, 143–144.
4. The senior positions are Speaker, floor leader, and whip, and the chairs of the conference, policy, and campaign committees. These same members are limited to a single committee assignment but may return to a previously held assignment without penalty if they leave one of these leadership posts.
5. House Rule X 6(c).
6. The changes are reported in Pamela Fessler, "Helms Sweeps Through Panel, Fires Nine GOP Staff Aides," *Congressional Quarterly Weekly Report*, January 11, 1992, 57.
7. Richard E. Cohen, "The Transformers," *National Journal*, March 4, 1995, 532.

8. A fourth agency, the Office of Technology Assessment, was abolished in 1995, and the staff of the General Accounting Office was substantially reduced.

9. For more detail on these subjects, see Steven S. Smith and Christopher J. Deering, *Committees in Congress* (Washington, D.C.: CQ Press, 1984), chap. 6.

10. For a complete discussion of how the role of a committee chair systematically varies, see C. Lawrence Evans, *Leadership in Committee: A Comparative Analysis of Leadership Behavior in the U.S. Senate* (Ann Arbor: University of Michigan Press, 1991).

11. House Republican leaders allowed moderates Gerald Solomon of New York to become chair of the Rules Committee, Jim Leach of Iowa to become chair of Banking and Financial Services, and Bill Goodling of Pennsylvania to become chair of the Economic and Educational Opportunities Committee. The committees abolished at the outset of the 104th Congress—District of Columbia, Post Office and Civil Service, and Merchant Marine and Fisheries—all had a distinctively constituent character to them.

12. See, for example, Kirk Victor, "Trust Me," *National Journal*, March 11, 1995, 607–611; Dan Carney, "Committee Clamor Illustrates Extent of Partisan Divide," *Congressional Quarterly Weekly Report*, May 11, 1996, 1291–1292; and David Hosansky, "Shuster: A Winning Record and Ruffled Feathers," *Congressional Quarterly Weekly Report*, July 6, 1996, 1916–1918.

13. This practice was not automatically abandoned when Republicans gained control of the Senate in 1981. Bob Dole, (R-Kan.), kept nine subcommittees in the 97th Congress (depriving only one colleague of a chair) and Bob Packwood only reduced the number by one more subcommittee in the following Congress (depriving two colleagues of a chair).

14. These figures are derived from and elaborated in Christopher J. Deering, "Career Advancement and Subcommittee Chairs in the House of Representatives: 86th to 103d Congresses," *American Politics Quarterly* 24 (January 1996): 3–23.

15. Smith and Deering, *Committees in Congress*, 197–198.

16. Evans, *Leadership in Committee*, chap. 4.

17. Ibid., chap. 5.

18. Richard L. Hall, "Participation and Purpose in Committee Decision Making," *American Political Science Review* 81 (March 1987): 115; and Richard L. Hall and C. Lawrence Evans, "The Power of Subcommittees," *Journal of Politics* 52 (May 1990): 335–355. On these same themes see C. Lawrence Evans, *Leadership in Committee: A Comparative Analysis of Leadership Behavior in the U.S. Senate* (Ann Arbor: University of Michigan Press, 1991); Richard L. Hall, *Participation in Congress* (New Haven: Yale University Press, 1996); and Richard L. Hall and Gary J. McKissick, "Institutional Change and Behavioral Choice in House Committees," in *Congress Reconsidered*, 6th ed., ed. Lawrence C. Dodd and Bruce I. Oppenheimer (Washington, D.C.: CQ Press, 1997).

19. For additional background, see Christopher J. Deering, "Subcommittee Government in the U.S. House: An Analysis of Bill Management," *Legislative Studies Quarterly* 7 (November 1982): 533–546.

20. On the importance of floor "managership," see Barry R. Weingast, "Fighting Fire with Fire: Amending Activity and Institutional Change in the Postreform Congress," in *The Postreform Congress*, ed. Roger H. Davidson (New York: St. Martin's Press, 1992), 142–168.

21. A recent development in the House is the more frequent appearance of the majority leader as a bill manager. This is a byproduct of the greater frequency of multiple committee bills orchestrated by the central party leadership (a subject addressed in more detail in Chapter 5). Bills on drugs, education, trade, and other issues have been stimulated by the leadership, drafted by multiple committees, and then packaged into a single measure for consideration on the floor. The majority leader managed several of these bills during the 1980s, although the number is small relative to the large volume of measures considered on the floor (the tally for the majority leader is included in the "Others" category in Table 4-2). As we will see in the next chapter, this development is indicative of a general trend toward a more centralized decision-making process and less autonomous committees in the House.

22. Dole often shared bill management duties with his whip, Alan Simpson. One-third of the leader-managed measures were managed by Simpson in the 99th Congress. Byrd was far more self-reliant. George J. Mitchell, Democratic majority leader during the 102d and 103d Congresses, followed the Dole pattern by delegating floor management chores to Democratic Whip Wendell Ford of Kentucky. Indeed, Ford handled about 60 percent of the bills the two leaders managed on the floor.

23. It also should be noted that House Democrats have exhibited a trend toward increasing support for party positions since the mid-1970s (as have House Republicans). The trend is due primarily to the increasing party support among southern Democrats, although northern Democrats have become more supportive of party positions as well. In the 1980s, the gap between northern and southern Democrats remained, but was much smaller than in the 1970s. In light of these trends, the increase in party support among full committee chairs is notable because it far exceeds the increases found among southern Democrats.

24. Not-so-veiled threats are reported occasionally. In 1989, for example, John P. Murtha (D-Pa.), a new defense appropriations subcommittee chair, was put on notice that liberals in his party would be scrutinizing his behavior. See Richard E. Cohen, "Calling the Tune on Military Spending," *National Journal*, March 11, 1989, 605.

25. The events surrounding the Hatfield vote are reported in Donna Cassata, "GOP Retreats on Hatfield, But War Far From Over," *Congressional Quarterly Weekly Report*, March 11, 1995, 729–731. Passage of the new Republican Conference rules is reported in David S. Cloud, "GOP Senators Limit Chairmen to Six Years Heading Panel," *Congressional Quarterly Weekly Report*, July 22, 1995, 2147.

26. At the time of his election in 1985, Aspin is reported to have assured colleagues that he would modify his position on the controversial MX missile, which he had supported. Aspin later was criticized for reneging on his promises, although he contended that he never promised to alter his MX position. On Aspin's original election and his colleagues' concerns, see Steven V. Roberts, "Democrats Defy House Leaders; Price Loses Post," *New York Times*, January 5, 1985, 1, 7; and Nadine Cohodas and Diane Granat, "House Seniority System Jolted; Price Dumped, Aspin Elected," *Congressional Quarterly Weekly Report*, January 5, 1985, 7–9. On Aspin's initial defeat for reelection as chair, see Jacqueline Calmes, "Aspin Ousted as Armed Services Chairman," *Congressional Quarterly Weekly Report*, January 10, 1987, 83–85.

27. See Barbara Sinclair, *The Transformation of the U.S. Senate* (Baltimore: Johns Hopkins University Press, 1989), chap. 5.
28. Roger H. Davidson, "The Emergence of the Postreform Congress," in *The Postreform Congress*, ed. Davidson, 13–23.
29. See Dale Tate, "Retrenchment Too: Use of Omnibus Bills Burgeons Despite Members' Misgivings: Long-Term Impact Disputed," *Congressional Quarterly Weekly Report*, September 25, 1982, 2379–2383; and Allen Schick, "The Whole and the Parts: Piecemeal and Integrated Approaches to Congressional Budgeting," paper prepared for the Task Force on the Budget Process, House Committee on the Budget, Serial No. CP-3 (Washington, D.C.: U.S. Government Printing Office, 1987).
30. See, for example, Allen Schick, "The Ways and Means of Leading Ways and Means," *The Brookings Review* (Fall 1989): 23.
31. Jacqueline Calmes, "'Professor' Runs the Show at House Banking," *Congressional Quarterly Weekly Report*, September 8, 1984, 2203–2205.
32. See Tom Kenworthy, "Gonzalez's Pugnacious Populism," *Washington Post*, December 6, 1989, A1.
33. For more background on the emergence of powerful subcommittees, see Roger H. Davidson, "Subcommittee Government: New Channels for Policy Making," in *The New Congress*, ed. Thomas E. Mann and Norman J. Ornstein (Washington, D.C.: American Enterprise Institute, 1981), 99–133; Steven Haeberle, "The Institutionalization of Subcommittees in the U.S. House of Representatives," *Journal of Politics* 40 (1978): 1054–1065; and Lawrence C. Dodd and Richard L. Schott, *Congress and the Administrative State* (New York: Wiley, 1979).

   For background on the role of subcommittees on various standing committees, see David N. Farnsworth, *The Senate Committee on Foreign Relations* (Urbana: University of Illinois Press, 1961); Richard F. Fenno, Jr., *The Power of the Purse: Appropriations Politics in Congress* (Boston: Little Brown, 1966); Richard F. Fenno, Jr., *Congressmen in Committees* (Boston: Little Brown, 1973); George Goodwin, Jr., *The Little Legislatures* (Amherst: University of Massachusetts Press, 1970); Ralph K. Huitt, "The Congressional Committee: A Case Study," *American Political Science Review* 48 (1954): 340–365; Charles O. Jones, "Representation in Congress: The Case of the House Agriculture Committee," *American Political Science Review* 55 (1961): 358–367; John D. Lees, *The Committee System of the United States Congress* (New York: Humanities Press, 1967); John Manley, *The Politics of Finance: The House Committee on Ways and Means* (Boston: Little, Brown, 1970); William Morrow, *Congressional Committees* (New York: Scribner's, 1969); Norman J. Ornstein and David W. Rohde, "Shifting Forces, Changing Rules and Political Outcomes: The Impact of Congressional Change on Four House Committees," in *New Perspectives on the House of Representatives*, 3d ed., ed. Robert L. Peabody and Nelson W. Polsby (Chicago: Rand McNally, 1977), 186–269; Norman J. Ornstein and David W. Rohde, "Revolt from Within: Congressional Change, Legislative Policy, and the House Commerce Committee," in *Legislative Reform and Public Policy*, ed. Susan Welch and John G. Peters (New York: Praeger, 1977), 54–72; Ralph Nader Project, *The Agriculture Committees* (New York: Grossman, 1975); Ralph Nader Project, *The Money Committees* (New York: Grossman, 1975); David E. Price, *Who Makes the Laws?* (Cambridge, Mass.: Schenkman, 1972); David E. Price, *The Commerce Committees* (New York: Grossman, 1975); Catherine E. Rudder, "Committee Reform and the Revenue

Process," in *Congress Reconsidered*, ed. Lawrence C. Dodd and Bruce I. Oppenheimer (New York: Praeger, 1977), 117–139; Randall Strahan, "Agenda Change and Committee Politics in the Postreform House," *Legislative Studies Quarterly* 13 (May 1988): 177–197; Randall Strahan, *New Ways and Means* (Chapel Hill: University of North Carolina Press, 1990); Andree E. Reeves, *Congressional Committee Chairmen: Three Who Made an Evolution* (Lexington: University of Kentucky Press, 1993); Joseph White, "Decision Making in the Appropriations Subcommittees on Defense and Foreign Operations," in *Congress Resurgent: Foreign and Defense Policy on Capitol Hill*, ed. Randall B. Ripley and James M Lindsay (Ann Arbor: University of Michigan Press, 1993), 183–206; and C. Lawrence Evans, *Leadership in Committee*.

34. The limitation, which appeared in the Democratic Caucus rules in 1981, restricted committees of at least thirty-five members to eight subcommittees, with the exception of Appropriations, and small committees to six subcommittees.

35. The limit appears as House Rule X 6(d).

36. Smith and Deering, *Committees in Congress*, 131.

37. A 1981 rule of the House Democratic Caucus limiting the number of subcommittees made it more difficult to create such semipermanent task forces. Current House rules, which limit most committees to five subcommittees, define subcommittees to include "any panel (other than a special oversight panel of the Committee on National Security), task force, special subcommittee, or any subunit of a standing committee that is established for a cumulative period longer than six months in any Congress" (Rule 6 (c)).

38. In practice, House Republican committee leaders have some flexibility (and they may receive input from party leaders as well). They often suggest certain arrangements of subcommittee assignments to strengthen the party's position or retain experienced members on critical subcommittees.

39. At the start of the 100th Congress in 1987, the Democratic Caucus barred waivers of the subcommittee rule, except in two situations: (1) members serving on three full committees by serving on the less popular District of Columbia, House Administration, or Judiciary committees; and (2) members serving on a full committee with a temporary appointment (for one congress).

40. House Rule X 6(b)(2)(A). The rule is relatively easy to accommodate, of course, once the elimination of three full committees and numerous subcommittees is taken into account.

41. Senate Rule XXV(4)(b)(1) limits each senator to no more than three subcommittees on the two "major" committees on which she or he may sit (Appropriations excepted) and to no more than two on the one "minor" committee on which she or he may sit.

42. Judiciary Committee Rule V(3). Standing Rule XXVI(2) of the Senate requires each committee to establish and report its rules by March 1 at the commencement of each congress. These are gathered together and published by the Committee on Rules and Administration. See U.S. Congress, Senate, Committee on Rules and Administration, *Authority and Rules of Senate Committees, 1995–1996*, 104th Cong., 1st Sess., Document No. 104–2.

43. Finance Committee Rule 16(a).

44. Agriculture Committee Rule 7.5.

45. House committees uniformly have required that subcommittees consult with the full committee chair to avoid scheduling conflicts. During the 1980s, Energy and Commerce was the only House committee with an even stricter

requirement. Its rule required the "approval" of the full committee chair when scheduling meetings and hearings.

46. The use of subcommittees on most Senate committees has not changed much with recent changes in partisan control of the Senate in 1981, 1987, and 1995. Although, as noted earlier, some committees (Armed Services and Foreign Relations) did shift their practices somewhat for idiosyncratic reasons. On the 1981 switch in majority status, see Roger H. Davidson and Walter J. Oleszek, "Changing the Guard in the U.S. Senate," *Legislative Studies Quarterly* 9 (November 1984): 635–663.

47. Rule X 6(f). Six House committees took an additional step by adopting rules designed to limit their full committee chair's discretion in recommending conferees to the Speaker. Three committees, Education and Labor, Foreign Affairs, and Ways and Means, explicitly required the chair to recommend members from the appropriate subcommittee or subcommittees. The other three committees, Budget, Interior and Insular Affairs, and Public Works and Transportation, granted to the majority party members of the committee the right to approve or reject the chair's recommendations.

48. For additional discussion of the formation of conference committees in the 1980s, see Steven S. Smith, *Call to Order: Floor Politics in the House and Senate* (Washington, D.C.: Brookings Institution, 1989), chap. 7; and Lawrence D. Longley and Walter J. Oleszek, *Bicameral Politics: Conference Committees in Congress* (New Haven: Yale University Press, 1989).

49. For background on congressional committee staff, see Joel D. Aberbach, "The Congressional Committee Intelligence System: Information, Oversight, and Change," *Congress & the Presidency* 14 (Spring 1987): 51–76; and Joel D. Aberbach, *Keeping a Watchful Eye: The Politics of Congressional Oversight* (Washington, D.C.: Brookings Institution, 1990); David W. Brady, "Personnel Management in the House," in *The House at Work*, ed. Joseph Cooper and G. Calvin Mackenzie (Austin: University of Texas Press, 1981), 164–177; Christine DeGregorio, "Professional in the U.S. Congress: An Analysis of Working Styles," *Legislative Studies Quarterly* 13 (November 1988): 459–476; Susan Webb Hammond, "The Management of Legislative Offices," in *The House at Work*, ed. Cooper and Mackenzie, 186–189; Gladys M. Kammerer, *The Staffing of the Committees of Congress* (Lexington: University of Kentucky Press, 1949); Kenneth T. Kofmehl, *Professional Staffs of Congress* (Lafayette, Ind.: Purdue Research Foundation, 1962); Harrison W. Fox, Jr., and Susan Webb Hammond, *Congressional Staffs: The Invisible Force in American Lawmaking* (New York: Free Press, 1977); Michael J. Malbin, *Unelected Representatives: Congressional Staff and the Future of Representative Government* (New York: Basic Books, 1980); David E. Price, "Professionals and 'Entrepreneurs': Staff Orientations and Policy Making on Three Senate Committees," *Journal of Politics* 33 (May 1971): 316–336; Robert H. Salisbury and Kenneth A. Shepsle, "Congressional Staff Turnover and the Ties-That-Bind," *American Political Science Review* 75 (June 1981): 381–396; and Steven S. Smith and Christopher J. Deering, *Committees in Congress*, chap. 7.

50. See, respectively, *Business Week*, March 27, 1987, 90; *Washington Post*, January 18, 1981, A1; and *Washington Post*, February 12, 1980, A1; also see Hedrick Smith, *The Power Game: How Washington Works* (New York: Ballantine, 1988), chap. 10.

51. Quoted in Irwin B. Arieff, "Growing Staff System on Hill Forcing Changes in Congress," *Congressional Quarterly Weekly Report*, November 24, 1979, 2631.

52. This minority staffing guarantee remains as Rule XI 6 (a)(2) of the House but applies only to the professional or statutory staff of the committee.
53. Technically, the House Administration Committee also exceeded 200, but this is because the House computer center staff, which is quite large, is counted against their total.
54. The rule also cautions that chairs should see to it that the "minority party is fairly treated in the appointment of such staff" (House Rule XI 5(d).) A motion to return control of subcommittee staff to the subcommittee chairs was deleted during the Republican organizational meetings prior to the 105th Congresses.
55. Pursuant to S.Res. 281. That resolution also removed the Senate Appropriations Committee's exemption from the funding process. The Senate Ethics Committee, however, may hire staff as needed to fulfill its responsibilities.
56. Senate Rule XXVII leaves this choice in the hands of the minority and requires the majority to comply although it is permitted much time in which to do so with any such request. Although the rule doesn't state so explicitly, the division of funds apparently takes place after amounts used for nonpartisan support are excluded from the committee's total. A similar circumstance exists in the House and, in effect, creates a majority staff, a minority staff, and a nonpartisan committee staff.
57. The statistic is Spearman's r, a correlation coefficient for ordinal rankings.
58. Price, "Professionals and 'Entrepreneurs'."
59. Omnibus legislating has little effect on the distribution of staff. It may actually increase the relative frequency of bill management by subcommittee chairs on some committees, as measures otherwise managed by the full committee chairs are included in larger packages.
60. As useful as an overall index of subcommittee orientation has proven, a caution is in order. In our effort to draw general characterizations of committee practices, we do not mean to imply that each subcommittee of a committee is treated identically. Variations in the salience and controversy of subcommittee jurisdictions, along with factors such as personal skills and human relations, shape the relationship between subcommittees and their parent committees. It certainly would be fallacious to assume that the general patterns we have reported accurately represent the experience of individual subcommittees. An excellent treatment of the experiences of House Ways and Means subcommittees can be found in Randall Strahan and R. Kent Weaver, "Subcommittee Government and the House Ways and Means Committee" (Paper presented at the annual meeting of the Southern Political Science Association, Memphis, November 1983). Nevertheless, we are confident that a more detailed analysis would support the view that variation in subcommittee orientation between House committee types and between the chambers exceeds the variation within most committees. Reliance on subcommittees for initiating legislation, patterns of bill management, and the independence of subcommittee staff do not vary greatly within most committees.
61. See Davidson, "Subcommittee Government," and Norman J. Ornstein, "The House and Senate in a New Congress," in *The New Congress*, ed. Mann and Ornstein, 367–369.
62. For examples of the limits of subcommittee chairs' power on an important committee, see Ronald Brownstein, "Trench Warfare," *National Journal*, September 14, 1985, 2047–2053, on the problems of a House Energy and Com-

merce subcommittee chair in gaining the approval of his subcommittee and
committee for legislation authorizing the Superfund, a federal program to
fund the cleanup of hazardous wastes; and Christopher Madison, "Midair
Collision," *National Journal*, October 7, 1989, 2491, on the problems faced
by another Energy and Commerce subcommittee chair in clean air legislation.

CHAPTER 5

Committees in the Postreform Congress

Committees do not operate in a vacuum. Indeed, it should be clear that committees, whether more or less autonomous, are inextricably entwined with their parent chambers. But what is the character of this relationship? How has it changed, and what does that mean for the power of committees? In the previous chapter we saw that full committees in both the House and Senate lost power in the aftermath of the reforms of the early 1970s.[1] In the House, power shifted to subcommittees while in the Senate it devolved to the rank-and-file members. In both chambers we observed a decentralization of power. But we also observed in Chapter 4 that a countertrend has since developed with very noticeable effects, particularly in the House. Simply put, committees have lost power. They are no longer as central to the decision-making processes of their parent chambers as they once were. In this chapter we will look at the effects of this countertrend on committees in Congress. What are its sources and how has it altered the relationship of committees to their parent chambers? We also will examine the impact of the recent shift in party control on committee politics and ask what this will mean for the role of committees in Congress.

AGENDA AND PARTISAN CHANGE

The character of the congressional policy agenda changed in important ways during the 1960s and 1970s as new issues appeared on the congressional agenda.[2] Energy, the environment, consumer protection, civil rights, and many other issues that had not been subject to national debate or had been suppressed emerged to create new demands for congressional action. These issues failed to fit neatly into the jurisdictional confines of a single committee, and many, like energy and the environment, became interconnected in new ways. Moreover, as the agenda grew in size it also became less predictable and recurrent. Issues died and new ones

were born in rapid succession. More members, particularly recently elected ones, insisted on having a voice in decisions concerning the wide range
of new issues before Congress. And, of course, aggressive committees
defined issues in ways that would allow them a share of the action.

Under such circumstances, a system of fairly autonomous committees was inconvenient, to say the least. Outsiders and junior committee
members resented the dominance of senior committee members on policy decisions, and committees vied with each other in seeking jurisdiction
over the new and complex issues facing Congress. By the late 1970s and
1980s, concern about the federal budget deficit began to dominate policy
making. Most other domestic policy issues were set aside or reinterpreted
largely in terms of their budget consequences. The result, as Roger H.
Davidson has argued, was an era of "cutback politics": a contracted agenda that is driven by budget concerns, and leads to increased partisanship,
fewer but larger pieces of legislation, blame avoidance, and a willingness
to tolerate stronger leaders.[3]

While the policy agenda was expanding and then shrinking, the
political alignments among members shifted.[4] In the 1970s, disagreements over how and where to expand the role of the federal government
continued to divide congressional Democrats. Liberal northern Democrats
generally favored an expanded federal role; they were opposed by conservative southern Democrats. Republicans experienced similar divisions
within their ranks. But in the 1980s and into the 1990s electoral changes
and a new agenda saw the party coalitions become far more cohesive. Not
least among the factors contributing to this trend was the "tidying up"
that occurred within both parties. In the South, conservative Democrats
were replaced by Republicans. Indeed, by the outset of the 104th Congress the number of Republicans representing southern congressional districts exceeded the number of Democrats representing these districts for
the first time in this century. The remaining southern Democrats in Congress became more supportive of their party leaders while the new southern Republicans proved highly partisan Meanwhile, the moderate northern wing of the Republican party declined as the party's center of gravity
moved south and west,[5] and Democrats from all regions were on the
defensive, producing more party-line votes in the face of budget cuts. The
effect was increased homogeneity in both parties.

By the mid-1990s a more consolidated and interconnected policy
agenda had combined with more partisan political alignments to dramatically alter the context in which committees operated. The legislative
workload had contracted, core budget decisions constrained other policy
decisions, and the parties were in a position to act more cohesively on key
policy decisions. The propositions set out in Chapter 1 suggest that committees would not be granted as much autonomy under such conditions.

A system once dominated by fairly autonomous committees and characterized by weak parties had become one ripe for strong party leadership.

Development of stronger parties and weaker committees is exactly what came to pass in Congress during the 1980s and the 1990s. The decline in committee power was greater in the House than in the Senate, where committees had less autonomy to lose, but a decline in committee autonomy is noticeable in the Senate as well. Not all committees have experienced the same changes, and, in the case of the House, some steps have been taken to stop or even reverse the decline in committee autonomy. Nonetheless, the place of the House and Senate committee systems in the legislative process has changed in ways that make them less central to policy outcomes than they were three or four decades ago.

Throughout the balance of this chapter we will focus on committees in relation to their parent chambers. First, we will examine a set of agenda-setting and agenda-constraining devices that affect the power of congressional committees—party caucuses and leaders, multiple referral, summits and task forces, and budget politics. We will then look at the ways committees operate on the chamber floors. Finally, we will assess the role of conference committees.

MANAGING THE AGENDA

In many parliaments around the world the legislative agenda is established by the majority party or coalition—frequently as a result of elections in which platforms are formed—and then presented as the "government's" program. Were Congress to follow this approach, committees would be almost wholly without power, forced instead simply to do the bidding of the majority party. For most of the twentieth century, at least, the U.S. Congress has allowed agenda control to rest with the committees rather than with the parties. And there has been rather limited leadership involvement. Hence, the negative power of committees has been considerable.

As we have seen, however, changes in the external agenda and shifts in the characters of the two parties have caused members to alter their attitudes toward the negative power of committees. During the last three decades we have witnessed a variety of enhancements to the ability of party leaders and the chambers to control committee agendas. Indeed, by one estimate the involvement of party leaders in agenda setting, shaping legislation, structuring the choices available to members on the floor, and vote mobilization more than doubled between the 1970s and the 1980s.[6] As we will see, party leaders in both chambers gained both the resources and the incentives to become activists.

Although we will look at a variety of specific techniques in the sections that follow, there are, fundamentally just two ways to overcome the negative power of committees. First, committees could be relieved of their authority to write legislation and the job given to someone else. This option is fraught with peril, however, as it strikes at the heart of committee power and expertise. Nonetheless, party leaders have used ad hoc committees, summits, and task forces to do just this. A less-threatening and thereby more common approach is to concede the committees' preeminence in drafting legislation, but only under constraints that induce or even compel positive committee action. In this way, leaders, parties, and the parent chambers become driving forces in setting and managing the legislative agenda.

PARTY LEADERS AND CAUCUSES

The single most prominent source of declining congressional committee autonomy was the revitalization of the House Democratic Caucus in the late 1960s.[7] The Caucus was an engine for the reform of committee procedures during the 1970s and also became the site of serious discussion about the party's position on important policy issues. Using powers that had been dormant for half a century, the Caucus even instructed various committees to report bills it considered desirable but that had been bottled up or to alter bills unreflective of the Caucus's opinion.[8] The most important change within the Democratic Caucus at that time, however, concerned the enhanced role of the leadership and the Caucus in determining who would gain the committee chairs. These changes—reinforced by the series of successful challenges—forced committee chairs to pay closer attention to the agenda preferences of the party as expressed by party leaders.

Throughout the 1970s and 1980s Democratic party leaders also set more or less formal agendas. Under Speaker Thomas P. "Tip" O'Neill the leadership team became the joint authors of a series of "leadership programs." In 1986, just after being nominated Speaker, Jim Wright of Texas expanded this practice by articulating a complete agenda for the coming session that included a wide range of bills on taxes, highways, trade, clean water, welfare, and agriculture. And he succeeded in getting much of it enacted. Although Wright's tenure as Speaker was brief, the aggressiveness of his leadership was unmatched until Newt Gingrich (R-Ga.) became Speaker at the outset of the 104th Congress. Even Wright's successor, Democrat Thomas S. Foley of Washington, by nature a less aggressive and more conciliatory leader, continued to lay out a program for House Democrats. Foley's reluctance to rein in certain committee chairs did not please all of his party colleagues, but as he explained it:

Unlike most Speakers of the immediate past, I have been a committee chairman. I have a certain sense of how the job and responsibility is looked upon from the chairman's viewpoint, and their sense and desire to have the leadership and the Speaker support them but on the other hand not intrude internally.[9]

By the 104th Congress, of course, Foley and the Democrats had been defeated and the new majority party came to power with a widely publicized and very specific agenda—the Contract With America. If the new majority party had done nothing whatsoever to alter the power of their party leaders, the presence of the ten-item Contract would have had a profound impact on the congressional agenda and the relationship of the committees to the Conference. But Republican leaders did not stand pat. Under new Conference rules the Republican leader has enhanced influence over the naming of committees and committees chairs. The leader has the authority to designate certain issues as "leadership issues," which require "early and ongoing cooperation between relevant committees and the Leadership as the issue evolves."[10] Conference rules further state that committee chairs have "an obligation to ensure that each measure on which the Republican Conference has taken a position is managed in accordance with such position on the [f]loor. . . ."[11] Beyond this, Speaker Gingrich created the Speaker's Administrative Group, comprised of senior leaders and trusted colleagues, which helps to plan legislative tactics from week to week and assist in long-range legislative strategy and agenda planning, and an informal budget steering group that includes the floor leader and the chairs of the Appropriations, Budget, and Ways and Means committees.[12] Thus, both formally and informally, the Speakership and the Conference are organized and managed with an eye toward enhanced agenda control.

In the Senate, Majority Leader George J. Mitchell (D-Maine) rejuvenated the role of the party organs in Senate decision making after gaining his post in 1989.[13] Former majority leader Robert C. Byrd (D-W.Va.) preferred to deal personally and directly with committee chairs and bill managers, and he held few meetings of the Democratic conference, Policy Committee, or whips. Mitchell changed course, as he had promised to do, after being elected majority leader. He shared important party posts with more Democrats, encouraged the new party leaders to help set a direction for the Senate on important issues, and began to call more regular meetings of the party conference. In 1989, the Conference played an important role in promoting his antidrug program over competing plans, including one sponsored by an Appropriations subcommittee chair.[14] Mitchell also appointed Tom Daschle (D-S.D.) co-chair of the Democratic Policy Committee, a post that, if used aggressively, can help to establish legislative priorities. After Mitchell retired, Daschle replaced him as floor leader in the 104th Congress, a move that allowed him to become chair of the policy committee. In addition, Daschle has enhanced the role of the old but strictly seniority bound steering committee and renamed it the Steering and Coordination Committee. He also created a new party committee on Technology and Communications that is intended to improve the public's awareness of the party's policy positions.

Senate Republicans also have enhanced the role of their leader in the agenda setting process. During the first months of the 104th Congress, the controversy surrounding Mark O. Hatfield's (R-Ore.) vote against the balanced budget amendment (reported in Chapter 4) caused then-majority leader Robert Dole (R-Kans.) to appoint a task force to review the Republican conference's rules. That task force, directed by Sen. Connie Mack (R-Fla.), returned with eight proposed rule changes that would tie committee chairs (or ranking members) more closely to the party. Although the package was moderated significantly, it broke important new ground by limiting Republican committee leaders to a maximum of six years in their posts, provided for secret-ballot conference votes for selecting committee leaders, and established a process for creating a Republican agenda at the beginning of each Congress.[15] The agenda will not be binding on floor votes, and the Republican leader was not given the power to nominate committee leaders. But these changes send an unusually strong message to committee leaders that they should pay heed to their party colleagues when discharging their duties.

MULTIPLE REFERRAL IN THE HOUSE

A development that directly bears on the autonomy of individual committees is the referral of legislation to more than one committee. In 1974 the Speaker of the House was granted the authority to send legislation to committees jointly or sequentially, or by splitting it into parts. Prior to this, the Speaker had been required to assign legislation to the single committee that had predominant jurisdiction for the contents of a bill, a practice that guaranteed monopoly referral rights to a single committee in each policy area. In the Senate, multiple referral always has been possible but never common—averaging just 2 to 4 percent of the bills introduced in that chamber—perhaps because it is so easy for committees to protect their jurisdictional interests by seeking to amend legislation on the floor.[16] In 1977 the House rule was expanded to allow the Speaker to set deadlines for the consideration of multiply referred bills. In practice, though, only sequentially referred legislation has been subjected to such time limits. Under the current rule, the Speaker is encouraged to recognize overlapping jurisdictions and the desirability of coordinating the decisions of committees on complex issues. At the outset of the 104th

Congress the Speaker's option to refer a bill to several committees simultaneously was rescinded, but sequential referral with time limits and split referral were reinforced.

In the 94th Congress (1975–1976), the first in which multiple referral was permitted, 6 percent of all bills introduced in the House received this treatment. By the 101st Congress (1989–1990), the proportion had increased to 18 percent of all bills.[17] During more recent congresses, more than a third of the workload for the average House committee is multiply referred legislation.[18] But there is sizable variance in the impact felt by various committees. For example, in the 102d Congress the Ways and Means Committee had a relatively low percentage of multiple referrals (29 percent) but only Energy and Commerce could rival the raw number of multiple referrals (582) received by the tax committee. Not surprisingly, committees with less fragmented jurisdictions experienced fewer multiple referrals in both proportional and absolute terms—the now defunct District of Columbia Committee and the Veterans' Affairs Committee, for example. By the early 1990s, nearly one in three bills were important enough to warrant a special rule—which established how long a bill may be debated and whether it can be amended when it reaches the floor—and about the same proportion of major legislation originated in two or more committees.

Multiple referral has several important implications for committee autonomy in the House.[19] First, sharing jurisdiction with other committees directly undermines the autonomy of a committee. The multiple referral rule has encouraged committees to stake jurisdictional claims on a wide variety of issues and almost guarantees that conflict between committees will frequently arise. Since the mid-1970s, many committees have developed informal understandings about areas of shared jurisdiction that reduce open conflict, but these arrangements represent perforations in the autonomy of the committees that once enjoyed sole jurisdiction over those issue areas. In some policy areas, then, interdependence has replaced autonomy in intercommittee relations.

Second, conflict between two or more committees enhances the importance of others in shaping policy. Sometimes that conflict spills onto the House floor, where votes on a series of amendments may impose a resolution on the contesting committees. And party leaders may be encouraged to intercede between committees to avoid open conflict on the floor between fellow partisans of different committees. Committees have recognized that they may be better off resolving their differences before the legislation goes to the floor. The Rules Committee has encouraged such pre-floor compromises by granting special rules limiting floor amendments and by allowing a compromise version to be taken to the floor as a substitute for the competing committee proposals.[20] The process may help committees fend off unfriendly floor amendments, but it also some-times involves compromises of committee positions that might not other-wise have been necessary.

Finally, and perhaps most important, the multiple referral rule and associated practices substantially strengthen the Speaker's influence on committee decisions. The Speaker determines, without appeal, the origi-nal referral of legislation to multiple committees. Moreover, since 1981 the Speaker also may re-refer a measure if it has been amended by a com-mittee in a way that affects another committee's jurisdiction. Thus, the Speaker is central to the process of resolving intercommittee conflict when it arises and may structure a multiple committee arrangement when it suits policy purposes. Speakers have taken such initiative on many important pieces of legislation in recent years, including legislation on international trade, drug importation and abuse, homelessness, South African apartheid, oil spills, health care reform, and, in the 104th Con-gress, several elements of the Contract With America.

Furthermore, the Speaker may set deadlines on committee decisions when legislation is subject to multiple referral—a process tantamount to a preemptive discharge. When the referral is sequential, a series of deadlines normally is set. Under the current rule, the Speaker is required to refer all bills to a committee of primary jurisdiction but can set a deadline for its consideration if additional committees are to receive it subsequently. The Speaker may informally announce the intention to proceed with a bill at a certain time and require that committees report legislation by that time if they want to contribute to a large package. In the 104th Congress, for example, the various elements of the Contract—whether multiply or singly referred—were all held to the 100-day deadline promised by the leadership and to shorter interim deadlines to ensure orderly floor consid-eration. In designing such arrangements, the Speaker is in a position to confer advantage on some committees, speed or delay committee action for strategic purposes, and send strong signals about policy preferences.

In sum, the new and still evolving techniques of multiple referral substantially reduce both the traditional negative and positive sources of committee power. On the negative side, committees receiving a referral subject to a deadline established by the Speaker effectively lose the option of reporting no legislation. If a committee fails to report its recommenda-tions by the specified deadline, the Speaker is free to discharge the com-mittee. On the positive side, more committees have access to legislation, but they now must formally share responsibility to determine the content of legislation taken to the floor. The net result of the increasing number of areas where committees share jurisdiction is declining autonomy, increasing interdependence among committees, and greater control of committee actions by the majority party leadership.

SUMMITS AND TASK FORCES

By the end of the second month of the 104th Congress (1995–1996), Speaker Newt Gingrich had established five temporary and ten permanent task forces and working groups on a variety of issues facing the first Republican-controlled Congress in forty years. Five of these task forces were organized to promote key elements of the Contract With America— regulatory reform, crime, term limits, welfare, and legal reform. The remainder were directed to consider specific issues, such as immigration or disabilities, or simply to reach out to specific constituencies or potential constituencies of the party, such as the entertainment industry (chaired by Rep. Sonny Bono of California) and minorities (chaired by Rep. James C. Talent of Missouri and Rep. J. C. Watt of Oklahoma). These groups bring together members from different committees with different points of view. They are intended to shortcircuit the turf-conscious committee system and to fashion either legislation or legislative coalitions that might otherwise be bottled up in committee or formulated in ways that suited committee members but not party members. As the Speaker's primary spokesman, Tony Blankley put it: "We envision using task forces a lot . . . as a device for finessing some institutional obstacles to decision-making."[21]

Finessing institutional obstacles is not unprecedented. During the 95th Congress (1977–1978), the first of President Jimmy Carter's administration, a huge package of bills on energy policy was submitted to Congress. Utilizing new powers that had been granted to the Speaker only a couple of years earlier, Speaker Tip O'Neill formed an ad hoc committee on energy to consider and bring to the floor the hundreds of discrete components embraced by the Carter administration's new policy. O'Neill, who was then being characterized as the strongest Speaker since Joseph G. "Uncle Joe" Cannon, succeeded in getting the House to adopt the legislation. As with the Contract With America in the 104th Congress, a much less benign fate awaited the energy legislation when it moved to the Senate. Parts of it were ignored, savaged, or altered virtually beyond recognition. Most importantly, legislators found that portions of the energy legislation just didn't stand up to close scrutiny because of the haste with which it had been thrown together.

The formation of congressional task forces also is not new.[22] During the late 1970s, Democratic Speakers appointed task forces of twenty-five or thirty fellow partisans to assist the leadership in gaining House approval for most important legislation. Now a matter of routine, task forces represent whip systems specialized in both policy and political strategies. The members appointed to task forces have a special interest in the legislation and often are chosen for their ability to work with contending factions.

Most often they are used to help the party leadership secure a House majority for a measure reported from committee, and so they reflect a partnership between leadership and committee. But there have been several occasions when task forces have produced policy proposals on their own, usually in the form of floor amendments. In a few instances, with the blessing of party leaders, task forces have pressured committees to produce legislation to their liking or even written legislation themselves. Minority party Republicans, and now minority party Democrats, also have employed task forces to shadow and blunt their opponents' messages.

A more recent development in the House is the creation of bipartisan task forces by the joint leadership or the inclusion of "like-minded" minority party members on majority party task forces. In the first session of the 101st Congress (1989–1990), bipartisan task forces on the reform of congressional ethics and campaign finance held many hearings and, in the case of the former, eventually devised legislation.[23] Partisan differences over campaign finance practices proved too deep for that task force to overcome. In the 104th Congress, Republicans announced that task force membership would be available for selected Democrats. Gingrich's task force on immigration included a handful of conservative and moderate Democrats.[24]

Senate majority leader George Mitchell followed the House lead by creating several Democratic task forces to address issues that crossed committees' jurisdictional lines—on rural development and government ethics, for example. And in the 105th Congress Republican majority leader Trent Lott (Miss.) established six ad hoc task forces to help shape the agenda, but not to draft bills, on education, the environment, campaign finance reform, retirement security, health care, and the workplace. As Sen. Robert F. Bennett (R-Utah) put it: "The cement is a little more liquid in a task force. It hardens later on."[25]

Committee and subcommittee chairs become nervous when task forces begin to look too much like committees—when they have formal membership rosters, appoint leaders, hold hearings, and propose legislation, for example.[26] Task forces cannot, in a formal sense, draft and report legislation to their parent chamber. For the most part, they remain opportunities to build bridges, brainstorm, and advertise positions. But critics have bemoaned their secrecy, partisanship, and, in some cases, the close but exclusive links they forge with organized interests. And they can also expose party splits and create hostilities. For example, in March of 1996 Speaker Gingrich formed a task force to formulate a Republican legislative strategy on the environment. When it came time to appoint task force members, House Resources Committee chair Don Young (R-Alaska) skipped over H. James Saxton (R-N.J.), who chaired a relevant subcommittee, to suggest Richard W. Pombo (R-Calif.), a more junior member of the full committee. That move, which underscored a split between eastern and western Republicans on a variety of environmental issues, did not sit well with Saxton.[27]

By the end of the 104th Congress, Gingrich and his fellow party leaders were feeling the heat from committee chairs. Gingrich recognized the problem but did not give up hope: "I would like to simultaneously strengthen the committee chairs and the task force system, and do it in a way that [produces] a very sophisticated , integrated system. Whether or not that's possible, I'm not sure yet."[28] It was not possible. At the outset of the 105th Congress, Gingrich narrowly won reelection as Speaker and was forced to backtrack on his efforts to deprive committee chairs of their independence. There were no new efforts to empower task forces and Republican party leaders made it clear that, on most matters, committees would be allowed to shape initial legislative proposals without leadership dictation. As Judiciary chair Henry J. Hyde of Illinois put it: "I think there is a general mood of granting more autonomy to the committee chairmen. I think there will be fewer dictates and fewer mandates."[29]

One additional development of the 1980s worth noting is the use of domestic policy summits and commissions. Summits are meetings of committee leaders, congressional leaders, and top executive branch officials designed to get over impasses on important policy problems. Summits have been used effectively to handle budget and social security problems. But they can also fail to achieve positive results. The probability of a summit's success appears directly related to the level of political disaster awaiting policy makers who emerge with no agreement.[30] Once summit groups reach agreements, their recommendations carry tremendous weight in the legislative process. Those in Congress who seek to alter or block the recommendation before it becomes law generally risk disapproval and blame if no legislation results. Although committee reactions are anticipated, committees and their leaders find that their freedom to design legislation as they see fit is severely limited by the terms of summit agreements. Summits have the effect of shifting the proposal power to party leaders and administration officials and reducing the blocking power of committees. Commissions are similar to summits but they are more formal bodies created by statute or executive order and designed to find bipartisan solutions to difficult policy problems. Commissions on the federal deficit, health care, and social security have been created in recent years, but none have proved successful in bringing forth bipartisan recommendations.

BUDGET POLITICS

The most important change in the political agenda during the last two decades has been the ascendance and continuing preeminence of budget politics. Passage of the Congressional Budget and Impoundment Control Act of 1974 marked the beginning of this trend, though by comparison to the 1980s and 1990s, budget politics during the 1970s was a staid affair. In addition to redefining national politics by highlighting sharp distinctions between the two parties, budget politics reshaped the character of politics inside Congress, enhanced the role of leadership in the legislative process, and undermined the power and autonomy of congressional committees.

During most of this century, committees set the agenda for their parent chambers. While committees always have had to be concerned with various formal constraints, such as time deadlines set in law for the expiration of programs or spending authority, they have had few conditions imposed on them by their parent chambers concerning the substance of the legislation they were to report. Committees, of course, dislike formal restrictions. The imposition of enforceable constraints in advance of committee action would greatly alter the sequence of decision making in Congress and reduce committee power. Adoption of the 1974 Budget Act created the possibility of rearranging the usual sequence and placing the initiative for policy change in the hands of members not serving on the committees of relevant jurisdiction. That threat was realized in the 1980s when policy changes, partisan shifts, and interbranch disputes all collided with massive budget deficits. The budget process entered a state of flux as contending forces—committee, party, leadership, and executive branch—jockeyed for advantage. And three additional "reforms" were passed that substantially altered the character of the budget process—the Balanced Budget and Emergency Deficit Control Acts of 1985 and 1987 (also known as Gramm-Rudman-Hollings, or GRH I and GRH II) and the Budget Enforcement Act of 1990.

Committees resisted developments that put their power in jeopardy, but they were not able to avoid the added complexity of the process and additional compromises to their autonomy. Four components of the budget and spending legislation noted above must be understood to appreciate the implications of budget politics for committee autonomy. First, *reconciliation* instructions provide orders to committees to recommend legislation that achieves specified spending savings. Second, the *Byrd Rule*, which allows parliamentary objections to "extraneous" matter included in reconciliation bills in the Senate, recaptured some of the ground lost in the reconciliation process. Third, *appropriations caps*, sometimes called 602(b) allocations after a revised section of the 1974 Budget Act, provide spending guidelines for appropriations bills. And third, *continuing resolutions* provide budget authority for federal programs when regular appropriations bills are not passed by the beginning of the fiscal year. Developments in each of these areas redistributed power among the parent chambers, party leaders, and committees, as well as among the various committees. And they continue to shape committee autonomy in the 1990s.

RECONCILIATION.   The 1974 budget process was designed to supplement and coordinate the decisions of the standing committees. A first budget resolution was to be adopted in May, setting targets for spending and revenues for the next fiscal year. Individual authorization, appropriations, and revenue bills would be passed during the summer months, to be followed in September by a second budget resolution. Used aggressively, the first budget resolution could be used to shape the legislative agenda for each session—with the second budget resolution serving as an enforcement mechanism. According to the budget act, the second budget resolution, which was binding, could be used to order certain committees to report legislation that achieved specified spending savings or revenue enhancements. Such reconciliation legislation—so named because it was originally intended to reconcile the differences between committee decisions and the second budget resolution—was to be adopted before October 1, the beginning of the new federal fiscal year. Responsibility for writing the budget resolutions and supervising the reconciliation process fell to a new budget committee in each chamber. Responsibility for devising the detailed legislation required for the reconciliation bill rested with the individual committees.

Unfortunately, at least from the perspective of those who devised the new process, it has never worked quite the way it was laid out. During the 1970s, the decisions of the summer months on appropriations and authorization legislation were allowed to stand under the terms of second budget resolutions, despite the fact that many of those decisions were not consistent with the targets of the first budget resolutions. During that period, no reconciliation instructions were imposed, with the one exception of instructions to a few Senate committees in 1979. Although the Senate's Budget Committee was more aggressive than the House committee, the new budget process proved to be accommodating rather than threatening to the interests of the appropriations and authorizing committees.[31]

Large budget deficits dramatically altered the context of budget politics in the 1980s and produced an important change in the sequence of congressional decision making. In 1980, an unexpectedly large deficit led both chambers to include reconciliation instructions in the first budget resolution to give the budget process new teeth. By including reconciliation instructions in the first resolution, the various committees were provided with binding instructions before they even had an opportunity to report legislation. Moreover, by noting how they had devised the reconciliation figure for each committee, the budget committees were indicating which programs might be cut to achieve the specified level of savings. Committee chairs protested this infringement on their jurisdictions, arguing that the budget committees had no business making suggestions about individual programs within the jurisdiction of authorizing committees. The budget committees insisted that taking programs into account was the only way to devise reconciliation instructions appropriate to each committee. An amendment to the resolution that would have deleted the reconciliation instructions was easily defeated. Reconciliation has been a central component of the budget process ever since.[32]

In 1981, House Republicans, still in the minority but allied with a group of conservative southern Democrats, and the new majority Republicans in the Senate succeeded in passing a budget resolution containing reconciliation instructions for fifteen House committees and fourteen Senate committees. A reconciliation bill, which contained significant programmatic changes, united the same coalition in the House to defeat majority Democrats. After 1981, reconciliation lost some of its bite but reconciliation instructions continued to be included in the first budget resolution. The House, in fact, decided that the use of reconciliation instructions in the first resolution obviated the second budget resolution; it dispensed with separate action on second resolutions.

By the mid-1980s, then, the budget process had been substantially revised, at least in practice, placing the decisions on individual pieces of appropriations and authorizing legislation a step behind the adoption of meaningful budget resolutions. The potential existed, and was realized in 1981, for the autonomy of the appropriations, authorizing, and revenue committees to be eviscerated by first budget resolutions written by the budget committees and party leaders and approved by the parent chambers. But stalemate on the shape of the budget prevented such a disaster for congressional committees between 1982 and 1985.

In the meantime, many committees found reconciliation legislation a convenient vehicle for unrelated authorization legislation. Hitching such legislation to the necessary reconciliation bills was a way to guarantee that authorization legislation opposed by the other chamber would get to conference.[33] In addition, reconciliation legislation usually went to the floor in the House with a special rule that restricted amendments, giving the authorizing committees some insulation from unfriendly floor amendments that they might not have if they reported separate legislation. In the Senate, reconciliation bills are protected from nongermane amendments and subject to a limit on debate. While Senate rules do not protect reconciliation bills from germane amendments, the limit on debate allows committees to include provisions that otherwise might be subject to a filibuster, thereby giving Senate committees an ounce of autonomy they would not have if the provisions were handled in separate legislation.

Thus, while the restructured budget process threatened committee autonomy, many House and Senate committees actually gained some insulation from their parent chambers through the reconciliation process.

Reconciliation acquired some additional bite in 1985 with the adoption of the Gramm-Rudman-Hollings procedure—named after its primary Senate sponsors.[34] The procedure provided for across-the-board spending cuts—a process labeled *sequestration*—if certain deficit reductions were not attained in each of the following five years. The purpose of the sequestration procedure was to motivate Congress and the president to achieve deficit reduction, thereby reinforcing the reconciliation process. For most committees, it was thought, failure to achieve the deficit reductions and suffer across-the-board spending cuts would impose a worse outcome than an adequate deficit reduction that they devised for themselves. As it turned out, though, GRH failed because committees never feared the sequestration process—either because accounting procedures kept them out of harms way or because the programs they handled, mostly entitlements, were exempt from the cuts.[35]

THE BYRD RULE.   Although sequestration was a failure, certain rules adopted by the Senate as a result of Gramm-Rudman-Hollings were particularly tough on Senate committees. Under the Byrd Rule, named after Sen. Robert C. Byrd (D-W. Va.), reconciliation bills are protected from "extraneous" provisions. The rule is enforced by allowing any senator to raise a point of order, a parliamentary objection, to any provision that is not related to the central purposes of reconciliation (cutting spending and raising revenues). The rule is effective because sixty votes must be obtained to override a ruling by the presiding officer on such a point of order (the same number required to invoke cloture to stop a filibuster). Therefore, a committee seeking to include extraneous provisions in its reconciliation package must either avoid a point of order or have enough support to overturn the decision of the presiding officer. The Byrd Rule limits the ability of committees to attach legislation to reconciliation bills and therefore reduces the value of reconciliation bills as a means for preserving committee autonomy.[36]

In 1995, a variety of Senate committees controlled by the Republicans found their efforts to load a massive reconciliation bill with numerous programmatic changes shortcircuited by their Democratic opponents. The policy areas affected were as diverse as state department reorganization plans, Medicare, banking reform, and most significantly, welfare reform legislation. Although Byrd Rule challenges were anticipated, Republican leaders and committee members decided to risk a major welfare reform package as part of the reconciliation bill that came to the Senate floor in October. Forty-five provisions of this huge bill were stripped because of Byrd Rule objections. Senate Republicans were dismayed at the outcome. As Sen. Rick Santorum (R-Pa.) lamented at the time: "You have gutted the welfare bill." Senate Republicans were left to try and recoup their losses in the House-Senate conference committee that followed shortly thereafter.

APPROPRIATIONS CAPS.   Although the earliest reconciliation instructions focused largely on the appropriations committees, their contemporary impact is much more keenly felt by the authorizing and revenue committees. And yet one of the major purposes of the 1974 Budget Act was to set overall spending levels as a guide to subsequent appropriations decisions. Put differently, the act was intended to limit the autonomy of the appropriations subcommittees and their ability to be advocates for those who benefited from their spending bills.[37] Yet even when budget resolutions do not specify reconciliation instructions for authorizing and revenue committees, they must provide guidelines for appropriations decisions if they are to have any meaning.

The federal budget is organized into twenty budget functions, or categories, that bring together roughly similar activities. The appropriations committees are organized into thirteen subcommittees that bear some resemblance to the budget's functional categories. Once broad spending levels are set for the functional categories, those sums must be allocated to the various committees, and then to their subcommittees. This two-step process is prescribed in sections 602(a) and 602(b) of the Budget Act.[38] Thus, after the appropriations committees receive their 602(a) allocations, they are required to translate the functional allocations into subcommittee allocations and report the result. The subcommittees are then prohibited from reporting legislation that exceeds their reported allocation. Once allocations have been made, the Congressional Budget Office is responsible for determining whether appropriations bills are consistent with the budget resolution, an accounting process known informally as *score keeping*.

During the 1970s, when first budget resolutions were nonbinding, the allocation process created some friction between appropriations and budget committees.[39] This friction was greater in the Senate, where the Budget Committee was more assertive and the Appropriations Committee more prone to exceed the allocations in the bills it reported. But in neither chamber was the allocation decision of the appropriators viewed as strictly binding and there were no rules enforcing the caps. In fact, numerous appropriations bills passed that exceeded allocation ceilings set by the appropriations committees themselves. Other than operating on a faster schedule, as provided in the Budget Act, the appropriations process in fact changed very little, perhaps with the exception that appropriators now could use the allocation caps as an argument against floor amendments proposing more spending.

Making the 602(b) allocations binding became an issue when federal deficits increased in the 1980s.[40] To enforce the caps, the 1985 Gramm-Rudman-Hollings package added an enforcement procedure to the 602(b) process. The new rules made the 602(b) allocations binding on *individual* appropriations bills rather than on just the budget totals in the resolution. They also authorized points of order against individual bills reported to the floor.[41] Like the Byrd Rule, overcoming challenges on the Senate floor requires sixty votes; otherwise the challenge is sustained by the presiding officer. Thus, the 602(b) allocation process has added bite to budget constraints in recent years. The more rigid constraints have reduced the autonomy of the appropriations committees. But at the same time appropriators have retained control over the 602(b) allocations, permitting them some discretion in identifying the specific spending limits for each appropriations bill. Moreover, the constraints also apply to floor amendments to appropriations bills, which means that appropriators can raise points of order against amendments that push a bill beyond the spending limit. This is particularly important in the Senate, where appropriations bills have almost routinely been made more expensive through floor amendments. As a result, within the constraints imposed on them by the process, the appropriations committees have gained more control over the details of their bills.

The remaining, more difficult question is: Are the appropriations committees more powerful as a result of the binding 602(b) process? The answer goes both ways.[42] With respect to their ability to make decisions according to their own policy preferences and by processes that suit their own needs, the appropriations committees have lost a great deal of autonomy. They are constrained by budget decisions negotiated by party and budget committee leaders and imposed by the parent chambers. They are more constrained in their ability to meet the demands placed on them by their colleagues and constituencies. In the long run, this will substantially reduce the influence of these committees. With respect to determining legislative details *within the constraints* of the binding 602(b) allocations, however, the appropriations committees have gained insulation from outside forces. When the committees do include in their bills funding for projects or programs desired by colleagues and constituencies, they are in a better position to protect them from unfriendly floor amendments. And they are also in a better position to set priorities as they see fit.

CONTINUING RESOLUTIONS.   Congress uses continuing resolutions to provide funding for federal agencies and programs when one or more of the regular appropriations bills have not been enacted by the start of the new fiscal year.[43] Traditionally, these brief resolutions provided a continuation of funding through a formula based on the previous year's rate of spending—hence, a *continuing* resolution. The CRs, as they are frequently referred to on the Hill, were short term—they expired in a few days or weeks when the regular appropriations bill was adopted. And they concerned only the one or two regular appropriations bills that Congress and the president did not manage to enact. Continuing resolutions were considered unfortunate, largely innocuous necessities.

Budget conflict and the resulting strategies and delays associated with the appropriations process transformed continuing resolutions in the 1980s. Disputes between the House and Senate and between Congress and the president delayed approval of budget resolutions and the appropriations bills dependent on those resolutions. The key continuing resolutions of these years became full-year funding measures—obviously comprehensive, including hundreds of pages of text rather than just a formula—and took on great political importance. These resolutions ceased to be simple, albeit enormous, extensions of preexisting spending authority. Instead they became a battleground for budget priorities, programmatic changes, and deficit reduction.

These developments had several implications for the autonomy of both appropriations and authorizing committees.[44] At the most general level, reliance on continuing resolutions came at the price of sharing decision-making functions on appropriations with party leaders, who were the only members in a position to negotiate effectively for their caucuses. But in other ways reliance on continuing resolutions increased the power of the appropriations committees at the expense of their parent chambers and the authorizing committees.

Greater control over appropriations details was the product of several aspects of the way continuing resolutions were handled. First, because the massive continuing resolutions of the 1980s were considered under severe time constraints, they were protected on the House floor under special rules that restricted or barred floor amendments. This encouraged appropriators to delay their regular bill and include it instead in the continuing resolution to avoid unfriendly floor amendments. Second, the size of some continuing resolutions makes them difficult to challenge. They were so large that only a few elements received much scrutiny on the floor. If they had been considered as separate bills, days or weeks apart, more issues normally could have been raised. Finally, the strict time constraints increased the difficulty of defeating the conference report on the continuing resolutions, giving the appropriators who were conferees greater leeway in writing the report. Conference reports on continuing resolutions were not insulated from defeat, of course (the House turned one down in 1983), but it usually was their aggregate cost and nonspending features, not their appropriations details, that got them into trouble.

An even more important concern to members of Congress not sitting on the appropriations committees was that continuing resolutions infringed upon authorizing committees' jurisdictions. Unlike regular appropriations bills, continuing resolutions could include any kind of legislation, such as legislative authorizations not within the jurisdiction of the appropriations committees. Continuing resolutions of the 1980s became vehicles for authorizing legislation. In some cases, authorizing committees asked friendly appropriators to include their legislation in a continuing resolution to force the other chamber and the president to consider and agree to it. Many large authorizing measures were included in continuing resolutions in this way. In doing so, however, appropriators gained a voice in shaping legislation that they otherwise would not have had, particularly in conference. And the continuing resolutions gave appropriators—as well as nonappropriations members through appeals to appropriators and through floor amendments—an opportunity to pursue legislative matters without the consent and cooperation of the affected authorizing committee.

Leaders of authorizing committees complained bitterly about the use of continuing resolutions for nonappropriations matters. Even when policy outcomes suited their needs, authorizing committees realized that they were not in control and worried about unsatisfactory future outcomes. They risked becoming supplicants to the appropriations committees on matters within their own jurisdictions. And the lobbyists and constituencies traditionally dependent on authorizing committees shifted their attention to appropriators when the action shifted to continuing resolutions, further undermining the value of membership on the authorizing committees. In short, for authorizing committees the long-term price of legislating through continuing resolutions a trophy in their policy-making role.

Adoption of the Budget Enforcement Act of 1990, which was achieved through a protracted and contentious budget summit, brought this phase of budgeting to a close. CRs once again reverted to their traditional "stopgap" use and new rules refocused members' attention on budget walls and discretionary spending caps. For four years after the 1990 agreement, between 1991 and 1994, the budget process resumed a measure of quietude unseen in more than a decade. During the 102d Congress (1991–1992) the budget agreement reached between President George Bush and the Democratic Congress maintained a tenuous peace and both sides seemed to await the outcomes of the 1992 elections.

The election of President Bill Clinton diminished the prospects for interbranch conflict and led to two more years of relative calm, with neither CRs nor reconciliation playing much of a role. A return to divided party government in the 104th Congress, however, also meant another protracted budget battle as majority party Republicans used every tool at their disposal to shape a balanced budget *and* a significant tax cut. After some negotiation, the Republicans did succeed in getting the president's signature on a large *rescission bill*—legislation used to cancel previously approved spending in a current fiscal year. But the two sides disagreed on just about everything else, with the Republicans unwilling to meet the president's demands and the president content to veto most of what Congress sent to him. As a result, a series of continuing resolutions once again became the focal point for policy discussions and programmatic changes. Although the first of these, which extended virtually all government operations into November, generated little controversy, a much tougher second continuing resolution was vetoed by President Clinton on November 13, 1995, leading to a huge government shutdown. Not until April 25, 1996, did the episode come to an end. In all, Congress passed fourteen temporary spending bills before finally agreeing to an omnibus bill that cleaned up the last of the unfunded government activities—with less than half the fiscal year remaining.[45]

Continuing resolutions are likely to remain the product of inter-branch disagreement rather than a legislative fixture. Authorizing committees have some short-term incentive to allow appropriators to muscle them aside. "A lot of it is time," House Commerce Committee chair Thomas J. Bliley, Jr., (R-Va.) explained. That is, allowing authorizing to appear on faster moving appropriations vehicles "buys a pause" and permits the authorizing committees to "do it the way it ought to be done" during a subsequent legislative cycle.[46] In addition, authorizing language has to be constantly revisited, since appropriations are repeated each year. Appropriators also gain some short-term advantages through the process. But neither has reason to allow it to continue in the long run because both lose power to party leaders and summits.

COMMITTEES ON THE FLOOR

We have seen that parties and party leaders have a number of ways to shape the legislation that committees consider, to control their agendas, or to circumvent them entirely. We also have seen that partisan and inter-branch disputes can alter the decision-making environment of the various committees. But in the midst of all these pressures, committees still produce legislation, albeit not as much as they once did. When that legislation reaches the floor it faces its ultimate test. It may be of little concern to the parent chambers and sail through on its way to a presidential signature. It may reflect party or chamber preferences already, in which case similar safe passage is assured. But if it lacks partisan or chamber support, or faces some entrenched partisan or other minority waiting to alter or dismember it, then the floor phase of the legislative process can be particularly harrowing, or even deadly, for a bill. In the face of such a possibility, the following questions naturally arise: To what extent are committee bills amended? What protections, if any, do they receive? And how do the chambers differ in these regards?

Traditionally, the ability of committees to attract support on the floor and to fend off unfriendly amendments has rested on sources of positive power—the ability to induce others to accept committee recommendations even when they oppose them (see Chapter 1). In most circumstances positive power is the product of extraprocedural resources of committees. Committee leaders usually have an advantage in information about policy substance and political circumstances. Their expertise is acquired from personal experience, formal hearings, relationships with interest groups and executive agencies, expert staff assistance, and close ties to the party leadership. Committees' specialized staffs place committee members in a better position than others to define issues to their advantage, monitor the activity of their opponents, and respond promptly to opponents' political maneuvers. Due to their standing relationships with lobbyists and executive officials, committee leaders usually are in a good position to orchestrate external pressure on their colleagues.

These sources of positive power were reinforced by informal norms, at least before the 1960s.[47] An *apprenticeship* norm provided that new members refrain from active participation in policy making until they had served several years and gained political and policy experience. A *specialization* norm provided that members should concentrate their efforts on matters under the jurisdiction of their assigned committees and matters directly affecting their constituencies. In practice, this meant that committee recommendations, which were the handiwork of senior committee members, deserved *deference*. That deference, in turn, was *reciprocated* when other committees' legislation was on the floor. Apprenticeship, specialization, deference, and reciprocity formed a coherent set of informal norms that enhanced the autonomy of committees in policy making.[48]

Many of these committee advantages have weakened since the 1950s. Junior members, majority and minority, now have substantial personal staffs and office budgets; improved office technology for information retrieval and dissemination; expanded access to strengthened support agencies, such as the Congressional Research Service and the General Accounting Office; and extensive relationships with experts in the swelling community of interest groups in Washington. Thus, the net informational advantage for committees diminished and the rationale for deferring to committees when their recommendations were brought to the floor weakened. Moreover, many of the new interest groups and growing constituencies placed demands on members to champion their causes when legislation affecting their interests reached the House and Senate floors. And just as important, many new members were elected to Congress with an established commitment to have an immediate impact on policy. By the early 1970s, few members considered deference to committee recommendations a viable norm.

Weakening committee autonomy is reflected in the record of floor amending activity since the mid-1950s.[49] Amending activity steadily increased in both chambers during the 1950s and 1960s, then shot upward in the 1970s.[50] A spectacular surge in House floor amending activity during the 92d (1971–1972) and 93d (1973–1974) Congresses coincided with the adoption of recorded electronic voting in the Committee of the Whole, which appears to have increased the political incentives for members to offer floor amendments. The increase in floor amending activity was not merely a function of the congressional workload, since the *proportion* of measures adopted in the House and Senate that were subject to at least one floor amendment also increased in the 1960s and 1970s.

It is important to note that, from a committee's perspective, floor amendments can cut two ways. A fairly constant 10 to 15 percent of all amendments are *second-degree amendments*—that is, amendments to amendments—supported by committee members and designed to weaken the effect of unfriendly first-degree amendments.[51] While the majority of first-degree amendments represent legislative contributions that committee members find acceptable, a significant number are unwanted by committees. These amendments can critically alter and in some cases even be fatal to the committee's legislation. Thus, the increase in floor amendments represents weakening committee autonomy if for no other reason than that it reflects a shift in the location of policy initiative from committees to outsiders.

COMMITTEE DIFFERENCES

The pattern of change in floor amending activity is not identical for all committees. Consider the House first. The number of floor amendments per measure offered to each House committee's legislation in selected congresses since the 1950s is reported in Table 5-1. The data show that the surge in House amending activity occurred disproportionately among prestige and policy committees. That is, the most powerful committees witnessed the greatest increase in threats to their autonomy. The move to limit House floor amendments is visible for most committees in the drop in floor amendments in the 96th (1979–1980), 99th (1985–1986), and 103d (1993–1994) congresses.

House Appropriations stands out in Table 5-1 as a committee faced with heavy amending activity. In fact, the appropriations committees long have been the leading targets for floor amending activity, measured on a per bill basis. In part this is because they report relatively few separate

TABLE 5-1   Number of Floor Amendments per Measure in the House, by Committee (Selected Congresses)

Committee type	Congress					
	84th (1955– 1956)	88th (1963– 1964)	92d (1971– 1972)	96th (1979– 1980)	99th (1985– 1986)	103d (1993– 1994)
Prestige committees						
Appropriations	2.6	2.4	3.6	9.5	4.4	7.7
Budget	—	—	—	16.5	0.5	4.3
Rules	a	a	a	a	0.1	0.1
Ways and Means	0.1	0.1	0.2	0.8	3.1	0.4
Policy committees						
Banking, Finance, and Urban Affairs	0.6	0.8	2.2	7.2	10.2	0.6
Education and Labor	2.1	6.6	4.1	3.0	2.1	5.3
Energy and Commerce	0.4	0.8	1.1	3.0	0.4	0.5
Foreign Affairs	0.3	2.9	0.9	10.1	3.4	1.4
Government Operations	0.8	0.9	0.7	2.7	0.3	0.7
Judiciary	0.2	1.5	0.8	3.4	0.4	0.4
Constituency committees						
Agriculture	0.4	2.0	1.0	2.2	4.1	1.2
Armed Services	0.3	0.4	0.8	2.6	19.1	7.0
Merchant Marine and Fisheries	0.2	0.5	0.4	0.9	0.2	1.1
Natural Resources	0.1	a	0.4	1.0	0.2	1.0
Post Office and Civil Service	0.6	1.3	0.3	0.5	0.1	0.2
Public Works and Transportation	0.3	0.3	2.3	2.1	1.8	0.3
Science, Space, and Technology	—	1.2	0.7	3.1	0.9	4.5
Small Business	—	—	—	1.7	a	1.3
Veterans' Affairs	0.2	0.1	0.1	0.1	0.1	a

Source: Data collected from the "Index" to the *Congressional Record,* debates reported in the *Record* itself, and the *Calendars of the United States House of Representatives and History of Legislation,* for the various congresses.

Note: Includes only amendments to measures reported to three or fewer committees.

[a] Fewer than 0.1 amendments per measure.

bills. Each bill is fairly important and must, in some form, be considered each year. The appropriations committees, unlike most other committees, do not have the luxury of reporting dozens of noncontroversial measures. In addition, because their bills cover most federal spending, many substantive controversies find their way into debates on appropriations bills. Spending decisions themselves often are controversial, of course, and they are made even more so when they are used as vehicles for legislative provisions that might not survive the scrutiny of the authorizing committees.

A notable exception to the overall pattern of proportionately smaller increases in amending activity among constituency committees is House Armed Services, historically no more than an average constituency committee with respect to floor amendments. The traditional deference to the executive branch and the committee that generally reflected the policy preferences of the executive branch disappeared during the 1970s in the aftermath of the Vietnam War. In the 1980s, sharp differences between the Democratic House and the Reagan administration regarding defense policy and spending, as well as other priorities, sharpened the differences between Armed Services and the Democratic majority. This is reflected in the very high level of amending activity on Armed Services measures in the 99th Congress (1985–1986), which was fairly typical of the congresses of the 1980s. By the 103d Congress—which featured unified Democratic control—amendments dropped sharply once again but went higher than the norm for constituent committees and higher than the level experienced in the 96th Congress.[52] The Senate's Committee on Armed Services shows a similar pattern, except that during the 103d Congress its bills attracted little attention on the floor.

The Education Committee also deserves brief mention. During the long period of Democratic control in the House, Education and Labor (now called Education and the Workforce) consistently ranked among the most liberal committees in the chamber. It is not surprising, therefore, that it ranked first among policy committees as a target for floor amendments in four of the six congresses examined in Table 5-1. From the 1960s to the 1980s the committee routinely dealt with issues that sharply divide the two parties. During that period committee Democrats, with help from moderate Republicans, frequently reported bills that even their own party colleagues found unacceptable. Although the shift to Republican rule moved the committee sharply to the right (see Figure 3-1) it remains among the most partisan panels in the House.[53]

As in other areas, differences between committee types are not as tidy in the Senate as in the House (see Table 5-2). Nevertheless, the major policy committees faced a large number of floor amendments and, with the obvious exception of Appropriations, displayed larger increases in the 1970s than constituency committees.

THE USE OF SPECIAL RULES IN THE HOUSE

Although committees used second-degree amendments, monopoly control of the conference delegations, and even preemptive concessions to

TABLE 5-2   Number of Floor Amendments per Measure in the Senate, by Committee (Selected Congresses)

Committee type	Congress					
	84th (1955–1956)	88th (1963–1964)	92d (1971–1972)	96th (1979–1980)	99th (1985–1986)	103d (1993–1994)
Policy committees						
Budget	—	—	—	20.3	33.0	58.0
Foreign Relations	1.1	2.4	3.7	2.2	4.8	1.6
Governmental Affairs	0.2	0.1	1.4	0.7	0.4	1.9
Judiciary	0.1	0.2	0.1	0.3	0.2	0.3
Labor and Human Resources	0.1	1.8	5.1	3.0	1.4	5.1
Mixed policy/ constituency committees						
Armed Services	0.2	0.3	1.7	1.8	10.8	13.5
Banking, Housing, and Urban Affairs	0.9	1.1	2.4	6.5	0.4	2.1
Finance	0.7	1.1	10.1	2.7	12.7	1.4
Constituency committees						
Agriculture, Nutrition, and Forestry	1.1	1.4	0.6	1.4	12.1	0.4
Appropriations	2.7	3.6	3.1	11.8	17.9	21.0
Commerce, Science, and Transportation	0.2	0.4	1.3	1.1	1.0	1.6
Energy and Natural Resources	0.1	0.2	0.3	1.3	0.4	0.3
Environment and Public Works	0.5	0.2	2.0	1.4	2.5	0.7
Veterans' Affairs	—	—	a	3.1	0.9	0.3
Other						
Rules and Administration	0.5	0.2	0.6	0.2	0.6	10.2

Source: Data collected from the "Index" to the Congressional Record, debates reported in the Record itself, and the Calendars of the United States House of Representatives and History of Legislation, for the various congresses.

Note: Includes only amendments to measures reported to three or fewer committees. Data prior to the 96th Congress is for a committee's closest antecedent.

a Fewer than 0.1 amendments per measure.

opponents to combat unfriendly amendments, they needed additional tools to overcome the challenges they faced on the House and Senate floor. The problem was especially acute in the House, where committee autonomy traditionally was stronger than in the Senate. Eventually, the majority party Democrats in the House were compelled to pursue new strategies: increased use of suspension of the rules and expanded use of special rules to restrict and structure amending activity in the Committee of the Whole.[54] Both procedures had been employed for decades, but new conditions pushed House Democrats to discover novel uses.

The rule providing for a motion to *suspend the rules* limits debate to forty minutes, bars amendments, and requires a two-thirds vote to adopt (simultaneously) the motion and measure. Use of the procedure by a committee requires the cooperation of the Speaker, who must recognize a representative of the committee before the motion can be made. The procedure was designed to expedite the consideration of minor legislation. Before 1973, motions to suspend the rules were in order only two days each month. By 1977, the majority party Democrats had amended the rule to allow suspension motions two days each week. As a result, the number of measures considered under suspension increased from fewer than 200 between 1967 and 1972 to more than 400 in three of the four congresses between 1977 and 1984, and then to over 500 in those between 1987 and 1992.[55] Thus, committees more frequently enjoyed insulation from unfriendly floor amendments. One byproduct of this development was greater discretion for the Speaker in determining when and how legislation is considered on the floor. Such discretion occasionally has given the Speaker some leverage in gaining policy concessions from committees seeking to avoid the floor amending process. But even suspension has its limits as a mechanism for circumventing the floor because it requires an extraordinary majority for passage: two-thirds of those present and voting.

Starting in late 1979, the House majority party leadership and the Rules Committee began to employ special rules more frequently to restrict floor amendments in some way. *Special rules* (usually simply called "rules," sometimes "special orders") are resolutions from the Rules Committee that provide for floor consideration of legislation and, by supplementing or supplanting the standing rules of the House, may structure the amending process in the Committee of the Whole. They are necessary for most major legislation and so offer a regular opportunity for the Rules Committee to bar amendments, order the consideration of amendments, or even allow amendments that otherwise would violate the rules of the House. They also give majority party leaders, who control their party's contingent on the Rules Committee, an opportunity to structure floor consideration of legislation in a manner that meets the needs of the party and of the standing committees that the party controls. The majority leadership's increased use of these restrictions exacerbated the emerging battle between the two parties in the House.

Special rules long had been used to limit amendments on tax and social security measures from the Committee on Ways and Means. In fact, tax bills from Ways and Means generally received *closed rules*—that is, rules that barred amendments altogether. The justification for this special treatment was that Ways and Means measures were very complex substantively and very fragile politically. The decision to expand the use of restrictive rules to measures originating in other committees represented a clear break with the past practice of preserving each member's right, under the standing rules, to offer germane floor amendments in the Committee of the Whole.

The change in the content of special rules in the 1980s was dramatic. Between the 94th (1975–1976) and 97th (1981–1982) Congresses, the percentage of special rules that restricted amendments in some way increased from 15.7 to 28.8 percent. In the 99th Congress (1985–1986), 44.6 percent of all special rules limited amendments. By the mid-1980s, nearly everyone assumed that a controversial measure would receive a special rule that restricted and structured amending activity to some degree. In fact, in the 99th Congress 65 percent of floor amendments were offered under special rules that limited or structured amending activity in some way, up from just over 13 percent in the 96th Congress (1979–1980).[56]

Restrictions on amendments take many forms. Some restrictive rules merely require that eligible amendments be printed in the *Congressional Record* in advance, giving committee bill managers and party leaders time to react to the proposals. But in many cases restrictive rules bar amendments to certain sections or even specify the particular amendments that would be in order in the Committee of the Whole. In the 1980s, between two-thirds and three-fourths of special rules identified the particular amendments that would be in order, up from one-third or less in the congresses of the mid-1970s. Furthermore, special rules can be used to alter relations among amendments, such as barring second-degree amendments or allowing third-degree amendments, making the consideration of an amendment contingent on the adoption or rejection of another amendment, and requiring adoption of an amendment without a separate vote, among other things.

Special rules need not bar unfriendly amendments altogether to achieve a committee's goal of preventing their adoption. For example, in 1991 the Rules Committee approved a rule for a compromise civil rights bill that President Bush was expected to veto. The rule first allowed a vote on a *substitute*—an entirely different piece of legislation—preferred by liberals in the House. Next, a vote was permitted on a version that Republicans preferred. Finally, the compromise version was put to the test. Under the rule, whichever version passed last, regardless of how many votes it received, would be declared the winner. Thus, the order of consideration was crucial here and was designed to allow the compromise version to prevail but also to permit members to say they had voted for an alternative not preferred by the leadership. Rules such as this are called "king-of-the-hill" rules.[57]

The innovations in special rules were, in most instances, the fruit of a partnership between the majority party leadership, Rules Committee Democrats, and the committee originating the legislation. Majority leaders and the Rules Committee often cared most about an orderly, efficient, and predictable consideration of legislation, while committee leaders sought to reduce uncertainty about the timing, sources, and content of unfriendly amendments to their bills. Indeed, committee bill managers began to demand advantageous special rules once they learned of the possibilities. To a large degree, then, restrictive rules helped House committees regain some of the autonomy they had lost during the 1970s.

In some cases, though, majority party leaders take charge of designing a rule and impose a structure on floor debate to suit party needs, even when party needs are inconsistent with committee interests. One Rules Committee Democrat put it this way:

> We do what the Speaker wants. If he has a keen interest in a piece of legislation and sends us a message he wants thus and so, that's what we do. We'll go back to him sometimes and say, "Mr. Speaker, we think it should be done this way" and sometimes he'll agree with us and sometimes he won't. Of course, the Speaker doesn't take a direct interest in every piece of legislation or certainly every amendment.[58]

Party leaders regularly play a central role in crafting rules for budget resolutions and reconciliation bills that are very important to the party and the chamber. Thus, while special rules usually are a product of the majority party leadership and committee majorities working together, there are times when the expanded and more flexible use of restrictive rules has increased the influence of the majority party leadership at the expense of committee autonomy. It is reasonable to hypothesize that the leadership's new uses of special rules have caused committees to anticipate more carefully the reaction of the majority party and its leadership and to become more responsive to leadership and party policy preferences in writing legislation.

As noted earlier, the use of these rules alienated minority party Republicans during the latter half of the 1980s and into the 1990s. Indeed, during that time Republicans began to publicize the unfairness they perceived in the use of restrictive rules by circulating data on the decline in open rules in the House under the majority party Democrats. Republicans claimed they would "open up the process" once again when they became the majority party. "We're going to have fair rules . . . free and open debate. We're going to let the House work its will," said incoming Rules Committee chair Gerald B. H. Solomon (R-N.Y.).[59] And by their definition, they did. By their own count, Republicans reversed the trend toward more restrictive rules by allowing 72 percent of the bills considered on the floor under a rule to be open or "modified open" during the first few months of the 104th Congress.[60] Unfortunately, they also became impatient with amending marathons and threatened the new Democratic minority with restrictive rules of their own (see Box 5-1). To preserve at least the appearance of openness, new majority Republicans avoided restrictions on amendments and enforced strict time limitations instead. Thus, Democrats complained, they could offer amendments freely but they had no time to do so since even roll call votes are counted against the limits. Either way, the new use of special rules tends to reassert some protections for committee bills once they reach the floor.

Not all committees require the protection of special rules that restrict amendments. In fact, only a few committees routinely receive restrictive special rules. The prestige committees and, to a lesser extent, the policy committees request and often receive special rules that limit amendments.[61] Their legislation is almost always controversial and perceived as vital to the interests of the majority party. A large part of it is necessary legislation (budget bills, continuing appropriations resolutions), and much of it is considered under severe time constraints. All of these factors help to justify limiting amendments. The majority of committees receive a restrictive special rule for only a small fraction of the legislation they report to the floor. Thus, innovations in special rules have helped the House committees that suffered most from the surge in amending activity regain some of their autonomy.

Innovations in special rules, however, have not allowed committees to recover all of the autonomy that is threatened by a more active parent chamber. Indeed, the available evidence suggests that rather than allowing committees to return to their presumably distributive ways, these rules have simply subjected them to greater party domination.[62] First, not all unfriendly floor amendments are barred by restrictive rules. Most rules still allow the important alternative proposals to receive a vote. Second, special rules must be adopted by majority votes on the floor—and those votes are frequently highly partisan in character. The House has rejected special rules from time to time—an average of one per year during the late 1980s and the early 1990s[63]—when a majority of members balked at the alternatives offered.[64] And third, committees sometimes must make policy concessions to the majority party leadership and Rules Committee Democrats to obtain a protective rule. To a significant degree, then, House committees no longer are in the business of picking their own fights. In designing special rules, leaders and Rules members help to shape the battle, too.

Under Open Rules . . .

House Republicans are finding out very quickly that freewheeling debate carries a high price. After years of seething under Democratic rules that restricted how often House members could speak and what amendments they could offer on the floor, the new Republican majority promised to do things differently in the 104th Congress.

Even before taking the reins of the House, the GOP vowed to reverse their Democratic predecessors' penchant for closed rules limiting floor debate and amendments. In the 103d Congress, for example, only 31 of 104 rules—30 percent—governing floor debate were so-called open or unrestricted rules down from 85 percent, 179 of 211, in the 95th Congress. Upon taking control of the House, Republicans promised to use more open rules, though they took no steps to formalize the promise in the sweeping package of institutional changes passed on Congress's opening day.

"You get a far better quality of legislative product under open rules rather than closed rules," remarked Robert S. Walker, R-Pa. "It [a closed rule] under-mines and destroys the quality of the legislation. That's what happened in the last few years. They, more and more, had the impression of insider Washing-ton deals."

In its first test case, the House plodded for five days on legislation designed to curb the federal government from imposing mandates on state and local governments without providing money to pay for them. Some 168 amendments were proposed. The House was able to dispose of only 22 before the bill was set aside temporarily Jan. 25 to clear the way to debate a constitu-tional amendment requiring a balanced budget. Action resumed Jan. 27.

With the reality of an open rule looking far less attractive than the idea, Republicans are now signaling that they may be forced to revert to limiting debate in order to complete work on their agenda. "It looks like we're going to have to increasingly restrict rules if the Democrats won't cooperate," warned House Rules Committee Chairman Gerald B. H. Solomon, R-N.Y.

Indeed, Majority Whip Tom DeLay, R-Texas, has warned that the future of open rules may in fact rest with the Democrats. "We certainly could revisit the openness of the House," DeLay said. "It would only come as a result of these dilatory tactics." House Republican leaders even warn that if Democrats con-tinue to use open rules to stall, the GOP may not find time to consider the $40 billion Mexican aid package Republican leadership backed by President Clin-ton.

. . . Republicans believe that the Democrats are using the new process to prevent the House GOP's "Contract With America" from being considered

BOX 5-1

... *Discord Rules*

within the first 100 days of the new Congress, as promised. For their part, Democrats insist they're simply expressing legitimate concerns about the unfunded mandates legislation and are not abusing floor procedures.

"This is a very fundamental issue," said Vic Fazio, D-Calif., chairman of the House Democratic Caucus. Federal mandates deserve the attention they're getting. If you're going to rewrite the entire federal-state relationship in one bill, you're going to have to give people time to wrestle with these issues."

The upshot of all this is that the American people, fed up with gridlock and political bickering, are being treated via television to watching the GOP-controlled House operate at a snail's pace—the same slow speed that once was the exclusive province of the Senate.

House Republican Conference Chairman John A. Boehner, R-Ohio, saw a silver lining in all this. He said the spectacle of Democratic delay will reap political advantages for Republicans in the 1996 elections. "There is a concerted effort in the House and Senate to obstruct, to delay, to cause us to miss our commitment to the American people," Boehner said. "I think it will become evident. If they want to obstruct every day, it may work to our [political] advantage."

... Democratic lawmakers said it was their duty to raise questions about the Republicans' legislative agenda. They said the more questions they raised, the more the public will know, and, in their view, the less likely the proposals will win public support. "We are voting on slogans," Fazio said. "The longer people ponder these issues, the more they're going to have doubts. But that's what the legislative process is all about."

As debate resumes on the unfunded mandates bill, the Democrats show no signs of backing down. "They don't want to give us the time to fully debate a very important piece of legislation," said Harold L. Volkmer, D-Mo.

The Republicans, meanwhile, are willing to put up with the Democratic strategy—to a point. "They're going to test the limits and push the limits," Walker said. "I hope they're not going to be destructive. It would be very destructive if it was seen as a political opportunity to try to destroy the concept of open rules."

Source: Jonathan D. Salant, "Under Open Rules, Discord Rules," *Congressional Quarterly Weekly Report*, January 28, 1995, 277.

THE SENATE RESPONSE TO THE SURGE IN FLOOR AMENDMENTS

The floor amendment stage is particularly troublesome for Senate committees. Apart from budget matters, Senate rules do not bar amendments that are nongermane or irrelevant to the subjects addressed in a bill reported from committee. Thus, senators may seek to attach an amendment on any subject, even the text of a whole bill, to a bill before the Senate. For example, the dramatic and widely felt Gramm-Rudman-Hollings deficit reduction act was added to a debt ceiling bill on the Senate floor in 1985. Or, for an example of less significance but even more dramatically different subject matter, consider a July 1989 amendment to allow for easy eviction of tenants from public housing that was added to a bill authorizing the activities of the State Department.[65] The absence of a general germaneness rule makes it very easy for senators to circumvent Senate committees by bringing issues directly to the floor.

In contrast to the House, however, no Senate strategy to control floor amending activity and enhance the autonomy of the committees has emerged. Efforts to make it easier to block nongermane amendments, which allow senators to circumvent committees, and to prevent unlimited debate, have failed. Adjustments in the cloture rule, through which debate is limited and a final vote on a measure is assured, have made it marginally easier to limit debate and impose a germaneness requirement on remaining amendments, but cloture still requires an extraordinary majority (three-fifths of all senators) to go through. Even so, cloture use has risen and repeated cloture votes on a single measure also have increased. Indeed, cloture has become a normal feature for the consideration of many important bills on the Senate floor. That said, use of such a blunt instrument cannot completely shield committee bills from unfriendly amendments. Thus, only on reconciliation measures has the Senate moved effectively to limit debate and amendments.

Lacking any formal rules and facing the ever-present threat of filibusters, Senate leaders turned to unanimous consent agreements to structure amending activity and bring debate to a close. *Unanimous consent agreements*, as the name implies, are agreements adopted by the Senate that require unanimous approval. These agreements may supplement or even supplant the standing rules of the Senate in much the same way that special rules do in the House. As a result, unanimous consent agreements may be used to restrict or order the consideration of amendments and to specify times for votes, limit debate, and provide for a final vote on measures. They are useful tools for adding some predictability to the flow of business on the Senate floor and often streamline the consideration of measures and amendments. But because the agreements require unanimous consent, any senator who wants to preserve his or her privileges under the standing rules can prevent restrictions from being imposed. In general, therefore, there is no way for a majority of senators to insulate committee bills from unfriendly or nongermane amendments whose sponsors are committed to offering them.

The possibility of objecting to unanimous consent requests to limit debate and amendments gives senators a source of leverage with floor and committee leaders. An objection to a prospective unanimous consent request is known as a *hold*. Holds are communicated privately to the floor leaders and usually have the effect of preventing floor action on a bill (see Box 5-2). In 1996, for example, a promising bipartisan proposal regarding health insurance was delayed in the Senate for months because of holds placed on it by unknown opponents.[66] Floor leaders may call a senator's bluff now and then, but they generally cannot afford to risk creating a legislative logjam by calling for the consideration of a bill and stimulating a filibuster. Consequently, the increased dependence on unanimous consent agreements to streamline floor debate reinforced the obstructionist power of individual senators. Thus, as the House was moving with special rules to recover some of the autonomy its committees had lost to the floor, the Senate was moving in to further entrench individualism at the expense of committee autonomy.

CONFERENCE COMMITTEES

Decision-making processes within each chamber affect not only committee autonomy, but also the manner in which differences between House and Senate versions of bills are resolved. This post-passage stage creates one last opportunity for members to alter the legislation before it is sent to the president. The changing role of subcommittees in conference delegations and the importance of conferences for the power of subcommittee members were discussed in Chapter 4. The assumption made there was that committee members—whether organized by subcommittee or not—have dominated conferences for more than a century and a half. In fact, committee domination of conferences has weakened somewhat in the last two decades.

The procedures for resolving House-Senate differences on legislation grant committee members important advantages. First, much controversial legislation goes to a conference committee after initial House and Senate passage. The differences between the chambers are usually too important and complex to be resolved through informal discussions and an exchange of amendments between the chambers. Second, conference delegations are composed, usually exclusively, of members of the committees that originated the legislation. Conference appointments are made by the Speaker

Eliminating Holds . . .

As Congress looks for ways to make itself more efficient, some would-be reformers are taking aim at a custom that gives each and every senator enormous power to hogtie the Senate—almost effortlessly. At issue is the Senate's informal system of "holds," which allows any senator, with the stroke of a pen, to delay action on legislation or executive branch nominations. They can be as effective as a filibuster without the bother of extended debate.

"It is a form of filibuster—a silent one," said Lawrence J. DeNardis, a former GOP House member from Connecticut who wrote a doctoral dissertation on Senate delaying tactics. Senators put "holds" on bills by writing to their party leader asking for advance notification of floor debate on a bill or nomination. But the significance of those simple requests is far broader: It usually means that a senator will filibuster the matter if it comes to the floor, all but forcing the leadership to delay action.

Senate leaders periodically rail against abuse of this prerogative. House members who have seen their bills die in the Senate have become increasingly critical. Now, senators on the Joint Committee on the Organization of Congress say that their panel's proposal to reduce filibuster opportunities would weaken the grip of holds. However, some say the Senate would not necessarily be a better place without holds, because they give Senate leaders early warning of time-consuming controversies.

"They are in many ways a favor to the leadership by letting them know how senators feel about a bill," said Robert B. Dove, a former Senate parliamentarian who now is an adviser to Minority Leader Bob Dole, R-Kan. "It lets them know how to plan their time."

In an era when smoke-filled backrooms supposedly have been opened to the sunshine of public scrutiny, few aspects of the Senate are more mysterious than holds. They are nowhere described in Senate rules. Their origins and history are obscure. Senators can register holds anonymously. But they are a routine part of the daily life of the Senate. This month, Mitch McConnell, R-Ky., blocked five diplomatic nominations for three weeks to force the Clinton administration to respond to reports that the State Department had improperly perused personnel files from George Bush's administration.

Last year [1992], Larry Pressler, R-S.D., put a hold on more than 30 nominations by George Bush because the administration had not filled a federal judgeship in South Dakota. Howard M. Metzenbaum, D-Ohio, routinely puts holds on legislation he wants more time to examine. His practice is so estab-

BOX 5-2

. . . Or Busting the Silent Filibuster

lished that, during busy end-of-session periods, the form that clears bills for floor action has included checkoffs for the leadership, committee chairmen—and Metzenbaum.

The roots of the system go back a generation to a time when members only occasionally asked their leaders to delay consideration of legislation. What began as an occasional courtesy evolved into a powerful political weapon, said Donald A. Ritchie, associate Senate historian. The hold became a more potent tool of obstruction in the 1970s because Senate leaders, faced with a growing workload, turned increasingly to a new method of expediting bills: the use of unanimous consent agreements to limit debate. Because those agreements could be blocked by a single objecting member, the hold gained new meaning as a way to signal objections.

The use of the hold "grew like Topsy," said William F. Hildenbrand, secretary of the Senate from 1981 to 1985. Staff got involved, and it turned out many times the member did not know he had a hold on a bill. Stalling nominations became an especially powerful tool for putting pressure on the executive branch—often, as in the cases of Pressler and McConnell, on issues wholly unrelated to the nominations being held. Every so often, senators rise to complain that holds are getting out of hand, and urge the leader to call up a bill to see if opponents are serious about filibustering. David L. Boren, D-Okla., co-chairman of the Joint Committee, said he thought holds would decline if the Senate adopted the panel's proposal to eliminate the right to filibuster on motions to proceed to legislation. Without such filibuster threats, he contends, the leadership would have little incentive to honor requests for long delays.

But senators could still filibuster a bill once it is on the floor. What's more, the Joint Committee proposal would not affect nominations, on which holds are common. Senators' enthusiasm for eliminating holds may be tempered by the fact that most of them love the power when they use it and loathe it when their adversaries do. Indeed, Boren himself was behind a memorable Senate stall. He held up the 1984 nomination of Edwin Meese III to be attorney general to pressure Ronald Reagan's administration to address problems in the farm credit system.

Source: Janet Hook, "Busting the Silent Filibuster," Congressional Quarterly Weekly Report, November 13, 1993, 3095.

and the presiding officer of the Senate, who generally rely on lists provided by committee chairs. And third, the primary products of conference negotiations, conference reports, are given special treatment when they are sent back to the two chambers. A conference report is returned to the chambers after a majority of conferees from each chamber have signed it. But amendments may not be offered to the report from the House or Senate floor—the report must receive a simple up-or-down vote.[67]

The conference process endows committee members, as conferees, with important sources of negative and positive power. On the negative side, conferees may strip away unfriendly provisions added on the floor as long as the modified measure is acceptable to the other chamber's conferees and to a majority of both chambers. In some cases, committees may even repeal provisions they originally favored to punish members who voted against them on the floor.[68] Because this negative power constitutes a sort of veto after the floor stage is completed, some scholars refer to it as the *ex post veto*.[69]

On the positive side, conferees may take advantage of conferences to introduce provisions not included in the original committee bills reported to the House and Senate floors, subject to the condition that House and Senate majorities will support the conference report. The ability to include new provisions is circumscribed by House and Senate rules that limit conferees to subjects addressed in at least one of the chambers' bills and restrict the conference agreement to the scope of the differences between the bills. These rules must be enforced by a point of order and majority vote when the conference report is considered in the House or Senate. Many new provisions are tolerated or simply go undetected. Moreover, the House and Senate versions may differ in so many ways—as when one chamber adopts a substitute version—that the scope of the differences is broad enough to allow any provision remotely related to the subjects addressed in either bill to be included in the conference report.

The strategic advantages bestowed upon committee members by the conference process exist for both House and Senate committees. In fact, in many circumstances the ex post veto is just as viable in the Senate as in the House. Senate committees may suffer during initial floor debate from nongermane amendments, unlimited debate, and the absence of protective special rules, but they may recover in conference much of what they lost. Yet Senate conferees do operate under a constraint that House conferees do not: senators may filibuster a conference report and force supporters of the report to garner an extraordinary majority to overcome the filibuster and bring the report to a vote. In 1995, for example, senators Byron L. Dorgan (D-N.D.) and Bob Kerrey (D-Neb.) threatened to veto the conference report on a major rewrite of the nation's telecommunications laws if the compromise bill failed to allow the FCC to compel providers of data and video services to reach remote areas.[70] Thus, threatened filibusters often give individual Senate nonconferees leverage that their House counterparts do not have.

Several developments in the conference process, particularly in the House, suggest that committee autonomy at the conference stage is not as strong as it was in the 1950s and 1960s. Changes in the rules and practices related to the composition of conference delegations, new rules governing the procedures and discretion of conferences, and increases in the challenges to conference recommendations on the House and Senate floors are all evidence of diminished autonomy. We will consider each in turn.

COMPOSITION OF CONFERENCE COMMITTEES

The appointment of conferees is a critical point in the legislative process because the conferees are usually the last group of members who may alter the details of legislation. The Speaker of the House and the presiding officer in the Senate are responsible for appointing conferees, but they generally follow the recommendation of the appropriate committee chair and ranking minority member. Much behind-the-scenes maneuvering occurs at this stage as the contending factions seek advantage in gaining committee leaders' recommendations.[71] Sometimes party leaders must step in to referee disputes, especially in the House, where the Speaker has a formal role to perform in the appointment process.

Under a rule adopted in 1946, the Speaker and the Senate's presiding officer are obliged to appoint conferees who have demonstrated support for the measure in their chambers. In practice, the rule is difficult to enforce.[72] Determining which members support the legislation, and to what degree, is nearly impossible. In the 1950s and 1960s the rule usually was ignored. In the 1970s the House moved to tighten the conference appointment rule, reflecting the view that committee chairs should not be able to exercise unchecked control of naming conferees. The rules now require that "the Speaker . . . appoint no less than a majority of members who generally supported the House position as determined by the Speaker" and that "the Speaker . . . name members who are primarily responsible for the legislation and . . . to the fullest extent possible, include the principal proponents of the major provisions of the bill as it passed the House." The new rules imply that members who did not sit on the committee originating the legislation but who sponsored important provisions in the House-passed version are entitled to appointments to the conference. The Senate has not adopted similar rules.

Changing attitudes about rights to participate in conference deliberations produced major changes in the number and type of members appointed. In the 1950s and 1960s, the modal conference was composed of five representatives and five senators, usually the three most senior majority party members and the two most senior minority party members from the committee, or sometimes the subcommittee, of each chamber. The mean size of the conference delegation in the 88th Congress (1963–1964) was just 5.8 in the House and 6.4 in the Senate. By the 96th Congress (1979–1980), the mean was 10.5 in the House and 9.2 in the Senate, excluding the large conferences for reconciliation bills and a few other measures originating in multiple committees. In the 99th Congress (1985–1986), that mean had increased further to 11.8 in the House and 10.1 in the Senate. In those two years, 71.2 percent of House conference delegations and 43.1 percent of Senate delegations had eleven or more members, up from just 2.4 percent and 4.5 percent, respectively, in the 88th Congress.

This expansion in delegation size resulted from reaching deeper into committees for conferees. In the House, this meant including nearly all subcommittee members on most delegations. In the Senate, where the average committee has only seventeen or eighteen members, a majority of full committee members gained appointment to most conferences. In fact, the expansion of conference delegations reinforced the democratization of intracommittee politics that occurred in the 1960s and 1970s. Because a majority of each chamber's delegation must approve the conference report, a few senior committee members cannot dictate conference outcomes. Nor do a few senior members monopolize information about what took place in conferences, making it easier for the parent chambers to hold conferees accountable.

Committee outsiders also gained a greater voice in conferences after the new House rules were adopted. In the 92d Congress (1971–1972), only 2 of 150 House conference delegations included members not sitting on the committee originating the legislation, but by the 96th Congress (1979–1980) the number had increased to 27 of 154. Senate delegations also seldom included committee outsiders before the 1970s, with the exception of a few members of authorizing committees who were ex officio members of appropriations conferences specified in a Senate rule. The rule was dropped in 1977. But the Senate continues to appoint fewer outsiders to conferences than the House. In the 96th Congress (1979–1980), only eight Senate delegations included outsiders; in the 99th (1985–1986), only eleven included outsiders.

The expansion of delegation size and the addition of more committee outsiders commonly made conference negotiations more difficult and time-consuming. Committee leaders and staff were forced to consult with more members, delegations tended to be less cohesive, and committee outsiders often had little long-term commitment to maintaining good working relations with committee members from the other chamber. It did not take long for committee leaders to look for ways to limit the role of some conferees, particularly committee outsiders. Limitations arrived in two forms: additional conferees and exclusive conferees.

Additional conferees are eligible to consider and vote on only specified subjects or sections of legislation. In contrast, *general conferees* participate in all matters. Conference agreements on the specified subjects or sections require the support of a majority of conferees, general and additional, who have jurisdiction. Additional conferees who are committee outsiders with an interest in only a few subjects or sections will likely find this arrangement acceptable. The general conferees retain unfettered control on all other matters.

Exclusive conferees are the sole negotiators for their chamber on specified subjects or sections. General conferees are not allowed to vote on those subject or sections unless they also are named among the relevant exclusive conferees. Only a majority of the named exclusive conferees may approve a conference agreement on the specified subjects or sections. Thus, exclusive conferees have a virtual veto over both policy within their jurisdiction and the entire conference report that depends on House-Senate agreement on all items. The relative influence of committee and non-committee members on an exclusive subconference therefore depends on the number of each that are appointed and the policy preferences they hold.[73]

The appointment of limited-purpose conferees, additional or exclusive, was rare before the late 1970s. Since then, about half of the instances of use of limited-purpose conferees have involved measures originating in multiple committees. In fact, use of limited-purpose conferees represents an effort to reduce intercommittee conflict and preserve committee autonomy. Assigning members of a committee with jurisdiction over just one section of a bill as exclusive conferees, as usually happens, allows that committee to retain control over negotiations with the other chamber without interloping on and perhaps hampering the efforts of other committees. The process sometimes makes it more difficult to trade provisions in one section for provisions in another, but it is more likely to produce coherent legislation than the alternative of considering separate bills, each from a different committee. Complex arrangements of additional and exclusive conferees became standard practice in the 1980s for large, multiple committee conferences on budget reconciliation, trade, and drugs, to name a few. The use of limited-purpose conferees to limit the role of committee outsiders is now common in both the House and Senate.

The developments in the appointment of conference delegations have produced many strange conferences. In 1995, for example, a conference on a large and complex bank deregulation bill was composed of eight senators from two committees (five from Banking, three from Finance) and more than seventy-five House members from seven committees—Banking, Education and Labor, Energy and Commerce, Foreign Affairs, Judiciary, Small Business, and Ways and Means. On the one hand, Senate Banking chair, Donald Riegle (D-Mich.) had established a practice of deliberately keeping his delegations small to facilitate negotiations on the large, complex bill. And the participation of the three Finance conferees was limited to negotiations on the bill's tax provisions. On the other hand, House Banking chair Henry Gonzalez (D-Texas) felt that he had to include nearly all members who wanted a voice in the conference. Even so, Gonzalez, with the consent of the Speaker, was able to structure the House conferees into subgroups for particular sections of the bill. During 1989, a conference committee strikingly similar in composition to the 1995 committee had created quite a stir among House members, who complained about both its composition and operating procedures. But in each case conference reports were eventually adopted by both chambers.[74]

CONFERENCE PROCEDURES AND DISCRETION

New rules governing conference appointments in the House were part of an effort to make conference committees more responsive to the parent chamber. Concern about conference representation extended to the Senate as well, but there it produced less dramatic changes in formal rules. Two additional sets of rules that affect the autonomy of committees in conference warrant attention.

First, the two chambers moved in 1975 to open conference meetings to the public. Previously, most conference meetings had been held in closed sessions. The rationale was that closed sessions eliminated grandstanding and facilitated compromises on difficult issues. But closed sessions meant that outsiders, even other members of Congress, were in a weak position to evaluate the performance of conferees. The new rules required that conference meetings be open to the public unless the conferees of either chamber voted in open session to close the meeting for that day. But the House, displeased with the decisions of a few conference delegations, required in 1977 that the House itself approve closure of conference meetings. The major exception to the rule has been conferences on legislation dealing with national security matters; in those cases, explicit permission for members of Congress to attend is included in the motion to allow a closed meeting.

Since 1977, most formal meetings of conferences have been held in public session. Yet conferees have found ways to circumvent the rules. Informal meetings of committee leaders and staff can help to resolve many of the issues facing complex conferences. In some cases, very small meeting rooms can be used to limit the number of outsiders who may attend. For example, the 1989 conference on the savings and loan industry bill met in a room so small that no television cameras were allowed; only print reporters were present, and they had to stand. The general public could not attend at all.[75] In a few cases, the two delegations have met in separate rooms so that their meetings did not constitute formal conference sessions. Negotiations were then carried out via staff members who shuttled between the rooms or by arranging hallway meetings of two or three members.

A second set of rules concerns the exercise of discretion by conferees. An issue particularly troubling to the House has been the addition, in conference, of provisions on new subjects. The chambers have no opportunity to amend these nongermane additions before they are faced with a take-it-or-leave-it decision on the entire conference report. The problem is most acute when one chamber adopts a substitute version of the other chamber's bill that differs in structure and scope as well as content. In such cases the longstanding rule that the conference report be restricted to the scope of the differences between the chambers is not very limiting. The problem became more severe in the 1960s as substitutes became more common.

Although both chambers had longstanding rules barring nongermane modifications to legislation in conference, these rules were frequently ignored. The House, however, resisted nongermane provisions more strenuously, particularly those added by the Senate to a House bill, consistent with its traditionally stronger concern for germaneness and the jurisdictional territories of committees. In 1971 the House sought to strengthen its rule barring the addition of new subjects in conference by requiring that "the introduction of any language in [the conference] substitute presenting a specific additional topic, question, issue, or proposition not committed to the conference committee by either House shall not constitute a germane modification of the matter in disagreement." But this rule, like the Senate's less specific rule, had to be enforced by a successful point of order. And a point of order is a very blunt instrument because it defeats the entire conference report. The risk for members objecting to the nongermane provisions was that a new conference report might be less acceptable in other ways than the original, or that it would not be possible to negotiate a new version with the other chamber. Thus, in 1972, the House granted itself the right to "surgically" remove nongermane provisions added by the Senate or the conference committee. The rule allows the House to vote separately on a nongermane provision after a successful point of order has been made against the provision.

These and related developments were part of the reform efforts to limit the control of committee chairs and a few senior committee members over conference outcomes.[76] Pushed by liberal Democrats, the House moved more aggressively than the Senate because of concerns over the power of a few conservative chairs who could thwart the will of the majority party and of the House itself. Much of that concern had dissipated by the late 1970s after many of these chairs had been replaced by members more in tune with the party, and as the composition of conference delegations themselves began to change.

ROLL-CALL VOTE CHALLENGES TO CONFERENCES

The 1970s' efforts to curb committee autonomy in conference through rules changes were accompanied by more frequent challenges to conference recommendations. During the 1950s and 1960s, the vast majority of conference reports were approved by the House and Senate by voice votes. Only one in five in the House and one in ten in the Senate faced a recorded vote on the motion to adopt the report. Even fewer conferences were subject to motions to instruct the conferees to adhere to a specified policy position or to recommit the report to conference.

By the end of the 1960s, more and more recorded votes occurred on the various motions related to conference deliberations, especially in the House. In the 91st Congress (1969–1970), more than 34 percent of conference reports were subject to a recorded vote on adoption in the House, compared with just 7 percent in the 84th Congress (1955–1956). In the Senate, the frequency increased from 2 percent in the 84th Congress to more than 15 percent in the 91st. Voting procedures cannot account for the increase because no changes in voting procedures had been adopted by that time. The frequency of challenges continued to increase during the 1970s, reaching a peak of 61 percent in the House during the 95th Congress (1977–1978) and 27 percent in the Senate during the 97th (1981–1982). A recent surge in motions to instruct conferees has been sponsored by House Republicans. They have turned to this tactic as a way to force votes on difficult issues, establish a party position of symbolic value, and increase the pressure on conferees to adhere to a House-passed version.[77] Successful motions to instruct are not binding on conferees, but they make compromises on the chamber's position very conspicuous and sometimes more difficult to justify.

Few challenges to conference reports succeed. This is because conferees anticipate the reaction of the two chambers and often act in advance to make sure the conference report will be acceptable to a majority in both chambers. When a defeat does occur, it may be the result of an error in judgment on the part of the conferees. In 1989, for example, a conference report on a supplemental appropriations bill was defeated in the House, much to the surprise of the conferees and the majority party leadership.[78] Despite the fact that the bill included appropriations for veterans' medical facilities that were about to close for lack of funding, Republicans voted against the bill to avoid a subsequent vote on whether it should include antidrug funds, and some Democrats voted against it because they disapproved of certain extraneous projects that were included. Cases such as these put conferees on notice that the parent chambers will not defer on important matters.

Changes in conference delegation composition, new formal constraints, and more floor challenges all suggest that committee autonomy in conference is no longer certain. The prescriptive norm of deference to conference recommendations has disappeared. The committees have responded, of course: they have sought restrictions on outsiders' participation in conference deliberations, found ways to circumvent the open meeting rule, and so on. But the necessity of playing such games reflects how much the rules have changed. As committee outsiders have become more assertive and less indifferent to conference negotiations, the autonomy of committees at the post-passage stage has weakened considerably.

PERSPECTIVES ON COMMITTEE POWER REVISITED

Committees are unique, resilient, and almost certainly permanent features of the United States Congress. But they are not immune from assault, diminution, or circumvention. Power in committees reached its lowest ebb since the beginning of the century during the first 100 days of the 104th Congress. As House committees worked to implement the promise of the Contract With America, leaders and members were required to shape the sometimes complex pieces of legislation entrusted to them in various bills at a breakneck pace, perhaps unmatched in terms of the scope of committees involved. But this achievement did not come without costs.

After the Contract and the first 100 days had been successfully negotiated, the Speaker and his new Republican majority did not rest on their laurels. Speaker Gingrich continued to take a strong and direct interest in what his committees were producing. He circumvented the Ways and Means and Commerce Committees to form an ad hoc group on Medicare policy; he ignored a bill produced by the Appropriations Committee's District of Columbia Subcommittee and, in effect, ordered that a new one be written; and he rejected portions of a telecommunications bill crafted and passed by the Commerce Committee. For the most part, Republican committee chairs tolerated the intrusions as a necessary cost of success. Said Bill Archer of Texas, chair of the Ways and Means Committee: ". . . I accept that because that's part of making something happen. In the end, you have to be part of the process. You don't run out there like the Lone

Ranger and do whatever you want to do."[79] They have been tolerant, but not always entirely happy. After having his appropriations bill dumped, D.C. Subcommittee chair James T. Walsh (R-N.Y.) said: "[Speaker Gingrich] brings an awful lot to the table, so you may have resources, financial and otherwise, that you didn't know you had. The down side is, you do your best to put a bill together going through the normal process and all of a sudden it's not the normal process anymore."[80]

Committees, which are ultimately procedural and structural institutions, thrive on "normal process." Like most institutional arrangements they provide predictability and stability. In the House more than the Senate, committee routines have become a defining characteristic of a relatively efficient but typically decentralized organizational structure. Put somewhat differently, committees are conservative in a bureaucratic sense. High levels of partisanship, centralized leadership, and effective agenda setting all compromise committee autonomy, as we have seen. But these circumstances, at least in their intense form, tend to be ephemeral. And in fact, during the second session of the 104th Congress, some slack appeared in the tight reins Gingrich had held on committee activity. Committee leaders used leadership meetings to complain about the use of task forces. Rep. Bill Goodling (R-Pa.), chair of the Economic and Educational Opportunities Committee, expressed some of this frustration: "I think the chairmen as a whole have been saying, 'It's our work to do, let us do it.' The committee process works very well if you just allow it to."[81]

At this point our the discussion has reached full circle. We should now be able to answer the question: Which perspective on committee power fits best today—the *distributive committees perspective*, the *party-dominated perspective*, or the *chamber dominated perspective*? At first glance, the answer seems to be that if anything committees are party dominated. But party dominance has raised tensions within the two institutions, and we know that the parent chambers have difficulty tolerating extended periods of partisanship. At the very least, we should be able to discard the distributive committees perspective. Yet didn't the Republican leaders look the other way when their election-imperiled colleagues added special projects to various appropriations bills? And wasn't that fisheries act reauthorization considered in light of its impact on coastal states? In fact, examples of distributive politics-as-usual still abound. The fact is, we cannot answer the question because, as stated above, it is wrong.

The most important lesson imparted by Richard Fenno in his seminal work on committees is captured in the oft-quoted first lines of *Congressmen in Committees*: "This book rests on a simple assumption and conveys a simple theme. The assumption is that congressional committees matter. The theme is that congressional committees differ."[82] Among all the advantages that the "perspectives on power" debate has going for it, it does have one drawback: it *tends* to focus on committees as an institutional arrangement rather than as separate institutions. We want to reaffirm Fenno's wisdom regarding committee differences without simply throwing up our collective hands and saying that each is unique. We also want to emphasize that committees should not be viewed with a static model that captures today's essential features but ignores how committees change. We conclude, then, by returning to the conditions that shape the role of committees in Congress.

If the majority party is highly cohesive on the issues and most issues are salient, then that party will be in a position to impose policy decisions by virtue of numbers, and a system of party-dominated committees will then develop. During the early days of the 104th Congress, committee chairs felt bound to deliver on the promises of the Contract. By the end of the 104th Congress, however, fissures had appeared in the Republican coalition, leaders were somewhat less united than they had been, and committee chairs felt freer to stray from the wishes of their party generals. These developments were caused by fallout from the previous year's budget deadlock with President Clinton, internal party disagreements about how to handle pressing agenda items, the plummet of Speaker Gingrich's own public support, and the approach of the 1996 elections. "All the factions are equally unhappy," said Rep. Thomas Petri (R-Wis.).[83] But these developments also say something about the staying power of institutions and the personal *and* collective value members derive from them. The haste with which the Contract legislation was produced, and its Senate fate, is reminiscent of the events surrounding House adoption of the Carter energy policy. Congress simply does not work at that pace as a matter of routine. Revolutions can be very tiring; that's why they are so difficult to sustain. Rep. Fred Upton (R-Mich.) seemed to agree: "We've had a long legislative session, between last year and this year, and you have a lot of frayed nerves out there."[84]

Changes in policy agendas and political alignments that encourage committee-dominated or party-dominated decision making are not reflected as rapidly in the Senate as in the House. Senate committees remain permeable. The defining institutional arrangements of that chamber— unlimited speech and lack of a germaneness rule—force committees, parties, and leaders to accommodate wider participation. It is not always easy. Only a month after taking on his role as majority leader, Sen. Trent Lott (R-Miss) was already publicly frustrated. A former *House* Republican Whip, Lott was used to losing while he was in the minority party; but he tended to lose with a certain degree of dispatch. No so in the Senate. "We've got work to do," Lott said on the Senate floor in July 1996, "and we're completely balled up . . . and it's not my fault."[85] The Senate too, is conservative, but because of the power of individual members rather than the role of its committees. However frustrated Lott might have been on that occasion, he still knew quite well what his colleagues in the House sometimes failed to grasp. The Senate is different, and just because the House decides to do something does not mean the Senate has to go along. "The House still struggles with understanding the Senate, and I fully understand that. I used to damn the Senate when I was in the House." Lott said. "The thing that they cannot comprehend is the filibuster and the cloture vote."[86]

The larger the agenda, the more separable the issues, the more frequently issues recur, and the less salient the issues, the more Congress relies on committees and the less it relies on parties or the parent chambers to make decisions. The preceding suggests that events of the past few years, perhaps even the past two decades, should be viewed with caution. Most importantly, we should not leap to the conclusion that committees are best viewed through a partisan lens—any more than we should be seduced into accepting the immutability of the distributive committees perspective. The partisan intensity of the 1980s was a break from the less partisan Cold War era. And the shift in party fortunes produced by the 1994 elections was dramatic by any measure. But these events will also fade, and institutions, by their nature, tend to weather such changes or adapt to them. During the 104th Congress, the House and Senate grappled with major legislation on farm subsidies, telecommunications, banking, fisheries, welfare, and a host of other issues. Those issues will remain. And while they may be viewed through a partisan lens, and parties may heavily influence how committees deal with them, the intensity of the partisanship response to solving them cannot be sustained over a long period of time.

Committee power in the House and Senate will continue to ebb and flow. And it will continue to reflect chamber influences, party influences, and the parochial influences of communities and interests throughout the country. Committees and their role in the House and the Senate are not immutable. Rather, the role and influence of these critical structural elements are constantly changing. Committees today may have less autonomy than they have experienced at any point in this century. But that too will change. Committees are important. They are unique. And they remain critical to our understanding of the Congress of the United States.

NOTES

1. On this theme, see Roger H. Davidson, "The New Centralization in Congress," *The Review of Politics* 49 (Summer 1988): 345–363; Roger H. Davidson, "The

Impact of Agenda on the Post-Reform Congress," (Paper presented at the annual meeting of the American Political Science Association, Atlanta, August 31–September 3, 1989); Kenneth A. Shepsle, "The Changing Textbook Congress," in *Can the Government Govern?* ed. John E. Chubb and Paul E. Peterson (Washington, D.C.: Brookings Institution, 1989), 264; Barbara Sinclair, "House Majority Leadership in the Late 1980s," in *Congress Reconsidered*, 4th ed., ed. Lawrence C. Dodd and Bruce I. Oppenheimer (Washington, D.C.: CQ Press, 1989), 3–7, 29; Barbara Sinclair, "The Changing Role of Party and Party Leadership in the U.S. House" (Paper presented at the annual meeting of the American Political Science Association, Atlanta, August 31–September 3, 1989); and Steven S. Smith, *Call to Order: Floor Politics in the House and Senate* (Washington, D.C.: CQ Press, 1989).

2. For a discussion specific to the postreform era see Roger H. Davidson, "The Impact of Agenda on the Post-Reform Congress," (Paper presented at the annual meeting of the American Political Science Association, Atlanta, August 31–September 3, 1989). Also see Bryan D. Jones, Frank R. Baumgartner, and Jeffery C. Talbert, "The Destruction of Issue Monopolies in Congress," *American Political Science Review* 87 (1993): 657–671; and Frank R. Baumgartner and Bryan D. Jones, *Agendas and Instability in American Politics* (Chicago: University of Chicago Press, 1993).

3. Roger H. Davidson, "The Emergence of the Postreform Congress," in *The Postreform Congress*, ed. Roger H. Davidson (New York: St. Martin's Press, 1992), 14–22.

4. David W. Rohde, "Electoral Forces, Political Agendas, and Partisanship in the House and Senate," in *The Postreform Congress*, ed. Davidson, 27–47.

5. See William F. Connelly, Jr. and John J. Pitney, Jr., *Congress' Permanent Minority? Republicans in the House of Representatives* (Lanham, Md.: Littlefield Adams, 1994), chap. 2; and James G. Gimpel, *Fulfilling the Contract: The First 100 Days* (Boston: Allyn and Bacon, 1996), chap 3.

6. Barbara Sinclair's data is for major legislative measures in the House, an average of just under 50 bills per congress examined. She finds that the leadership's share of the agenda is lower in the first year of an administration and much higher later in an administration. Her examination of "leadership involvement" shows an almost uninterrupted rise from the 91st Congress (1969–1970) to the 101st Congress (1989–1990). See Barbara Sinclair, *Legislators, Leaders, and Lawmaking: The U.S. House of Representatives in the Postreform Era* (Baltimore: Johns Hopkins University Press, 1995), chap 4.

7. For background on the caucuses, see Don Wolfensberger, "The Role of Party Caucuses in the U.S. House of Representatives: An Historical Perspective" (Paper prepared for the annual meeting of the American Political Science Association, Washington, D.C., September 1–4, 1988); on its revival see Diane Granat, "Democratic Caucus Renewed as Forum for Policy Questions," *Congressional Quarterly Weekly Report*, October 15, 1983, 2115–2119. For additional coverage of recent changes, see David W. Rohde, *Parties and Leaders in the Postreform House* (Chicago: University of Chicago Press, 1991), chap 3; and Sinclair, *Legislators, Leaders, and Lawmakers*, chaps. 3, 4, and 5.

8. In 1972, for example, the Democratic Caucus directed the House Foreign Affairs Committee to report a bill setting a date for the termination of U.S. military involvement in Southeast Asia. In 1973, the Caucus instructed its members on the Rules Committee to vote against a closed rule—one that would bar floor amendments—-for a tax bill and to vote in favor of a rule that would

make an amendment on the oil depletion allowance in order on the House floor. And, in 1978, the Caucus voted to urge the Ways and Means Committee to report a measure that would stall an increase in the social security payroll tax. For details on these and other incidents involving the Democratic Caucus, see James L. Sundquist, *The Decline and Resurgence of Congress* (Washington, D.C.: Brookings Institution, 1981), 383–387.

9. Chuck Alston, "The Speaker and the Chairmen: A Taoist Approach to Power," *Congressional Quarterly Weekly Report*, November 2, 1991, 3177. For more discussion on the Caucus's views of Foley see Sinclair, *Legislators, Leaders, and Lawmakers*, 272–274; and on the prospects for a "new" Foley during 103d Congress, see Ronald D. Elving, "Era of a Firmer Hand: Foley at the Fore," *Congressional Quarterly Weekly Report*, January 23, 1993, 194.

10. House Republican Conference, Rule 2.

11. House Republican Conference, Rule 14.

12. These developments are reported in Richard E. Cohen, "The Transformers," *National Journal*, March 4, 1995, 532; and Walter Pincus, "Centralized Republican Power House," *Washington Post*, September 6, 1995, A19.

13. Ronald D. Elving, "Mitchell Will Try to Elevate Policy, Predictability," *Congressional Quarterly Weekly Report*, December 3, 1988, 3423–3424; Richard E. Cohen, "Setting the Senate Democrats' Agenda," *National Journal*, February 25, 1989, 484; and Richard E. Cohen, "Making His Mark," *National Journal*, May 20, 1989, 1232–1236.

14. Jackie Calmes, "Fight Over Anti-Drug Funds Threatens Spending Bills," *Congressional Quarterly Weekly Report*, September 16, 1989, 2368–2369.

15. On the events leading up to the adoption of these changes, see Donna Cassata, "GOP Retreats on Hatfield, But War Far From Over," *Congressional Quarterly Weekly Report*, March 11, 1995, 729–731; David Hosansky, "GOP Conference Will Consider Limits on Seniority System," *Congressional Quarterly Weekly Report*, May 20, 1995, 1392; and David S. Cloud, "GOP Senators Limit Chairmen To Six Years Heading Panel," *Congressional Quarterly Weekly Report*, July 22, 1995, 2147.

16. For a study of multiple referral in the Senate, see Roger H. Davidson, "Multiple Referral of Legislation in the U.S. Senate," *Legislative Studies Quarterly* 14 (August 1989): 375–392.

17. See Gary Young and Joseph Cooper, "Multiple Referral and the Transformation of House Decision Making," in *Congress Reconsidered*, 5th ed., ed. Lawrence C. Dodd and Bruce I. Oppenheimer (Washington, D.C.: CQ Press, 1993), 211–234.

18. To be precise, the proportion for the 102d Congress was 36.8 percent of all bills referred to committees. This figure is calculated from data contained in Table 3 of *Background Materials: Supplemental Information Provided to Members of the Joint Committee on the Organization of Congress*, Joint Committee on the Organization of Congress, 103d Cong., 1st Sess., S. Prt. 103-55, 1993. Data reflected in the next two sentences are from the same source.

19. For recent discussions of multiple referral, see Young and Cooper, "Multiple Referral," 228–232; Roger H. Davidson and Walter J. Oleszek, "From Monopoly to Management: Changing Patterns of Committee Deliberation," in *The Postreform Congress*, ed., Davidson, 129–141; and Sinclair, *Legislators, Leaders, and Lawmakers*, 172–176.

20. For background on multiple referral and special rules, see Stanley Bach and Steven S. Smith, *Managing Uncertainty in the House of Representatives: Adap-*

tation and Innovation in Special Rules (Washington, D.C.: Brookings Institution, 1988), 18–23, 38–45, 59–61.

21. Deborah Kalb, "Government By Task Force: The Gingrich Model," *The Hill*, February 22, 1995, 3.
22. Barbara Sinclair, "The Speaker's Task Force in the Post-Reform House of Representatives," *American Political Science Review* 75 (June 1984): 397–410.
23. Janet Hook, "Far-Reaching Rule Reforms Aren't Easy to Come By," *Congressional Quarterly Weekly Report*, September 23, 1989, 2437–2438.
24. See Kalb, "Government By Task Force."
25. On Mitchell, see Cohen, "Making His Mark," 1236; on Lott, see Donna Cassata, "Lott's Task: Balance the Demands of His Chamber and His Party," *Congressional Quarterly Weekly Report*, March 8, 1997, 567–571.
26. See, for example, Tom Kenworthy, "House 'Bulls' See Red Over Task Forces," *Washington Post*, April 18, 1991, A19.
27. Allan Freedman, "Republicans Strive to Gain Environmental Advantage," *Congressional Quarterly Weekly Report*, May 18, 1996, 1384–1385.
28. Jackie Koszczuk, "Unpopular, Yet Still Powerful, Gingrich Faces Critical Pass," *Congressional Quarterly Weekly Report*, September 14, 1996, 2579.
29. Hyde is quoted by Allan Freedman, in "Returning Power to Chairmen," *Congressional Quarterly Weekly Report*, November 23, 1996, 3300.
30. On this specific point, and on summits more generally, see John B. Gilmour, "Summits and Stalemates: Bipartisan Negotiations in the Postreform Era," in *The Postreform Congress*, ed., Davidson, chap. 12.
31. See Allen Schick, *Congress and Money: Budgeting, Spending, and Taxing* (Washington, D.C.: Urban Institute, 1980), chap. 8
32. For a useful summary of the 1980 budget battle in the House, see Barbara Sinclair, *Majority Leadership in the U.S. House* (Baltimore: Johns Hopkins University Press, 1983), 181–190.
33. This was a strategy particularly useful to House committees controlled by Democrats who faced a Republican Senate and administration opposed to most new policy initiatives. But both House and Senate committees have taken advantage of reconciliation to force floor and conference consideration of legislation. For examples, see Ronald D. Elving with Jackie Calmes, "Tax, Health-Cost Disputes Slow Deficit Reduction," *Congressional Quarterly Weekly Report*, September 23, 1989, 2444–2445.
34. For background on Gramm-Rudman-Hollings, see John W. Ellwood, "The Politics of the Enactment and Implementation of Gramm-Rudman-Hollings: Why Congress Cannot Address the Deficit Dilemma," *Harvard Journal on Legislation* 25 (Summer 1988): 553–575.
35. A discussion of the failure of GRH can be found in James A. Thurber, "If The Game Is Too Hard, Change The Rules: Congressional Budget Reform in the 1990s," in *Remaking Congress: Change and Stability in the 1990s*, ed. James A. Thurber and Roger H. Davidson (Washington, D.C.: Congressional Quarterly, 1995), 132–133.
36. Extraneous provisions under the Byrd Rule are those that do not make changes (or make only incidental changes) in outlays (spending) or revenues, increase the budget deficit when the reporting committee has not met its deficit reduction target, are not within the jurisdiction of the reporting committee, or increase the deficit after the final year covered by the bill by an amount greater than the savings achieved by the same title. In 1995, the rule frequently forced Congress to consider free-standing legislation when a

majority preferred its inclusion in the reconciliation bill. Welfare reform legislation, which was successfully knocked out of the bill in 1995, is a good
recent example. For some details, see, Alissa J. Rubin, "Senate's Last-Minute
Changes Kept Floor Action Lively," and Jeffrey L. Katz, "Key Welfare Money
Provisions Remain in Budget Bill," *Congressional Quarterly Weekly Report*,
November 4, 1995, 3358–3361 and 3381, respectively. The rule can also
work in favor of a committee because it can be used to block amendments
that are opposed by a committee, although there are other ways to block such
amendments.

37. On the appropriations committees and subcommittees, see Richard F. Fenno,
    Jr., *The Power of the Purse: Appropriations Politics in Congress* (Boston: Little
    Brown, 1966); and, more generally on budgeting, Allen Schick, *Congress and
    Money: Budgeting, Spending, and Taxing* (Washington, D.C.: Urban Institute,
    1980); John B. Gilmour, *Reconcilable Differences? Congress, the Budget Process
    and the Deficit* (Berkeley: University of California Press, 1990); and Howard
    E. Shuman, *Politics and the Budget: The Struggle Between the President and the
    Congress* (Englewood Cliffs, N.J.: Prentice Hall, 1992).
38. The relevant sections were originally 302(a) and 302(b) but were renum-
    bered pursuant to the Budget Enforcement Act of 1990.
39. Schick, *Congress and Money*, 447–462.
40. For background on making 602(b) allocations binding, see Allen Schick,
    "The Whole and the Parts: Piecemeal and Integrated Approaches to Con-
    gressional Budgeting," Report Prepared for the Task Force on the Budget
    Process, Committee on the Budget, U.S. House of Representatives, Serial No.
    CP-3 (Washington, D.C.: U.S. Government Printing Office, 1987), 20-21;
    Richard G. Forgette and James V. Saturno, "302(b) or Not 302(b): Congres-
    sional Floor Procedures and House Appropriators," *Legislative Studies Quar-
    terly* 19 (August 1994): 385–395; and Joseph White, "The Functions and
    Power of the House Appropriations Committee" Ph.D. dissertation, Univer-
    sity of California, Berkeley, 1989, 460–492. The remainder of this section
    draws from White's excellent study.
41. As noted earlier, this same law provided rules regarding restrictions on debat-
    ing reconciliation bills. Indeed, by the mid-1990s there were at least two
    dozen budget rules that required sixty votes to waive. See Allen Schick, *The
    Federal Budget: Politics, Policy, and Process* (Washington, D.C.: Brookings
    Institution, 1995), 91.
42. Our conclusion is similar to that of Richard Forgette in "Constraint or
    Accommodation: The Congressional Budget Procedure's Effect on Appropri-
    ations Decisions," *American Politics Quarterly* 24 (January 1996): 24–42.
43. For historical background on appropriations and continuing resolutions, see
    Schick, "The Whole and the Parts," 33–39. This section draws heavily on
    Schick's discussion, as well as on White's discussion of House Appropria-
    tions in *The Functions and Power of the House Appropriations Committee*,
    492–553.
44. For additional background, see Joe White, "The Continuing Resolution: A
    Crazy Way to Govern?" *The Brookings Review* (Summer 1988): 28–35.
45. George Hager, "Congress, Clinton Yield Enough To Close the Book on Fiscal
    '96," *Congressional Quarterly Weekly Report*, April 27, 1996, 1155.
46. Bliley's quotes appear in George Hager, "As They Cut, Appropriators Add a
    Stiff Dose of Policy," *Congressional Quarterly Weekly Report*, July 29, 1995,
    2247.

47. On norms, see Herbert B. Asher, "The Learning of Legislative Norms," *American Political Science Review* 67 (June 1973): 508–509; Richard F. Fenno, Jr., "The House Appropriations Committee as a Political System: The Problem of Integration," *American Political Science Review* 56 (June 1962): 310–324; Richard F. Fenno, Jr., "The Freshman Congressman: His View of the House," in *American Governmental Institutions: A Reader in the Political Process*, ed. Aaron Wildavsky and Nelson W. Polsby (New York: Rand McNally, 1968); Irwin Gertzog, "Frustration and Adaptation" (Paper presented at the annual meeting of the American Political Science Association, Chicago, August 1966); Ralph K. Huitt, "The Morse Committee Assignment Controversy: A Study in Senate Norms," *American Political Science Review* 51 (June 1957): 313–329; Ralph K. Huitt, "The Outsider in the Senate: An Alternative Role," *American Political Science Review* 55 (September 1961): 566–575; Donald R. Matthews, *U.S. Senators and Their World* (New York: Vintage Books, 1960), chap. 5; David W. Rohde, Norman J. Ornstein, and Robert L. Peabody, "Political Change and Legislative Norms in the U.S. Senate, 1957–1974," in *Studies of Congress*, ed. Glenn R. Parker (Washington, D.C.: CQ Press, 1985) 147–188; Barbara Sinclair, "Senate Styles and Senate Decision Making," *Journal of Politics* 48 (November 1986): 877–908; and Smith, *Call to Order*, chap. 5.

48. In addition to the empirical literature cited in note 45, there are several formal treatments of legislative norms that bear on the role of committees. See, for example, Robert Axelrod, *The Evolution of Cooperation* (New York: Basic Books, 1984); Emerson M. Niou and Peter C. Ordeshook, "Universalism in Congress," *American Political Science Review* 29 (May 1985): 246–258; Kenneth Shepsle and Barry Weingast, "Political Preferences for the Pork Barrel: A Generalization," *American Journal of Political Science* 25 (February 1981): 96–111; Kenneth Shepsle and Barry Weingast, "The Institutional Foundations of Committee Power," *American Political Science Review* 81 (March 1987): 85–104; and Barry Weingast, "A Rational Choice Perspective on Congressional Norms," *American Political Science Review* 23 (May 1979): 245–262.

49. On the problems associated with making inferences about committee power from the roll-call voting record, see Keith Krehbiel and Douglas Rivers, "The Analysis of Committee Power: An Application to Senate Voting on the Minimum Wage," *American Political Science Review* 32 (November 1988): 1151–1174.

50. The counts of amendments noted in this chapter exclude committee amendments, and so are not inflated by routine and substitute amendments offered by bill managers that represent committee recommendations. For more detail, see Smith, *Call to Order*.

51. On the use of second-degree amendments to preserve committee recommendations, see Smith, *Call to Order*, 183–187; Barry R. Weingast, "Floor Behavior in the U.S. Congress: Committee Power Under the Open Rule," *American Political Science Review* 83 (September 1989): 795–815; and Barry Weingast, "Fighting Fire with Fire: Amending Activity and Institutional Change in the Post-Reform Congress," in *The Postreform Congress*, ed. Davidson, 142–168.

52. Data for the 100th through the 102d Congresses are not available. But amendments offered in the 103d Congress are below the level experienced in the 97th and 98th Congresses. See Smith, *Call to Order*, 217.

53. For an in-depth treatment of this committee and its leaders, see Andree E. Reeves, *Congressional Committee Chairmen: Three Who Made an Evolution* (Lexington: University of Kentucky Press, 1993).

54. Bach and Smith, *Managing Uncertainty*, chaps. 2 and 3.

55. Data for the first two periods are from Stanley Bach, "Suspension of the Rules in the House of Representatives," Report 86-103 GOV (Congressional Research Service, May 12, 1986); for the 1987–1992 period see, Joint Committee on the Organization of Congress, *Background Materials*, 1039.

56. See Bach and Smith, *Managing Uncertainty*, 75, 82.

57. King-of -the-hill rules are frequently used to order a series of substitutes to allow votes but help ensure passage of a preferred version. For coverage on House passage and the substitutes, which in this case were defeated, see Joan Biskupic, "Bill Passes House, not Muster; Chance Is in Senate," *Congressional Quarterly Weekly Report*, June 8, 1991 1498–1503.

58. Sinclair, *Legislators, Leaders, and Lawmaking*, 155.

59. Pat Towell, "GOP's Drive For an Open House Reflects Pragmatism and Resentment," *Congressional Quarterly Weekly Report*, November 19, 1994, 3320.

60. But they have fashioned categories somewhat favorable to their point of view and, as noted in the text, have used other devices to limit what the minority party may do on the floor. The data referred to in the text are from Donald R. Wolfensberger, the Rules Committee staff director, who has been kind enough to share his data with a variety of scholars interested in this process. They are reported in Gimpel, *Fulfilling the Contract*, 116.

61. Bach and Smith, *Managing Uncertainty*, 116–117.

62. See Barbara Sinclair, "House Special Rules and the Institutional Design Controversy," *Legislative Studies Quarterly* 19 (November 1994): 477–494.

63. Sinclair, *Legislators, Leaders, and Lawmaking*, 158.

64. In 1997, for example, the House defeated a rule providing for floor consideration of a bill to authorize funding for House committees. Some Republicans used the vote to express dissatisfaction with Speaker Gingrich's leadership. Jackie Koszczuk, "Gingrich's Friends Turn to Foes as Frustration Builds," *Congressional Quarterly Weekly Report*, March 22, 1997, 679.

65. See Helen Dewar, "Bill Gives Senators a Chance to Play Secretary of State," *Washington Post*, July 20, 1989, A6–7.

66. Judith Havemann, "Secret Senate Maneuvers Have Blocked Health Reform Bill Five Months," *Washington Post*, January 25, 1996, A15.

67. For background on conference procedures and politics, see Lawrence D. Longley and Walter J. Oleszek, *Bicameral Politics: Conference Committees in Congress* (New Haven: Yale University Press, 1989).

68. This threat is common for committees whose bills contain projects important to the districts or states of individual members, such as the appropriations and public works committees. For an example, see Paul Starobin, "Can Anderson Bridge Gap to Fill His Wider Role?" *Congressional Quarterly Weekly Report*, April 29, 1989, 955.

69. See Keith Krehbiel, *Information and Legislative Organization* (Ann Arbor: University of Michigan Press, 1991), chap. 6; Shepsle and Weingast, "The Institutional Foundations of Committee Power," 85–104; Keith Krehbiel, Kenneth A. Shepsle, and Barry R. Weingast, "Why Are Congressional Committees Powerful?" *American Political Science Review* 81 (1987): 929–945; Steven S. Smith, "An Essay on Sequence, Position, Goals, and Committee Power," *Leg-*

islative Studies Quarterly 13 (May 1988): 151–176; and Smith, *Call to Order*, chap. 7.

70. See Dan Carney, "Industry Assesses Impact Of Delay of Bill," *Congressional Quarterly Weekly Report*, December 2, 1995, 3651. This can occasionally be taken even one step further: during floor consideration senators may pre-emptively demand certain concessions with respect to conference negotiations as a condition for initial passage.

71. An example is the selection of conferees on a 1989 appropriations bill that included provisions on counting illegal aliens in the 1990 national census. See Kim Mattingly, "House Census Vote Will Affect Reapportionment," *Roll Call*, October 9–15, 1989, 1, 24.

72. In the House, the Speaker's list of conferees can be altered only by unanimous consent, making it virtually impossible to challenge. In the Senate, the list of the presiding officer (nearly always taken from the committee chair) may be modified by a debatable motion that must be adopted by majority vote.

73. A good example is the 1989 defense authorization conference. See Pat Towell, "Conference over Defense Bill: Test of Political Muscle," *Congressional Quarterly Weekly Report*, October 7, 1989, 2656.

74. On the 1996 conference, see Andrew Taylor, "Conferees Stall On Two Major Bills, Holding Up Banking Agenda," *Congressional Quarterly Weekly Report*, July 23, 1994, 2014–2017; and Andrew Taylor, "Conferees Iron Out Final Knots, Combine Two Major Bills," *Congressional Quarterly Weekly Report*, July 30, 1994, 2115–2117. On the earlier incident, see John R. Cranford, "102 Conferees Appointed on S&L Bailout Bill," *Congressional Quarterly Weekly Report*, June 24, 1989, 1530; Susan B. Glasser, "Members Critical of Size of Huge Conference on S&L Legislation, Set to Begin Tomorrow," *Roll Call*, July 10–16, 1989, 3; Kathleen Day and Sharon Warren Walsh, "Negotiations on S&L Bailout Bill Move Behind Closed Doors," *Washington Post*, July 19, 1989, F1; and Sharon Warren Walsh, "House, Senate Staffs Work on S&L Bill," *Washington Post*, July 20, 1989, F2.

75. See Sharon Warren Walsh, "S&L Conference's Cramped Quarters Will Squeeze Out the Public, Media," *Washington Post*, June 22, 1989.

76. The rules of both chambers were changed in 1970 to allow minority opinions greater expression when conference reports are debated on the floor. The old practice of granting control over all debate time on the report to the chair of the conference delegation sometimes meant that little time was given to minority views. The new rules guaranteed equal time for the majority and minority. The House went a step further in 1985 when it adopted a rule that requires one-third of debate time to be reserved for an opponent of the report in the event that the majority and minority party bill managers support the report. The House also adopted in 1970 a rule requiring a layover period of three days for conference reports to give members an opportunity to review them. The requirement does not apply during the last six days of a session and may be waived by a special rule.

77. Janet Hook, "GOP Conference-Report Moves Often Serve to Split Party," *Congressional Quarterly Weekly Report*, October 21, 1989, 2765.

78. Don Phillips, "House Defeats Compromise Emergency Spending Bill," *Washington Post*, June 22, 1989, A7.

79. Jackie Koszczuk, "Gingrich Puts More Power Into the Speaker's Hands," *Congressional Quarterly Weekly Report*, October 7, 1995, 3049.

80. Ibid., 3052.
81. Jackie Koszczuk, "Unpopular, Yet Still Powerful" 2579.
82. Richard F. Fenno, Jr., *Congressmen in Committees* (Boston: Little Brown, 1973), xiii.
83. Jackie Koszczuk, "For Embattled GOP Leadership, A Season of Discontent," *Congressional Quarterly Weekly Report*, July 20, 1996, 2019.
84. Ibid.
85. Helen Dewar, "Frustrated Lott Thwarted in Attempt to Break Senate's 'Slow-Rolling Gridlock,'" *Washington Post*, July 12, 1996, A15.
86. Jackie Koszczuk, "With Humor and Firm Hand, Armey Rules the House," *Congressional Quarterly Weekly Report*, March 2, 1996, 527.

Index

237